Journey Work

Crafting a Life
of Poetry and Spirit

Advance Praise

"For almost forty years I've been reading every word by Edward A. Dougherty I could lay hands on. His words bear witness for peace—and for the 'eternal apprenticeship' that is the poet's life. In Journey Work he tells his fascinating story and shows us a worthwhile way of approaching our own days. Highly recommended."

—Mike Aquilina, Poet & songwriter, and Executive vice-president, St. Paul Center for Biblical Theology

"Edward Dougherty traces his journey from college to grad school to Hiroshima Peace Park to professor/poet, describing his own life events and encounters with the great poets, from Williams, Rilke, Levertov, then Kurihara, Morishita and Yosano, the haikuists, Shiki and Basho, and Stryk, Hayden, Roethke, and others. His instruction of "read the lives of artists" and "work, work, work" and the observation that "each of us struggles to address questions of craft and of self" represent the quest and purpose of this remarkably interwoven work of poetry, analysis and memoir. Every creative writing student, indeed, every writer and poet intending to become a well-crafted one, should read this. It's one of the finest anthologies of exquisitely skillful poetry in the accessible form of memoir."

—Mary A. Hood, author of *All the Spectral Fractures: New and Selected Poems*

Journey Work

Crafting a Life
of Poetry and Spirit

essays by
Edward A. Dougherty

Apprentice House Press
Loyola University Maryland

Copyright © 2021 by Edward A. Dougherty

All rights reserved. No part of this book may be reproduced or transmitted in any form or by any means, electronic or mechanical, including photocopy, recording, or any information storage and retrieval system, without prior permission from the publisher (except by reviewers who may quote brief passages).

First Edition

Hardcover ISBN: 978-1-62720-327-2
Paperback ISBN: 978-1-62720-328-9
Ebook ISBN: 978-1-62720-329-6

Printed in the United States of America

Design: Sarah Thompson
Promotion plan: Kira Maher
Managing editor: Danielle Como

Published by Apprentice House Press

Apprentice House Press
Loyola University Maryland
4501 N. Charles Street
Baltimore, MD 21210
410.617.5265
www.ApprenticeHouse.com
info@ApprenticeHouse.com

I owe my spiritual and creative grounding to three women: my mother, Rita, my cousin, Kate, and the love of my life, Beth. I am deeply grateful to each of you.

Contents

Apprentice Days..1
    In Praise of Ointment 2
    Apprentice Days..6
    The Memorial Chain..40
    Haiku and the Heightening of Awareness................52

At the Crossroads 61
    Hiroshima's Peace Park..62
    1995 in the "City of Peace":
        Spirit of Boredom or Hope 72
    At the Crossroads: In Hiroshima at the Fiftieth
        Anniversary...79
    Memories of the Future: The Poetry of
        Sadako Kurihara and Hiromu Morishita.............93
    The Sculpture of Real Feelings:
        The Poetry of Akiko Yosano 108

Beyond the Fishbowl 121
    Lessons in Totalitarianism:
        Seeking the Path of Love-acted-out 122
    The Secret History of Our "Enemies" 138
    Imagining Creation: A Poet's View of Evolution........ 152
    A Writer, Not Writing 164

Laying It on the Wire 189
    Laying it on the Wire: Delighting in

Poetry's Form and Rhythm 190
Walking in a Flame: The Affirmations
    of Lucien Stryk 205
Robert Hayden, American Master 225
The Making of a Poem 240

Acknowledgements 269
Bibliography 271
Endnotes.. 276

Apprentice Days

In Praise of Ointment

The piggy, greasy sound of the word makes it fun to say. The first part rises then makes a quick disappearance at the end.

Most of my apartments through college and after were basement units, being cheaper. And the first of those was on South Allen Street in State College, when I was at Penn State. Four of us shared it, each with our own room, with a tiny common area and a narrow galley kitchen. My bedroom never saw light. It was so cold that I crumpled newspapers as insulation, filled the window well with them, and pulled a shade down over the opening. I had to listen to the buzz of fluorescent light whenever I was in there, but most of my time was spent on campus anyway. I only ate and slept at the apartment.

But I didn't avoid my roommates. We shared many odd experiences. The four of us spent inordinate amounts of time (and money) at an arcade. Our favorite was Joust, a game where each player mounts a flying ostrich to do knightly combat. We also visited together the only walk-in humidor I ever experienced, and we sampled the cigars, too, the cheapest ones. We all nodded when Tom observed that smoking cigars was like roadkill got left in his mouth overnight. Having learned our lesson, we bought pipes. There's a picture of me somewhere in a green, crushed velvet hat and a corncob pipe reading *The Upanishads*. A proud academic moment.

In addition to cigars and video arcades, we sat around our living room and played a game where we'd ask each other, "What's your favorite word?"—two engineers, one a former engineer, and one budding poet. Usually, I'd pitch the words that held significance because of their meaning: *compassion, nonviolence, imagination,* etc. Mark once said, *ointment* using a falsetto that none of us ever recovered from. Our laughter was acute, prolonged, and painful. And from then on, pasta tasted like ointment, and this cigar was a stick of ointment.

Around this time, I recall standing in the stacks at Pattee Library, now much renovated and renamed, but at that time students could walk into the book collection, climb cramped half-level stairs, and wander the shelves. In the tight privacy of the stacks, I came across William Carlos Williams' *Pictures from Brueghel and Other Poems* with his work from the 1950s and 60s. Many of the longer poems walked through my mind in the three-step form he called a triadic line. It was an ordinary moment, just like the word "ointment" is an ordinary word, no different than "layup" or "cardamom." As ordinary as that moment could have been, I stood stock still and read page after page, and in that suspension, I sensed a recognition. Despite Williams being a towering figure in American poetry, and I was a goofy junior in college, a kinship lit up. Something in me asserted itself, saying, "I could do that." It was as strange as climbing onto a flightless bird to take into battle. *Ostrich*. A funny word. But soon it becomes as natural as walking up South Allen Street under the arching trees to Pattee Library.

"That moment of memorable, dramatic contact with an activity of fascination is known as a 'crystalizing experience,'" writes Scott Barry Kaufman and Carolyn Gregoire[1] in their book *Wired to Create: Unraveling the Mysteries of the Creative Mind*. I had gone to Penn State in order to study English and particularly Creative Writing and particularly writing poetry, so this stand-still moment in the stacks with Dr. Williams' book probably wasn't an *initial* crystalizing experience, "that first moment of falling head over heels for a creative activity," but I certainly felt tumblers hidden in a lock somewhere within me realign so that something sprang open. Maybe since I was already on the path of reading and writing poetry, this was what they call a *"refining* crystalizing experience" where "the creator goes deeper and discovers a particular instrument, style, or approach within their activity."[2] That makes it seem like there is something outside of us that suddenly becomes ours. The feeling was more resonant, a vibration of recognition that what Williams was doing with the language and with his experience was possible for me. There wasn't an outside and an inside, a *him* separate from *me*; instead, the disparate parts cohered.

I love the word "crystalize" in this sense. Scientifically, crystals are highly organized structures, whether of stone or ice, but they form in two processes. Imagine clouds floating in a winter sky. It seems like one blob of "cloud," but really they are just an area where water molecules have formed in the atmosphere. For them to form snowflakes, first they need a point of grit, some tiny solid core, which can be dust blowing in or the clustering of water into ice. This is the nucleation stage. And then the process of growth can occur, where the specific and unique development of the structure of ice can form as long as conditions occur. As a metaphor, this describes an artist's growth as well.

But "crystal" also is used for the multi-facetted glass that gleams and shines and sometimes rainbows light. As an artist begins to follow these initial fascinations, deepening these initial discoveries with actual practice, a whole variety of changes, both in one's life and in one's work. Following these led me to complete my degree at Penn State and master's at Bowling Green in Ohio, to collaborate with translators in Japan and with a composer, Will Wickham, in the US. Writing poems isn't just a hobby, something I do on the side, and it's certainly not my career, a job I do for money. It's deeper than that, and so it manifests in my hobbies, my work life, and in what I do on the side. As Kauffman and Gregoire say, "Ultimately, the individual and the activity become one and the same."[3] There is a clarity that emerges from this process, a singleness of purpose that makes life more vivid. And for me, playing with words, for meaning and texture, for sound and suggestion, has been one of the points where the activity of poetry writing and my own sense of identity are one. And I learned it that year of the basement apartment, on my own and with my roommates.

Before the end of that year, Mark ended up setting up residence in that basement living room, resting in a beanbag chair pointed at the TV, attending fewer and fewer classes. After our spring semester, I've never seen him since. He disappeared like *ointment*, a word which rubs itself out.

Apprentice Days

Heart Speaks to Heart

It was not a desk. Six handmade wooden crates, stacked two each. Two pine boards going one way, a single one spanning the other, making two sides of a square which I stepped into. It wasn't an office, but it was a workspace. Along one wall, the bench with a pegboard was idle and mostly storage. There, I placed some way of filling the air with music. That was always my first order of business wherever and whenever I moved. Set up tunes: receiver, turntable, tape player, run speaker wire. The components have shrunk over the past twenty-five years, but the presence of music has not. I probably got the stereo going even before unpacking the crates, leveling the planks with wads of folded paper, or carefully placing the glass desktop. In the shadows alongside the stairs stood the mechanical organs of the house: furnace and water heater. When I graduated from college with my degree in English, a Creative Writing major and a minor in Religious Studies, I moved into my parents' home and established my "study" in the basement. Even though I envisioned myself a Poet while at Penn State, I count that year at that desk my first writer's space as Year 01 in my apprenticeship as a writer.

There's no reason anyone should read on. As Emily Dickinson said, "I'm nobody."

I even had to quote her to say that.

In publishing terms, I still aspire to work my way up to becoming a mid-list poet. Like thousands of writers, I've published a couple of books and some chapbooks that few have heard of, fewer have read. I have at least five manuscripts in my files, unpublished, errr, I mean "looking for a publisher." I don't get invitations for my work, let alone my presence at conferences or reading series. And yet, isn't that the state of things for the majority of us? Most writers are nobodies. Framing the issue in marketing terms is false. I suspect even those who have household names can shout "Amen!" when Dickinson says, "How dreary to be somebody!" She says it's "like a frog / To tell your name the livelong day / To an admiring bog!" One *New Yorker* cartoon put it this way, "Sure, he can type the type but can he hype the hype?"

For all writers, the work is what's essential. And that requires becoming a person. From that struggle and in our anonymity, we reach out to each other. Right after declaring her nobody status, Dickinson asks, "Who are you? / Are you nobody, too?" Learning the craft of writing, for me, has been a way to grow in authenticity. And it always starts in the silence of our own private frog pond, or in my case, parents' basement.

I have kept journals since eighth grade, poured out heartfelt letters and love notes all through high school, even writing poems, mocking teachers and imitating textbook samples. I declared my major in English from the first week in State College, where I took up both the Creative Writing option and the Education component because, hey you need something to fall back on, right? With an insight I still don't understand, I saved workshops for when I'd read through my survey courses. But I thought of myself as a writer. More importantly, to me anyway, I thought of myself as a Poet. An Artist. I went barefoot to classes, carrying flip-flops in my backpack. I conformed to the extent of wearing them indoors. I sat under elm trees, reading: Thomas Merton and others on Christian contemplation, D. T. Suzuki's take on Zen, Wordsworth, T. S. Eliot, and E. E. Cummings—I wanted to perceive the heart of things. I wanted to be a mystic. Maybe all I wanted was to show how "sensitive" and "deep" I was. Maybe I had all of that going on, but I certainly didn't know how to craft the language or my own life to merge perception with expression. I was too busy venting and emoting.

After graduation, I gradually wrote less and less until I don't think I was writing very much at all. In my final semester, I'd taken three writing courses, and whatever else I was studying surely required papers. I was tired. I also had to move, get a job (*gasp!*), and begin managing in earnest the details of mature life. I owe a great debt to my father and mother who got me through college without saddling me with financial debt (and I was the seventh of eight to be so fortunate), who set me up with a used car as a gift (again, freeing me from further debt), and who welcomed me back into their house. I wasn't the only one who needed additional support in this way, coming from a big Catholic family, but I knew even then that being a poet is no money-maker. Managing the "worldly affairs" of a life of art would be another hallmark of my apprenticeship. But first I needed a "life of art" to balance with whatever else I was supposed to manage.

In the months after graduating, I wrote some poems over the summer and early fall, but soon the habit dropped away. So many beginning writers say they don't write much when they're happy, but give us depression! Give us anger! Give us the sweet flavor of feeling misunderstood! Then, words avalanche out of us, crashing loudly, an unstoppable force. In my post-graduation period of silence, I questioned whether I *was* a poet. Maybe I only wrote because it had been assigned. Maybe it was yet another way of expressing not a deep need within me, but a powerful desire to please others, to live up to their expectations.

I got a job at *The Cable Guide*, customizing the monthly magazine so viewers could program their VCRs accurately. We formed a creative bunch with many antics. But mostly that first year was shaped by my relationship with M, and our yearlong passion. We'd met at Penn State and moved within miles of each other outside of Philly. Each week, as we chose our destinies, as we chose to embody our values and personalities, we grew apart. Her degree in physics (along with her remarkable hard work and her startlingly acute mind) secured a fistful of job offers; she had accepted her position with General Electric even before we graduated. My English degree (and my penchant for "spontaneity,") did not open employment doors in quite the same way.

She bought furniture (new) to fill out her first apartment; I arranged copy-paper boxes for my bureau in college then, after graduation, I used my childhood furniture. Because of her security clearance, she could not tell me about her work at GE; not likewise limited, I held forth about the Pax Christi meetings seeking peace, in part through protesting GE's defense research. She could see into her professional future; I wasn't willing to plan our weekends. She thought I was "too Bohemian," and I thought she was remarkably acute. When we broke up, further silences emerged in my own life. I turned to literature. I returned to my own roots.

I began with William Pratt's *The Imagist Poem* and Mary Barnard's translation of Sappho. I turned to Rexroth's versions of Chinese and Japanese poems. Listening to George Winston, William Ackerman, or other acoustic instrumentals, I discovered how poetic words can be as full of energy as the classic rock I was reared on. The concentration of feeling in such literature resonated with my own heartbreak, but I loved how experiences hundreds of years apart spoke to each other. I also picked up the Gary Snyder volumes he signed when he came to Penn State, but whom I was too shy to actually speak to, though he sat in on our workshop. Reading his poems in this context, I felt a different relationship to my own landscape peeking up in my heart like a seedling. *Cor ad cor loquitor*, Cardinal Newman wrote. *Heart speaks to heart.* With such company, I didn't feel so alone in the world. My silences were filling with purpose and the community of writers, a community not bound by time or geography.

Down in my basement study, practicing calligraphy, I lettered those tiny poems, letting their images develop in my mind as I had to slow my mind down to lay down each stroke within each letter. I savored the lines, word by word. I relearned the principles of the Imagists, particularly the authoritative authority, Ezra Pound. I began writing description, striving to notice the subtle changes in daily light and seasonal shifts, but also striving to use fewer and fewer words. Well, not exactly. It was never a countable thing. If a phrase isn't needed, cut it, or if something could be said more economically, do it. But the discipline goes beyond such mechanical concerns. When I copied Sappho's or ancient Japanese poems—by hand, a practice I maintain to this day—I couldn't articulate what I was hoping for. What I didn't understand yet was that I love these kinds of poems because they evoke much from as few words as possible. There is a vastness to them, out of proportion to their printed scale. At their best, the concentrated image rises above mere description to meaning. Describing *things* allows inner states to be situated in the world so that the seemingly stable outer world gains the fluidity of emotional forces, personalizing it, while the individual's experience gains the context of the impersonal flow of nature.

With evenings and weekends free, a job that was a draining kind of busywork, I spent many hours in that basement. I'd lived underground in college (and later in grad school) since those apartments are cheapest, so the dark and the yellow buzz of fluorescent lighting was familiar, comforting. Most crucially, I was maintaining a productive solitude, a deepdown friendliness with myself, the person I wake to each morning and fall asleep with each night. Harmonious companionship with one's own self is utmost in any person's life, but especially an artist, since it is out of the sheer mountainside of the heart that all true art springs.

Throughout that year, I saved up money and planned two events. I set time aside for a two-part vacation and then, when I came back, I'd give my notice to the *Cable Guide*: the first week I'd fly out west, and the second, I'd go on retreat. The trip west was to Seattle to visit a former *Cable Guider*, who loved to haunt used bookstores, with a side trip to "meet" my cousin, Kate, living in a cabin by the Pacific, north of San Francisco. I'd only recently learned that Kate was a poet. This was like discovering gravity: a family member who *understands*! The world makes sense after all! We began a correspondence that I am still enriched by. I'd fly from Seattle to San Francisco, rent a car, visit Kate, and before heading back to Seattle, I'd go to City Lights Books. It'd be like a pilgrimage. It was a pilgrimage.

When I got home, I'd take a week-long silent retreat in Maryland, where I'd been on retreats all through college. My Catholic angel-wrestling about becoming a Christian Brother is a different apprenticeship story, but at this point I was still on the horns of my lifelong dilemma: a life of literature or a life of service/ministry? The question was should I pursue a masters in social work of some kind or should I go for an MFA in creative writing? These twin journeys helped begin unknotting that false polarity and set me on my discipleship as a writer.

Questions of Preparation

What's an apprentice need to learn? Between the first inklings about being a writer and through the many pages of what later is called "juvenilia," there is a period of formation that prepares for a life of writing. So what preparation is needed? What skills need to be honed? What knowledge is foundational? If the writing community knew the answers to this, there would be fewer how-to books, and if the academic community knew the formula, there would be less discrepancy in the types of writing programs—graduate, undergraduate, post-graduate, conference-for-credit, low-residency—and there'd be more similar orientation and foci.

Because "writing" is such a vast set of formal constructions with too many intended audiences to reduce to a simple formula, there's no way to standardize. Then there's the variable of the individual writer. I speak for the nobody I am, hoping the questions we entertain and the forces we engage with are similar enough. Each of us struggles to address questions of craft and of self, of the technical and mundane methods and of the philosophical elements. If we're lucky, these questions never resolve themselves completely or for long.

What are the forms I am most able to write in? What forms should I challenge myself to learn? How do I find and can I be found by ideas? How do I keep track of my submissions? What writers are my exemplars? What's a dangling modifier? How do I make a life of writing and maintain healthy relationships? What is "voice," and have

I found mine? What do I do with all these files, drafts, clippings, binders, and computer files? If I have an audience, how do I reach them? If I don't, how do I cultivate one?

After the *Cable Guide*, I took a job leading retreats for young people for the Archdiocese of Philadelphia. In that work, I used Rilke's advice to the young poet to be patient with all that is unresolved in one's heart and to love the questions, not the answers. In fact, he says, don't worry about the answers because you're not ready for them; instead, live the questions. While I was conscious of this effort to remain patient and to live the quest, I was not conscious of these exact writing concerns in my apprentice days. I just kept plucking along, unaware that I'd learned all that much until several events in 2005 helped me reflect. Only in retrospect—from the vantage point of nearly twenty years later—did I realize that I was no longer a beginner. Between the two was this story, which begins with Denise Levertov.

Form and Work

Flying home from my pilgrimage to my one known relative, who not only appreciated poetry but who wrote it herself, I read the two authors my cousin Kate recommended. I'd bought Robert Bly's translation of Rilke's poetry and Denise Levertov's *The Poet in the World*. In "Some Notes on Organic Form," Levertov's words struck the hollow of my secret intuitions, and they resonated with a truth that not only confirmed my experience but has been a source of musing ever since. She starts with a seemingly innocuous statement that behind her conception of organic form in poetry is the idea that "there is form in all things (and in our experience) which the poet can discover and reveal." Artistic creation is not separate from nor in essence different from any other creation. More than a fascinating concept to mull over while pulling my chin, such a conviction establishes a person's stance toward the world and experience, providing a meaningful continuity and a way to engage with it.

For some artists, the world of things and relations is chaotic, but through Protean effort the artist shapes the formless. Novelists know that life has no narrative arc, is full of extraneous details which no writer should leave in, and has been crammed with too many characters, and so the writer creates or at least transforms the meaningful bits so that they contribute to the revelation of personality, relationship, or action. However, Levertov's idea says that there is meaning and shapeliness in our interactions, and so, rather than willful creation, the artist needs receptivity most. A seemingly meaningless chat by the punch bowl at a company holiday party could bear within it the detail that reflects the many dimensions of a co-worker's life. Striving for this kind of attentiveness, I wrote a poem about a receptionist's face as she answered the phone on the anniversary of her son's death—it was exactly the mix of humdrum routine with the profound and emotional that I understood as the form I needed to acknowledge and honor. My stance toward experience has a genuflection in it.

Levertov illuminates her notion of innate form with an image, comparing the coalescing impressions that give rise to the language of a poem to a "constellation,"[4] which struck me a perfect metaphor. Better than "coalescing," certainly. I can imagine that I leaned my head back and gazed out the little plane window at the landscape or the cloudscape below, considering how this constellating occurs in my own life. It happens all the time. And still does. While reading, a lively phrase or startling impression expands in my mind beyond the confines of the page and often evokes emotions connected to completely separate experiences. Then, like stars that may be light-years apart, these varied and disassociated sensations take on a perceivable shape in relation to each other. For example, catching the sunset through silhouetted trees in autumn once during my commute during these years, I recalled a news story about the number of children who die a day of malnutrition, and the third "star," the experience that showed the outline of the poem was the melancholy of autumn, that particular sadness of evening that edges on rage. Or: flipping through a book of artwork, I sense the boundaries of the self blurring as I gaze at a Seurat, as if the man made of dots is my own personality, my own mixture of dark and light, muted and pure, and the language that emerges uses "I" but not the details of my life. Or: vague, leftover dream images of a train station, which have shed the story as well as the meaning (if I knew it) of the dream itself, but the image of the wood planks combines with remembered trips on the SEPTA trains and the imagined stance of my father on his commute into Philadelphia. This constellation could still be compelling enough and so, as Levertov says, it "wakes in [the poet] this demand: the poem."[5]

Rather than waiting on sufficiently "poetic" experiences or reserving writing for when emotions are overflowing so powerfully that I *must* write, Levertov says that paying attention to subtler influences may induce the same "demand." This new orientation marks a tidal shift of perception, one that many beginning writers do not make, especially poets. It moves from an understanding of writing as a means of expression to a means of discovery. Beginning with a description of the train station and ending with a poem about my father is unexpected, unpredictable, and exhilarating.

To engage in this process of attending to the liminal interaction between outer experience and inner impression, I took instruction from Rainer Maria Rilke's own example. He transitioned from poems of feeling (*The Book of Hours*, for example) to books of *things*, published in the two collections of *New Poems* from 1907 and 1908. And his mentor was the sculptor Auguste Rodin. Even now I have the image of Rodin pacing his studio as assistants worked on various components of *The Gates of Hell*, so perhaps one was polishing downward-pointing hands of *The Three Shades*, who overlook the suffering contained in those monumental doors; another was shaping the leaning back of *The Thinker* who ponders the scene also from above. Meanwhile, the master threads through all this activity, supervising, and as he does so, he takes clay in his hands, shaping it, and lays small figures here and there among all this production. Always working. How much of this is romanticized, half-remembered and half-created, I don't know, but the spirit of this artist motivates me to this day. When Rilke became

Rodin's secretary, the poet asked how he might improve his writing practice, how does an artist come up with material for his art? "*Travailler, travailler, travailler!*" shouted Rodin. Not by musing or waiting on inspiration, but "work, work, work." He suggested that the poet learn to observe things, not just look at them, but learn to see. "Go to the zoo," he instructed, "and observe the animals. Two to three weeks might not be enough."

The enterprise of learning to see a panther, for example, or a grasshopper, or the twist of hair on a woman's neck, or the changing light on a marble angel's wing—as Rilke's own poems were doing—took me to a continuing education class in drawing. I drew my hand, my guitar case, a jar of pencils, a rock on my desk. The objects themselves didn't make the artwork, I quickly realized, but the quality of the technique. Craft, not feeling. The material is as important as the content. I continued exploring the effects of line breaks and imagery, and now I knew I had to go deeper—yes, work more on the craft of poems, but I also had to learn how to shape my life to do that work.

Candles in the Hatband

The lives of artists were instructive. Rodin's example for Rilke continued, but I also learned how Cezanne created a two-dimensional patterning on canvas even while suggesting three-dimensional landscapes or how Van Gogh embodied his feeling in the thickness of paint and measure of brushstroke. From these biographies, I also learned the work of hauling your easel out into the open air to paint the mountain in storm-shadow and morning light, as Cezanne did, or to stick candles in your hatband to paint after dark, as Van Gogh did. "Work, work, work."

I subscribed to *The Writer's Digest*, which still features articles on how to characterize your villain in a detective story alongside how to write a query letter to an editor to get a contract for an article project, and get paid for it. Story after story chronicled the leap from paid work into the unknown of freelance writing, the difficulties and the thrills. Freelancers need a lot of tools. They research and produce the work, they get savvy about markets so they can sell the work, and they secure the contract and hopefully the payment. It's a job. In fact, it's at least three jobs. Thinking of "writing" as what we do with words is such a limited view of our work. I never harbored any illusions that I'd make a living as a poet, but I also had to admit that I thought those who successfully published books had it made. They were somebody while I was still a nobody. Far from it. The work never ends, if you're lucky.

As a poet, correspondence with the visual arts has been an invaluable part of my apprenticeship. At a very practical level, I was able to translate the easel in the fields to an ever-evolving "system" of notebooks and binders for keeping things straight. I didn't want any more napkin drafts. I wanted to be ready when I sensed the constellation taking shape, and I wanted to keep track of my various drafts, journaling, and notes on reading. I evolved various methods for revising poems from handwritten pages in notebooks to hand-cut ¾ sized pages (over and over) to typed versions in binders, which I then revised more. Once my poetry notebook was two hand-sanded thin boards a friend created for me, taking a break from building his own boat. He oiled the wood by hand to a warm glow. Seeing how devoted Tom was to the materials reminded me of the physicality of writing. I used rings that snapped closed, and so could replace the contents but have a permanent structure. Wanting to save paper—and to avoid the pressure that fine stationary can create to write something "worthy" of such materials—for years I used the back sides of computer paper in my notebook. Wanting to save on disposable pens, I bought my first fountain pen while at Penn State, and ironically once I plunked down $35 for a single fine writing instrument, I never lost it. Buy ten in a pack, and they were gone in a month. Now I buy recycled, sewn classroom copybooks (college ruled, only, please) which I wrap in a book cover given to me by the daughter of an A-bomb survivor I'd written about when I lived in Hiroshima. The material itself forms a network of meaning with echoes of associations from my life.

Despite models in the visual arts and great delight in these tools (and so a greater desire to actually use them), all this concern for a working system still embarrasses me. When I consider it within my own experience, I know that to honor the unexpected formation of "constellations" and to see work through with the dedication I observed in painters and sculptors requires regularity and practiced habits that encourage me to engage in the work. But whenever I speak of it to others, the shadow of obsession passes over, the specter of being perceived as weird or freakish chills me, and the many mouths of doubts come nibbling, asking if my so-called work deserves all this stuff and energy. These are simply the stones the village kids hurled at Cezanne as he lumbered out to paint his beloved Sainte-Victoire mountain. If inspiration was like being struck by lightning, artists need to wander around in thunderstorms, and we need some equipment to receive that burst of energy. I don't know a writer who doesn't work out their own beloved system for doing the work and keeping track of the various stages of all the projects.

Levertov, in "A Poet's View," answers these hecklers when she states her belief that

> *creative gifts confer on those who possess them the obligation to nurture them in a degree proportionate to the strength and demands of the gift (which, paradoxically, cannot be determined unless the opportunity for its development be provided, which may mean sacrifices and imbalances in other areas of life).*[6]

In addition, my early immersion in the working methods of visual artists gave me a way to enjoy paintings and sculpture in ways I never had access to. I'll never forget going to the Rodin Museum in Philly, a tiny, quiet haven that reminds no one of Rocky but is not far from where the famous southpaw ran up the steps. Outside the Rodin Museum, I craned my neck to gaze at all the twisted and twisting figures in *The Gates of Hell*. Inside, each pose in *The Burghers of Calais* carried a distinctive emotion; I was reading a short story in this seemingly static sculpture. The dramatic narrative of the visual arts confirmed for me the revelatory detail, the illuminated moment which suggested whole stories. In this way, the visual arts also brought me back to haiku and the Imagists.

The Work of Reading

Once I landed in Seattle, clutching my Rilke and Levertov, I traveled around with the best guide for this moment in my life. Mark hounded used bookstores like no one I've ever known; he once stared at me dumbfounded amid the piles of an Atlantic Book Warehouse when I agonized over spending a few bucks for a find. "Never," he declared as if he'd just come down the mountain in mystic robes, "never not buy used books!" He showed me Pike Place, where there was not yet a Starbucks but countless bookstores. There, I loaded up on all the black-and-white New Directions editions of Rilke, Levertov, and Gary Snyder I could find.

Having returned to *The Imagist Poem,* Sappho's fragments, and Asian poems, having dabbled in drawing to learn to see, and having dedicated myself to a notebook system that symbolized a commitment to my writing, I was ready for another important lesson. How to read. Of course, I read in college; I had to since it was assigned. Well, I read most of it. And some of that I even read well. Not much, I think now, but a little of my assigned and chosen reading I allowed to measure me, to lift my sights to what's possible. Many writing articles talk about how beginning writers need to discover "their voice," but that's wrong-headed. Not only do most writers have many voices, but we join a chorus, a conversation, an ongoing expedition to the limits of language where it returns into silence and the limits of human experience where mystery lives. An apprentice needs to find traveling companions. In my literature classes, professors urged us to learn the tradition, while in creative writing classes workshop leaders urged us to go beyond the past, to make it new. Over and over again, John Haag wrote "Read more" on my poems.

I had always scribbled in the margins of my textbooks, copying what teachers told me passages meant, footnoting ideas. In one Religious Studies course on Paul Tillich, I had to write notes just to keep track of those winding Germanic sentences and abstract philosophical language. That kind of engagement with the text is important—without an active pencil, I'd fall asleep bent over Tillich's *Systematic Theology*—but it can be merely functional. Once I entered my apprenticeship, I began to really take notes. I copied out of books the parts that engaged me. I allowed the words to pass through me, from eye to brain/heart, to hand. Just as food passes through the body, nourishing it as it does, this writing was how I devoured books. I copied examples of language leaping, of pulsating imagery, and of concepts that didn't need to be remembered for an exam but for the formation of my heart. Some are cryptic to me now because of the range of material I was dealing with. I copied words I didn't know ("spritely"), graffiti on an overpass ("I © Sue—#1 Sweetheart"), lyrics I'd heard for years but now stood in relief against the blank wall of radio songs, lines from Rilke's *Book of Hours*, quippy sayings on the back of cars ("I Hate Bumperstickers"), the quote I gave from Levertov's "A Poet's View," long passages from

Barry Lopez's book *Arctic Dreams*, pages and pages on artists, and scraps of poems by Theodore Roethke, Stanley Kunitz, Maxine Kumin, and others.

I had no idea how much this was preparing me for graduate school, but I was paying attention to my own experience. I was learning that a constellation can reveal itself out of discrete aspects of everyday experience to make the first demand of a potential poem; however, only those who obey that demand by stepping into solitude and following the first stumblings of language find their way into a poem. In a similar way, there is a momentary pause in the process of reading. In that hesitation, the tide shifts. No longer are words and ideas coming in, but a response goes out. That interaction of self with self is what I record. It is not merely receiving what I read but gathering ways my thinking and feeling extend along the shore of others' writing. I see it as grateful respect for writers, like me, who articulate truths I have not lived into or only intuited, and so they remain inchoate until put into words. This system of copying passages continued through grad school and to this day.

Taking notes on my reading, a process I call scribing, evolved into another working method that I consider essential to any apprenticeship. The method is not important, but the lesson and the practice is. With all the poems workshopped in all the creative writing programs all over the country, only one person in my undergraduate classes and only one in my grad classes ever discussed creating books. I am grateful to Maggie Anderson (who was a visiting poet at Penn State) and to Keith Wilson (who was a visiting poet at BGSU) for the clues they provided. But from their threads,

I had to find my own way through the labyrinth of writing books, not just individual poems. All writers have to. Just as I had no idea how helpful my method of scribing would prove to be, I did not set out to learn how to construct a collection. I was simply following my own instincts.

Within weeks of my return from bookstore hunting with Mark in Seattle and my pilgrimage to San Francisco to "meet" Kate and visit City Lights, I moved out of my parents' home, quit my deadening job at the *Cable Guide*, and moved in with two friends. This was about a year after graduating from college, and my apprenticeship was taking real shape now.

Frank and I had gone to high school together, and the two of us knew Christian from our mutual participation in the formation program for the Christian Brothers. Along with as many as 40 or so others, we all joined up for retreats throughout our undergraduate years; Christian and Frank went on for a year at the Novitiate. Christian spent those months we shared our Henry Avenue apartment in Philadelphia revising his novel. He made a contract with himself, even as he taught history at a vocational high school for the first time, that he would write for five hours a week. An hour a day, and if he missed a day during the week, he'd make it up on the weekend. He said this was how he drafted the novel the previous year. And he stuck with it. His example, which I witnessed up close, remains a model for me because of the way he accommodated visits from his now-wife, Mary, his teaching obligations, and all the other comings and goings of life, but through it all he stayed true to his commitment to his own work. Since Frank was also teaching, but also finishing a grad program and trying to keep a long-distance relationship going, Christian and I shared many meals together, countless conversations about the writing life (and other topics, of course), and many hours of quiet reading.

I was working as a retreat leader for the Department of Youth Services of the Archdiocese of Philadelphia. Our team created reflection experiences—many of them for one day—for school kids and those preparing to receive a new sacrament, like Confirmation or Holy Eucharist, but also weekend retreats for high school students. The writing life and the religious life may seem opposed, but they share a deep and relevant core. Religious experience and spiritual articulation is an exercise in imagination and metaphor, since what we encounter is literally beyond words, our language inevitably falls short of the ineffable. We traveled all over the metropolitan area in our work, which I loved. Our offices were forty-five minutes north of our apartment, so my commute was the reverse of most. I recall keeping a book on the passenger seat, and at red lights, I'd read a Merwin poem or part of one, holding in my mind as I drove the next stretch some phrasing. I was furnishing the palace of my mind with images and poetic forms.

When my two roommates began researching then applying for graduate programs, I was tempted, but I was still going back and forth about whether I'd study some kind of service/ministry or creative writing. The core may be the same, but the expression in any single person's life takes distinct forms. My schizophrenia about how to express my calling was embodied in my visit to both the University of

Washington, where I knocked on David Waggoner's door to ask what he meant when he scribbled "sorry to say no" on rejection after rejection from *Poetry Northwest*, and to the Seattle University which had a Pastoral Studies program designed to not only deepen one's individual faith but also prepare one for community service as well. Not ready for formal education, I opted not to go to grad school but continue my informal apprenticeship instead. We dismantled our apartment, said our farewells, and I moved closer to our Bucks County offices, taking a room in a house in Fort Washington.

There, I unpacked my boxes of books and lined them on my Ikea shelves across from my crate and pine board "desk" and was stunned by how little I could recall from these volumes I knew I'd read. Equipped with a word processer, not a computer, but typewriter that had a seven line screen and some memory—something like twelve pages—I embarked on a project to rectify this forgetting. I began writing my impressions of a collection once I'd read it. I included my questions and confusions, since these were like formal journal entries. I started with books I'd read before but couldn't conjure any of the themes. Of Sharon Olds, I wrote that "It's not that I don't like these poems…I feel incomplete, though." Commenting on Merwin's *The Drunk in the Furnace*, I admitted that at Penn State, where I first began reading his work, I found the poems beautiful, but I didn't understand them, so in this period I started again with the Copper Canyon edition of *The First Four Books*. "Finishing them, I felt as if I should have done my homework more in high school, and I had lots of reading to do just to see if I got the gist of these poems. Then came *The Drunk in the Furnace."* I've experienced such breakthroughs since then with T.S. Eliot's work, which I likewise read enjoying the music but finding the sense elusive, and some of Pound's work. John Haag was right: the more I read, the more I was prepared to read better. I wrote commentary about Anna Akhmatova (D.M. Thomas translation), Gary Snyder (both a book I'd read before and a new one), Pablo Neruda, Mary Oliver, and others I continue to read and learn from, including Carolyn Forché.

I'd read Forché's memoir of her work in El Salvador while in Maggie Anderson's class, but without making the connection I picked up *The Country Between Us* for $1.98 (in hardcover) at Atlantic Book Warehouse mostly because it was a hardcover collection of poems for less than two bucks. In my post-reading typed reflection, not only do I explain what I liked about the poems, but I could connect images across poems and see how they spoke to each other. I was learning to see not only how individual poems are constructed but also how collections are created. Is it Frost who said that if there are twenty-four poems in a book, the collection itself is the twenty-fifth poem?

Through graduate school I continued to jot these reflections, but soon I was directing them toward other readers, and thus I began writing book reviews. It was only after earning my MFA and after volunteering in Hiroshima for two and a half years that this practice of reflecting on whole books revealed the structure of a collection. I reviewed John Balaban's selected poems and could see how the poet's selection of work, the grouping into sections, and the sequence within them all composed meaning just as the images, rhythms, and lineation did for a poem. Maybe it was the fact that I was familiar with his work and knew how he changed the sequence that heightened my awareness. Nevertheless, the process of reading carefully and writing about others' collections made important principles and structures settle into place. It would be years still before I could use that recognition since knowledge precedes skill, but I believe I learned it from the inside out, beginning with a practice of typing up a few pages after reading a book I enjoyed. What begins in delight ends in wisdom.

Open Mic and Closed Audience

Through reading I was able to discover my own lineage in the tradition of American poetry, if I have one. While *The Imagist Poem* was a fine textbook for classes, it was only later that I sensed how the concerns of those Modernists melded with my own interest in the visual arts. And it was only by reading widely, attentively, and reflectively that I saw the connections from Pound and Asian poetry to Gary Snyder and Kenneth Rexroth, from William Carlos Williams to Levertov (and countless others, of course), and from Robert Bly and James Wright so-called Deep Image and surrealism. Forché and Levertov led me to Akhmatova and Neruda, who led me to Bly and Wright, and so on. Perhaps I could have saved lots of time by reading a single book that traced these influences—which I have since then—but discovering it myself was not merely knowledge but identity. I felt welcomed into the community, and I felt some responsibility. To what? For what? I'm still not sure I can articulate. The experience of finding in these people's work impulses and commitments that mirrored my own was more personally affirming than simply knowing what those artistic concerns were.

An apprentice situates himself or herself not only in relation to the world and to the structures of experience but also in relation to the community of culture. Art, like the idea of the "communion of saints" I grew up with in my Catholic imagination, helps us transcend time and geography to discover kinship with strangers from other eras, countries, and cultures. These are my people. In this company, I am not *strange* or *weird*, as I sometimes felt even in my supportive and loving family.

Likewise, beginning artists of all kinds need to wrestle with their relationship to their contemporaries. Who is my community now? Do I have an audience? Just as I waited to take creative writing classes until I had learned some literary history, I did not launch into giving poetry readings. This was before slams, "spoken word artists," and other contemporary ways poetry fills the air with the music of the human voice. Mostly there were open mics or reading series with a featured poet, followed by an open mic. Just as I didn't feel ready for formal education for years after graduating from Penn State, I felt I was not ready to take to the podium, and so my first experience reading a poem in public came after a long period of preparing.

Even though I was an English major all four years, I don't recall a very many poetry readings in that time. There were rumors that coffeehouse-style events were once held, and professors and students read and sang, but that era apparently was over; the generation of the MFA, with its grad readings and visiting writers, had not yet arrived. One event was held in the loungy English Department mail room. John Haag, with his white hair and bold moustache, sat at the edge of a counter by the cubbies, urging on another reader but never resorting to the tyrannies of a sign-up sheet. I still have an image of a poem by one of my profs from my very first term about waking "still webbed with dream." It was my first vivid experience of hearing a poem that became fully present within me—imagery full figured in my imagination, a concept that was clinched in the ending. I asked for a copy. Sensing something of a connection, I asked Edgar Knapp about his composing process. His response was inexplicable; he said he no longer wrote poems. In my adolescent mind, being a poet was permanent. I had to learn so much about the fluidity of identity, about the multiplicity of identities.

The other event was hosted by grad students, in my junior or senior year (1985 or 86), and it involved an actual podium, a microphone, and a clipboard for potential readers. I did sign up to read a couple of my own pieces; gratefully, my spiritual advisor from the Christian Brothers was in town, and his support enabled me to lift my tiny, shaking voice to an audible level. But my dominant impression of this formal event was that there was an in-group. Not only was I not in that circle, but part of me did not want to get too close even to the periphery. This was not my community. It seemed that there was too much self-congratulation, use of poetry to show off the writer's erudition, and lots of witty mockery that no one escaped except those whose own wit formed a cool protective bubble. There wasn't even the cloying self-expression of sincere feeling so common in open mic readings I've experienced since then. Well, if I leave my contribution out of it.

Readings were important, though, because the work, which has been labored over in solitude and over so much time, can directly and instantaneously encounter readers, who nod, smile, or say *hmm*. It is communal and dynamic. In an early workshop, I met a fellow student named John Fagan, whose poems at the time completely put me off. "Ziggurat Poems," a classmate called John's cool constructions full of mythologies none of us were familiar with. But John himself was open and authentic, and he believed that poetry was a means of heart-felt communion. He told me that he'd held living room readings, inviting friends to his own apartment for an evening of refreshment, and then he'd read. Following his example, I tried one. I used my awkward skills at calligraphy to make invitations, set up chairs, put on music, and read. Frankly, I don't know how it came off, but I never hosted another. Was it because it requires a more forceful promotion of one's self and one's work? Was it because I got negative or (even worse) lukewarm feedback? I know I felt too self-serving, but I still feel that when I encourage people to buy my books. Nevertheless, I love giving readings and knew I had to learn how to do it well.

In the years after Penn State, reading *Writers Digest* with its guidance that we all understand both our "markets" and their readers, I knew I needed to figure out this whole reading/self-promotion thing. I need to state as clearly as I can that I haven't yet. However, in 2005, I attended a panel at the Association of Writers & Writing Programs (AWP) Conference. Each panelist took on a different aspect of giving good readings, confirming what I had discovered; I even had a few things to contribute to the discussion that followed. It made me realize that one component of my apprenticeship was over. Between my living room reading and this affirmation from the community, though, were all kinds of events, one at a bar with a line of men's backs steeling themselves against our words, coffee house readings with espresso machines whining away constantly, one in a bookstore where the host used a stopwatch and cut off readers mid-sentence when their time was up, quite a few where the featured reader was given a free cup of coffee and whatever money listeners put into the hat or basket or cigar box (once a friend put his Visa card in for me), and countless open readings where most in the audience were flipping through their own folders just biding time until their five minutes at the mic.

Living on the fringes of the metro sprawl of Philadelphia, I thought there would be readings galore, but I had to search them out. Formal events—like W.D. Snodgrass at some college or Robert Hass somewhere in the arts community—were easy enough to find since the sponsoring organization has enough money to pay such a big name (in poetry, anyway) so they typically advertised. Listings in the classifieds helped. Finding a seat at these headliner events was sometimes the challenge. I remember listening to Robert Creeley, clutching my knees in a hallway, catching his voice through the open door but not catching many of his poems.

The informal readings were a little trickier. I did find one in a used bookstore that took me hours to get to, in a neighborhood I never returned to. I also found some at a bar, at an off-hour, so it didn't interfere with an actual crowd. Finding these events required networking, a process of knowing people and their concerns so that they can inform you of upcoming readings or introduce you to people you should know or give you the skinny on how to get on the list as a featured reader. Since I don't network well, this didn't happen for me. I attend readings, listen appreciatively, and leave. It's such a personal experience for me. Plus, some people's style of networking involves a great deal of egoism. It's not mutual; it's more take-and-take. Some writers are always on the make—some trying to score someone to sleep with and some trying to score their next reading, publication, or residency. To be more successful at networking, I'd have to develop more tolerance for this part of the dynamic—the po-biz—and work through it so I can arrive at the more truly communal aspect. It's alive and well, and I glimpsed it even then in the selfless work of the organizers, even the grizzled guy with the stopwatch. No one's getting paid, and no one's getting famous.

Still, most of what I learned was a kind of negative space, a what-not-to-do. Poet after poet showing off. Look at me, listen to me! Aren't I clever? Aren't I sensitive? Poem after poem that are really sermons, an attempt to convert. Christian, Wiccan, devoted atheism, and every other version of religious belief, of course, but also exhortations to convert us to some version of Earth-loving Hugabuggie or from the High Church of Consumerism or any number of political positions. Long Whitmanesque lists of grievances and offenses.

Conviction to a world-view, a vision of systems and relations, is not the problem, though these readings did feel far longer than their allotted time. The real problem is they assumed a great deal about the "you" or "us" in the poem. And that set the speaker/poet up as the expert, the priest, the righteous one laying out "our" error or "the truth." A self-contained world. If the reader/listener already lives inside the worldview, all is well, but if not, the poem doesn't convince, it bullies. This problem mirrors the personally self-absorbed work. Others have named and analyzed the pervasive experience of immature writers who spill their guts or "share" their anguish and angst, so there's no need to recount those experiences. Again, listening to evening after evening of these kinds of poems formed in me an important influence to wrestle with. There is value in honoring individual struggles and our common humanity. It's an exercise in empathy. But poetry can do more. It can create community. Still, these readings raised good questions to pose for myself. It was valuable. It's one thing to realize which influences to avoid, but how do we know which influences to follow? How do we learn the direction we need to go? If my poems were not going to be conclusions articulated, what could they be?

As an audience member myself, what do I *want* when I attend a reading? What do I hope for? What do I carry away from a good reading? At a practical level, witnessing the trembling papers distract even the reader or leaning closer and closer to just catch a few words of nervous poets who whisper or can't direct their voice toward the mic taught me what to avoid when I got my chance in front of the folding chairs. I had to learn to expect that nervous energy and make use of it. I learned to start with a poem I'm familiar with, one I like and know well enough not to rely on the page too much. Beginning with other people's poems helps me set the bar higher, to name what I aspire to, and so to keep me humble and focus on poetry, not on me. Overly-theatrical readers who came off insincere showed me that style is important but must enhance the drama and intensity of the language, not exceed it. This returned me again and again to the voice in the poem. Beyond typical amateur mistakes, feeling the aimlessness of a famous poet flipping through his book while applying Chapstick as he decided what will happen next made me seek to make a reading a whole, a complete experience. Excellent readings showed me that they could be more than a random set of poems, just as a collection could. If we are to actually give *a* reading, we could use the selection, order, thematic development, and even the patter between poems can create a whole composition. I think of it like a concert: don't musical artists put a great deal of effort into the playlist and rehearsals? Why not poets? Even jam bands and jazz ensembles practice their solos and improvisations.

Nearly twenty years after setting up that crate-and-board desk in my parent's basement, in 2005, not only did I attend the AWP panel on readings, but that year I was also the featured reader at a local poetry festival. In the audience, kids and their proud parents waited for their prizes in the awards ceremony that followed my reading. Other community members and poetry lovers filled out the room. Suppressing my desire to hog the mic (which is considerable), I knew that most listeners were not there to hear me, but they had a significant experience with poetry. Keeping audience in mind, I selected work that was largely narrative, mixing ones about my time in the Cub Scouts and other childhood experiences with a greenhouse poem by Theodore Roethke, Robert Hayden's perfect "Those Winter Sundays," and other "covers." I didn't realize it at the time, but this reading gave me the opportunity to put into action many the principles and structures I'd been developing all through my twenty-year apprenticeship.

Formal, Ongoing Apprenticeships

Eventually, I did apply to MFA programs and was rejected by most. Or, if accepted, I was not granted an assistantship, but I was not willing to go into debt for a degree in fine arts. Bowling Green State University accepted me and paid for my schooling. After three years out of school and into my informal apprenticeship, I was ready. I had a system for drafting and revising my work, for keeping track of submissions, and for reflecting on my reading. I was eager to explore styles and voices, traditions and lineages within the long history of poetry, to widen my timeless community.

While at BGSU, I learned from my fellow candidates as I took their influences and intentions seriously, trying their techniques and taking what I could from my many failures.

I attended the grad readings in Prout Chapel religiously. We organized a reading series at Grounds for Thought, a bookstore and coffee shop in town.

I am still grateful for several great influences during that time. Michael Mott, who led my first grad workshop, invited us to examine poems from the intention of the writer. Michael also oversaw my thesis, and despite nursing his dying wife, he honored my work by penciling suggestions on draft after draft. Another important influence was Keith Wilson, a visiting writer, who brought the living poetic of the Objectivists together with a mysticism that was itself luminous and had no need to convert others to. The third major influence was working on the *Mid-American Review* with Ken Letko, John Bradley, George Looney, and many, many others.

At the *Mid-Am*, individual readers would evaluate the submissions; if two said no, it was packed back in its SASE. For those with enough yeses, we'd gather as an editorial team, read them aloud, and discuss each poem. Passionate, ranging discussions. We honored the work. Even the proofreading respected the work. Once the proof pages were ready, we gathered in pairs, one reading from the writer's manuscript and the other looking at the proofs. We read each comma, all the capital letters, and every open-quote, close-quote. I am grateful for this formal stage in my apprenticeship and for the friendships that continue. My spouse and I left Bowling Green to become volunteers in Hiroshima, and then we moved back to the States, and eventually I become a community college faculty member.

My first and second books came out within a few months of each other, more than fifteen years after completing my MFA. Each cover is graced by artwork by people I know. Each collection has been praised for its haiku-like imagery, the long fulfillment of effort and discipline, of intuition and guesswork, of thousands of bad poems (hopefully learned from), and of the assistance of so many people despite there only being one name on the cover. By the time the collections were tangible objects in the world, some poems were decades old, and I was already working on new books.

All art enjoys a vast history as well as a vast interiority within each maker, so the work goes on. To remind myself of this truth, above my desk I display a quote by Theodore Roethke. I now understand it at a level I couldn't twenty years ago. "Eternal apprenticeship is the life of the true poet." Whether any one of us is a "true poet" or not may be up to others to decide, but I am committed to going on with my apprenticeship, nonetheless, a nobody among nobodies.

The Memorial Chain

Nineteen years after my father died at the end of May, from New Mexico, my sister Julie called our brother Michael, in Bucks County outside Philadelphia, who called me in upstate New York to say that we were going to make a "chain of stories" about our Dad to commemorate the anniversary of his death. One of my seven siblings would call, we'd exchange stories, and I'd contact the next one in line. Get something ready. June 4th was just days away.

What story should I relate?

The time he and I were driving to the Reunion and met up for lunch somewhere in Jersey with Moose? Afterwards, he and Moose, like leap-frogging teenagers, passed each other on the highway, heads rigidly straight and eyes riveted on the road. But one time Dad gave Moose a big fat finger as he zoomed by, and another time Moose cradled the trophy the Reunion golf tournament winner would go home with—the image already indicating who that prize was going to.

The time he slapped me? Right across the face. We lived in the Wayne house, so I had to be in primary school. It's not much of a story since I can't recall what occasioned it or what happened afterwards. What's remarkable, though, is that it's the only time I ever recall him raising a hand to me. Mom threatened when any of us got to be too much: "You wait until your father gets home," and we would then face the music. But being the seventh of eight kids, I got the mellower version of the Enforcer, and I remember him always being fair and reasonable. So that story won't work.

The message he wrote on a poem I'd sent him? A bad piece, thinking about it now, but as a son's letter to his father, it has a sincerity that doesn't embarrass me. Much. The poem starts, "You used to scare me" but lets him know that "I am drawn to you, learning." Written when I was in college, I may have been lifting my gaze from my own self to recognize and honor others' perspectives; I like to think so. The poem shifts to an awareness of my father's mortality and ends with an invitation to make new memories. He sent the original back to me, with that line about his death circled in a black flair, with this note: "Not to worry I talked to My Lord & He said I can't take it with me so I told Him I'm not going. Love Dad." That's the story. I started searching for this document; it was perfect. Dad's faith, humor, and distinctive communication style were all there.

His way of communicating suited his business career. My father worked for IBM for nearly thirty years, starting in the 1950s, when computers weren't quite as common as they are now. Big Blue, as IBM was known, was a family-oriented institution. Although it moved up-and-coming employees, like my dad, as regularly as the military, it also hosted picnics in the summer and holiday parties in December. IBM also meant lifetime employment, or at least that was the code, until relatively recently. Put these two together and you get a network of IBMers who stayed in touch professionally, took vacations together through incentive programs, and welcomed newly relocated members of the tribe to the area. Keeping in touch was very important to my father. Because his company was loyal to him, he was a company man. A salesman, like his father, he went on to manage sales teams. This IBM legacy carried into the next generation, too, so that at one point or another three of my siblings worked for the computer giant, and a fourth is an engineer but liaisons with sales teams for another tech-related outfit.

    The IBM and business world genes skipped me, though. My father and I are very different people. When I announced my desire to be a writer and to major in English, he urged that I study teaching as well. Just in case. Have a fallback. Or Journalism, he suggested. Actually, he didn't suggest exactly. His way of communicating often involved questions. It was a chess match, and he'd lead with something open-ended. "What do you know about journalism?" he'd ask, drawing out my queen. And when I had to concede that I knew nothing, he could point out that it was worth finding out. "You don't know it's not for you, then." Checkmate. Questions were his hallmark. Once, after dark in the summer, still around the long dinner table, now joined by some of my older brothers' and sisters' friends, my father elicited conversation, starting with his trademark declaration, "I've got a question." It could be anything from classics like "If you could have dinner with anyone living, dead, or fictional, who would it be and why?" to "When do you think a person is in 'the prime of life'?" That night, the sea air breezed through the jalousie windows, making candles flicker. I don't recall the question, but I know everyone chimed in, and he'd maestro the conversation, drawing people in, letting the shy know they were coming up and wouldn't escape. I was still in grade school, but he asked me what I thought. Who knows what I said. Inevitably, someone tried to turn tables, "Mr. Doc, what do you think? When do you think the prime of life is?" But he'd rope in someone else before answering, if at all. It went on for hours, if I remember right. The sunset light dimmed into actual night, and eventually my siblings and friends headed out. But they stayed and talked a long while. When he took his turn, he always answered that question the same way. "Right now," he'd say. "I'm in the prime of life right now." Years later, after my oldest brother's bachelor party, one of his friends recalled that summer evening on the porch, and said he'd never seen anything like it. Who hangs out with their parents like that? During the summer!? I remember his astonishment when he turned to me and underscored his point, saying that "he even asked you what you thought—and you were a kid."

Conversation was my father's art form. Long before restaurant servers started coming to the table to introduce themselves and welcome us like it was their house, pledging to "take care of you tonight," my father spoke to wait staff personally. He'd ask their name, and then address them, always by name. He'd also address cashiers, back when they had to key in each item's price, asking, "What do you like most about your job?" And he'd look at their tag and call them name when they answered. It was always, "What do you like most?" or "What are the top three reasons?" He engaged people personally and, with the deft gesture of an practiced craftsman, turned them toward the good.

He once told me about a technique he evolved to motivate a manager or other employee to buy into some project he wanted them on. Instead of telling them how it would affect their prospects for promotion or stressing the importance or urgency of the enterprise, he'd start by saying, "I need your help with something…"

At his funeral, my brother Chris eulogized him by noting that our father wasn't the kind found tinkering in the garage. We didn't learn to fix the lawn mower from him. He was fascinated by what makes people tick. He sought to discover what their goals and interests are. His people skills included a sense of humor. He had the kind of humor that included joke-telling that could match any situation to a story with a punch line. "That reminds me," he'd launch in, "of Stosh in the trenches of World War I." Or he'd ask if you'd heard about the guy who tried out for community theater. ("Hark! The cannons are roaring!") If someone offered him an after-dinner drink, port, say or sherry, off he went. ("Sherry, by all means…") But he also had the kind of wit that could jot a note on a poem and in few words express so much.

The problem with my contribution to the chain of stories that Julie proposed was that I couldn't find the copy of the poem with Dad's retort. I intended to scan and email it to whoever called, and so I put a physical link in the electronic chain. As I reflected on the poem—especially that bit in the middle about Dad dying—I recalled that, at times, I found his optimism relentless and social engagement exhausting. Maybe this is just a lingering feeling from the vantage point of a brooding teenager. And I did my share of brooding. But I hope there's something more to it than that. I hope I do more than "brood." In my writing, I seek to honor the world in ways that demand an honesty that honors "negative" aspects of life as death, deadening working conditions, and longing without relief. As I've grown to claim my temperament, I no longer see myself as moody or touchy, but reflective. But looking back I know I spent hours in high school and college in my room reading, journaling, strumming my guitar, or writing poetry. Confounding behavior for such a socially adept man as my father, I'm sure.

Maybe that poem and those mixed emotions wouldn't work after all. With folders and files spread out on my desk, I considered other stories I could share. I remembered an incident that had no real significance, except that it happened and, out of the countless daily occurrences of anyone's childhood, it's a little remarkable when one stands out in memory when so many others have drifted away completely. It was a Saturday, and I was in grade school, so the house was still full of my older siblings. Why he chose me to do errands, I don't know, but it was just the two of us. Such precious time. Whatever other stops we made in Wayne that day are lost to me, but we had to pick up dry cleaning, which was next to the drug store. In Wayne back then there was a Rexall's, which still had a counter with stools and actual fountain drinks, but we didn't go there. We went to the now-typical strip mall style drug store. It was in the same lineup as the Acme, and it was new and shiny, not like the worn down Rexall's over on North Wayne Avenue. The key to the whole story is the rack of candy at the checkout. In a family of eight kids, we didn't have chips or pretzels or candy lying around. My Dad bought a Heath Bar. A single one. Then he told me, "Heath's are my favorite, and the best thing about these," he said removing the brownish wrapper, "is that they come with two pieces." That's it, really. That's the whole story.

The story is brief, but it taught me a lesson that is so deeply coded in my nervous system, my very bloodstream, that I'm not sure I can name it. It has something to do with the fact that it was better to be sharing *his* favorite sweet than to have been given my own. It also marked me as distinctive in the family, special somehow, though both my mother and father were deliberate to reflect to each of us that we had our own God-given gifts and talents. Still, the light of his love shined on me that day, setting me apart from the others. No favorites, maybe, but I felt favored.

Having landed on my story, I waited for the call. But the anniversary of Dad's death came and went. Nothing. I made a half-hearted attempt to find the poem again, but I started thinking I wouldn't need it. The chain seemed to have been broken. Without Dad's shepherding, the project probably got abandoned. My father was an organizer; he was on the phone, making arrangements, checking people's progress. Quick, functional, but holding the network together. I still have one of his notes on IBM punch cards, from about a year before his death in 1991. He must have kept a stash of those old computer cards, which were about the size of a regular business envelope but rounded at the corners. Often he'd sign them "KIT, Dad"—Keep in Touch. Never a full letter, like I still do, but lots of these quick KIT cards. Another hallmark of his management of details. And relationships. On this particular note, he gave me the itinerary he'd arranged. We were going to have Thanksgiving in Florida, where he and my mom had started going in the winter. At first, they avoided the inconveniences of winter, but as Dad's lungs worsened with cancer, they sought warmth. Cold weather, even harsh air conditioning, would set him off coughing. The little note ends "It should be a great family get-together." No self-pity, not even any news of his health struggles. Just the efficiency of getting things done and bringing people together. In his absence, the family's attempts to network has passed from sibling to sibling, each coordinating in his or her own way. This time, though, I figured that organizing a chain of stories was just too much and had been abandoned.

And so, when my brother Tim did call, later in June, I was taken off guard. He traced the break and how Michael took it upon himself to mend it. Then I launched into my story of no significance that made me feel so special, even all these years later.

"Dad did the same thing with me once," he replied.

No dry cleaner, but the same Heath Bar.

I was stunned. A special childhood moment with my father wasn't all that special after all. Or maybe it was more important because with eight kids and a demanding work schedule, my father had to be more deliberate about making time for each child.

If it wasn't enough to have my "distinctive" memory echoed, what's more, we exchanged another similar experience with our father. Somehow it was just dad and his little son. For me, I traveled by train into Philadelphia, went to his office, then was toured around the city by one of Dad's co-workers. (At the top of City Hall, where visitors could go up to the statue of Billy Penn, formerly the tallest point in the city, I hugged the wall. There was some discussion about whether a penny dropped at that height would kill a person.) Tim's version had him arriving into the city via the airport from visiting relatives in Minnesota. We both ended up at Horn and Hardarts, which is like a Howard Johnson's or Cracker Barrel as far as I can remember, on our way to a Phillies game at Veterans Stadium. Pretty common experiences, I guess, but one detail sets it apart from the typical father-and-son-at-the-ballgame story, and it was exactly the same for Tim and me: we both were little boys with big headaches. I felt so terrible that I couldn't eat and had to lay down on the booth's bench-like seat. My father tried to cheer me by letting me in on a secret; they call this place Bugle and Soft-Arrow, he told me, not Horn and Hardarts. Again, his punning humor. And, again, I felt like I'd been initiated into a club. Of limited membership. But I still didn't feel well. Later, at the game, aspirin had upset my empty stomach, so Dad gathered me up, and we left the stadium before the ninth inning. Tim, too, recalls heading out of the Vet well before the game was over.

Hearing that my brother went through the same experience changed the memory, or at least the meaning of it. Relating these memories showed me that we are not video recorders that store and repeat experiences. Stories help reveal the meanings of what happens in our lives, and while the incident remains the same, these meanings change and grow. Maturing involves growing in sympathetic imagination, so that we can understand how another person feels in a situation, and this includes earlier versions of ourselves. As we develop the necessary distance to observe ourselves, we can add to our own perspective. I can still feel the pity party I want to throw as that let-down kid. This Phillies game story had always been How My Big Day with Dad Got Ruined. In addition, I can also feel the cool shadow of …what? Embarrassment before my father? Shame, even? It's a shadow cast by the doubt that I was a disappointment to him, being who I am rather than who I think he wanted me to be. Both Tim and I must share this flicker of doubt. How many others in the family? How many other adults generally?

Sharing these stories with Tim didn't cancel out these understandings but enhanced them, adding more. Knowing that my brother shared a similar experience and having grown older than my father was when these events occurred, I can imagine his perspective now, too. It's a sad little glimpse into our father's life. Here he was going to a ballgame, trying to make a special memory with one of his sons, and it turns out like a National Lampoon movie, minus the throwing up. Then, how many years later, he geared up again with his youngest son, and it happens all over again. I wonder if he thought he'd wasted his ticket money. Or maybe the Phils were tanking anyway, so leaving meant we wouldn't creep along on Packer Avenue. Knowing my dad, if the game meant anything to him, he was also moved by love for his sons. And maybe, since Mom did most of the childrearing, he felt a little out of his depths when it came to the care and comfort of his own children.

Stories are powerful in the way they connect us to the past, but by letting the meanings unfold, their power remains fresh in the present as well. Rexall Drug stores are gone. There's no more Vet, Horn & Hardarts, or computer punch cards. Even my father is gone. But the stories remain, in the living community that remembers and retells them. And the telling is also important. When Tim tells a joke that we all learned from our father, I still laugh. I enjoy Tim's style, how he weaves it into the conversation, his selection and emphasis of details, and the buildup to the punch line. I enjoy watching others enjoy the joke. And in this way, it becomes more than a story. In fact, it's not even about the joke: it's about the people gathered in the present situation and the continuity.

Tim revealed this dimension to these reflections when he noted that Dad's been gone for nineteen years, but here we were still telling stories about him. What a legacy. A sign of just how big a personality he was. And how much affection we still regard him with. Telling the stories not only opened me to remembering a host of incidents that had gotten dusty over the years, the chain linked me to my father in a whole new way. I related to him, not only as the boy in the story but as a man myself. As if that were not enough, the exercise linked me to my brother in a whole new way.

"I wonder if my kids will be telling stories like this when I'm gone," Tim mused.

"I'm sure they will," I replied, fully confident.

When Tim was at IBM, some people called him The Clone. Tim, too, creates networks of people, especially his family, enjoying their company and bringing out their best. He certainly also has features that distinguish him from my father. I can see them more clearly, in part, because we are of the same generation. But one similarity between them stands out. He's got my father's bottomless well of situationally perfect jokes, as well as a story-telling style that you'd pay good money to hear. And he's got a quick wit that sees the humor in a great many kinds of situations.

In fact, Tim's sons might tell the story of my Dad's twentieth anniversary memorial, one year after the chain was forged. Mom had arranged for a Mass to be said for my father, and we all came in for it. Liz from Jersey, Julie from New Mexico, me from New York. Dad's only surviving brother was there. Mom's two brothers were there. Scads of cousins, spouses, nieces and nephews—and now their spouses and kids. We took up at least three full pews. The priest invited us to pray for the person that the Mass was being offered for—I steeled my heart to hear my father's name—"Alejandro Jimenez." We glanced around. Were we at the wrong service? Did the priest take a name from the wrong list? We prayed for this stranger's soul to be at rest and silently offered one for Dad too.

Later, outside the church, as we hugged and greeted each other, some of us compared notes to find out what happened. We were at the right Mass, it turns out, but the priest made a mistake. In the hubbub, Tim sidled up to Mom and asked her a question: "Did you keep your receipt?"

Haiku and the Heightening of Awareness

One afternoon on a typical July day, the air grew suddenly, extraordinarily still. The piled-up clouds grew amber-colored, and light was a diffused apricot glow which brought out the rich summer-greenness of green grass, so full and deep. It seemed quieter somehow, too, so I walked out just to look, to experience this strange loveliness, and I stood in the back yard a long while just watching, my mouth open in amazement.

Just as that day's storm weather shifted my awareness, other kinds of circumstances call from us more concentrated attention. Those initial snowflakes that seem to float in winter's calm air. The slow-motion way time moves in hospital waiting rooms. A passing cloud-shadow—ooh, that relief!—on a sunny summer sidewalk. A cool cloth on your fevered forehead. After the thunderstorms knocked out the power and you don't have anything to do but listen to the hush and gurgle, the drip and patter of the water.

In June 1991, I had a moment like this when the situation invited my concentrated attention to detail. It was a day like no other. When I stepped onto the porch from my father's bedroom, I jotted these lines:

The Last Day

Mom brought the rose to me:
big as an open hand,
petals peeling back.

Last night's rain broke
the heat. August weather
the first week of June.
Cool air moves over my legs
like fog. In this calm,
Dad's breathing gurgles—
he is dying.

Mom put the flower
to my face. "Stop,"
she said, "stop and smell
the roses." Petals peeling back
like wings, like red wings.

Later that very day, my father died. Because of that context, the simple details of weather and a gesture that even contains a cliché can be fresh and evocative. Such moments are like knots of intense feeling, our emotion and physical surroundings are tightly related somehow— they're a brief glimpse of unity, the oneness of all things. That reality is always present, and so poems are lurking in all circumstances. The way of haiku encourages us to devote our attention, to sense that interrelatedness even in ordinary daily life.

The poet Masaoka Shiki (1867-1902) brought haiku into the twentieth century, reinvigorating the form so thoroughly that he's considered one of the top four Japanese haiku poets. When my spouse and I returned to Japan after being away for ten years, we traveled areas we'd never been to. I carried three books for my journey: my journal, a book by Basho (another of the top four), and Burton Watson's translations of Shiki. Here are some examples:

> *Getting lazy—*
> *taking my socks off*
> *after I get in bed*[7]

> *Winter rice fields—*
> *railroad tracks running*
> *a level above them*[8]

Sick in bed

> *Crows at four*
> *sparrows at five—*
> *and then the summer night is over*[9]

Even reading these tiny poems requires a different awareness. Listen for images, for specific things: socks, rice fields, train tracks, sparrows, crows. Then allow understanding to deepen into experience so you can picture the scene, the season, the situation. What do "winter rice fields" look like? How does landscape feel that time of year? Maybe in summer, you can't even see the tracks themselves because the green plants are high enough. So maybe in winter there is a silver gleam that contrasts the gray-brown fields, and so the mechanical seems stronger, more prominent than nature. Maybe that feels a little sad, or even lonely, intensifying the desolation of cold-weather farms.

Because they are so brief, haiku *suggest far more than they can name*, and so we have to be lively to unstated connections. Isn't that what we want in our daily lives, too? A heightened sensitivity to what one Quaker writer calls 'the Beyond which is within.' Listening to haiku in these ways practices being aware of unity.

Another book I carried with me was Sam Hamill's translation of Basho (1644-1694). This Japanese poet transformed haiku from just a part of a parlor game of linked verse where one person added lines to another's. In Basho's hands, the haiku became a form capable of conveying subtle sensibilities, good humor (and not just wit), and profound Zen insight.

> *The bee emerging*
> *from deep within the peony*
> *departs reluctantly*[10]

> *At dawn the brown faces*
> *of fishermen emerge from*
> *fields of white poppies*[11]

> *Along the roadside,*
> *blossoming wild roses*
> *in my horse's mouth*[12]

The slow departure of the bee from the sweet globe of the peony flower suggests my own reluctance to part with any delightful experience. The natural image finds its correspondence in the oneness of our longing, but in Buddhism such craving or clinging to experience causes us to suffer. Therefore, the natural scene in the haiku is a spiritual teaching, if I am listening to the poem well enough. While the fishermen's sun-darkened faces are clearer when they head to work (or home from the sea) because they contrast with the bright white flowers, the poem is more than a small painting of a scene. The faces seem to blossom as they emerge, but like flowers these men going off to work at dawn, grow up, and pass on. Life is fleeting, so be lively to beauty. Really attentive poets find images that embody resonate moments, like a bell's sound waves. For that to happen, you need a sharply-drawn image and something that strikes it.

I won't delineate the technical aspects of these poems—there are wonderful books available for that, like Robert Haas's *The Essential Haiku* or Clark Strand's *Seeds from a Birch Tree*. Instead, I will speak generally.

Small as it is, the haiku has even smaller parts. Usually two lines go together—the roses on the roadside—and then there is a pause, a turning of sorts, before another line that completes, contrasts or comments on the other two—the flowers are in the horse's mouth. Like a good joke, the punchline brings all the previous details together in a startling way. Our response to a good joke —laughter or a hard groan—is abrupt and uncontrolled. A joke explained is a joke ruined. If you have to say, "That's funny because…"

then you're already doomed because "understanding" a joke is very different from "getting" one.

Likewise, once we sense how the two parts of haiku strike together, our response can be below the level of thought, words, explanation, analysis. There is an immediacy and wholeness to our response. I have such a reaction to this haiku by Basho:

> *Whenever winds blow,*
> *the butterfly finds a new place*
> *on the willow tree*[13]

I attempt to write these poems because doing so encourages me to be on the lookout for such evocative constellations—details that seem unrelated but suggest so much more when combined. It also encourages me to be tender toward the intuitive, holistic, immediate responses to the world. Let me start with two of my attempts that I consider failures.

> *Still looking soft*
> *sprinkled with ice crystals*
> *—Lambs ear leaves*

I like the contrast of the leaves which in summer and fall are as soft as, well, a lamb's ear but in winter have become stiff, but that's all *in the poem*. Not so much suggestion. Plus when you only have seventeen syllables, you don't need redundancy like "ice" and "crystals." Does ice come in any other form? Writing such a poem and weighing its effects, like this, makes me more aware of my own perception and the way the language works—the two sides of every poem's energy.

Try this one:

> *All only a foot tall*
> *none thicker than my arm*
> *—stumps by the pond*

In this failed haiku, I like the physical image, a little too exact perhaps, but clearly focused. The poem does suggest what is not there: the gnawing beavers that stumped all those saplings. But that's more like a riddle, where details suggest a single answer. Once you understand it, you're done. It can be named, and so it's limited. Where's the feeling? What else does it connect with?

Even haiku that show their limitations are worth creating because to write these, I had to walk by the pond and through the woods, had to puff a little on the way back up hill and swing my limbs a little; I had to feel the cold and see the world in motion, even in winter. No downside to any of that!

Let me show a few that I think come closer to what haiku can do. But, of course, only you can tell if they are working:

> *ticking away*
> *like irregular seconds*
> *—falling maple leaves*

> *in the white morning*
> *the highway's loud around us*
> *—a single cricket*

> *Like waves, heat pours in*
> *each time the bus doors open*
> *—I could ride all day*

> *their shift done, men file*
> *out the front gates with lunchpails*
> *—the high prison wall*

Periodically, I "assign" myself haiku to regain sensitivity to the subtle shifts of activity in the world. It's like carrying a camera: if you strap a camera to your shoulder when you take a walk or you deliberately pick it up for the family picnic (instead of knowing that your phone *could* always take a picture, if circumstances deserved it), you look for possible pictures. Likewise, if you're cultivating haiku, you engage with surroundings differently. I get out of myself as I note the distinctive features of the season. My vision sharpens, and I sense more beauty, more harmonies which I usually overlook. And my fuller, more complex emotional responses come to the surface, having been pushed down by to-do lists and what's-next thinking. In short, I feel more alive.

I also try my hand at tanka, another Japanese form and the one that haiku evolved from. Tanka is much longer—instead of three lines of seventeen syllables, tanka have five lines of 31 syllables; it's like a haiku with two extra 7 syllable lines so you can blather on and on, if you need to. By even such small changes to the scope of the writing, I can sense how both my perception and expression need to adjust. Here are a few of mine.

> *The room is dark still*

> *outside the covers, it's cold:*
> *I draw my hands in.*
> *The alarm's music plays on*
> *but even the cats won't move.*

> *Next week's St. Patty's,*
> *a day for Irish ballads,*
> *green beer and long jokes.*
> *I tighten my scarf again*
> *and pull it close to my chest.*

> *Snow melts, freezes, thaws.*
> *It's almost time to straighten*
> *plow-bent poles, to find*
> *lost signs flopped down in the mud*
> *commanding the sky to stop.*

These small poems are responses to everyday moments when the material blends with the spiritual, when sluggish mornings mean savoring the dark and warmth of our bed, when winter is still harsh in mid-March, and when I can sense that "almost time" of a season's change. So, again, even if the poems themselves do not reach the profound levels of perception and insight of the greats, like Shiki and Basho, the practice is valuable.

As my father never tired of saying, it's important to stop and smell the roses, to pause and enjoy beauty. These forms of poetry do just that. And so they are celebrations—tiny, fleeting celebrations. It's difficult to write haiku or tanka and not feel grateful and delighted afterwards, regardless of the subject matter, regardless of how "successful" the poems end up being. It's hard to feel sad when you're on the lookout for beauty, and it's tough to feel lonely when you're sensitive to how your heart is answering the motion of life around you.

At the Crossroads

Hiroshima's Peace Park

We'd been in the city for weeks. My spouse and I had quit our jobs, sold our Corolla, put all our furniture in my brother-in-law's attic, and headed off to Hiroshima to serve as volunteers at a small peace organization. We served as directors of the World Friendship Center, and so it seems pretty important that we should experience the sites and memorials where the atomic bomb detonated over the heart of the city. Nevertheless, adjustments of all kinds kept us from Peace Park.

Michiko Yamaoka was shocked that we hadn't gotten there yet. And as a result, when we first went to Peace Park, she guided us herself. She was a young girl in 1945, and like many school children, she had been drafted by the military government to work in the city. Consequently, she was there when the bomb went off. It was imperative that the new directors of the Center witness that history, so imperative, in fact, that she herself hustled us off in a taxi and paid for everything. When she realized we didn't bring our camera, she zipped into a nearby shop and purchased a disposable one for us, making sure that she took our picture near some of the monuments.

The first picture in our album is slightly tilted. The two of us are standing on a cobbled walk in front of a ring of shrubbery and black iron fence about the height of our waists. Behind us, jets of water arc into a pool out of which a central fountain sends a spume upward. Beyond the fountain, there is a multi-story building that could be an office or hotel. Except for the Japanese kana on its side, there is no identifying feature that lets you know we stand in the first city in human history to experience nuclear war. We are small, as often happens with those throw-away cameras. We are smiling, so you might think we are tourists happy to be visiting a foreign plaza, its exotic fountain. Behind this photo is another, which Beth took. Yamaoka-san is smiling, but she is far enough away that you can't see her scars.

Yamaoka-san was a so-called Mobilized Student; she was just 800 meters from the hypocenter, the spot on the ground above which the bomb exploded. Over 8,000 students were laboring in Hiroshima that day. In the summer of 1944, as the burden of the ferocious war was turning fully against them, the government conscripted all students over a certain age. They were sent to farms and factories to help in the war effort. In Hiroshima, as in many other cities, buildings had been torn down to open spaces in the city because when a place was firebombed, the wooden houses burned quickly and intensely so that the fire spread fast. The Mobilized Students were forced to cart off the rubble to create fire breaks. And so, around 6,000 of them died. Yamaoka-san was fairly close to the bomb. The heat at the hypocenter has been estimated as 6,000° Celsius (10,800° Fahrenheit). For years, her body was so twisted, her face so scarred, neighborhood children pointed at her shouting, "Monster!"

Yamaoka-san directed the taxi to take us to the point near Shima Hospital above which Little Boy, the name given to the bomb, was born. We didn't know where the hospital was and couldn't read any signs, so we were clueless as to what stop was next or where we were at any moment. The streets follow a general grid pattern, but with the rivers, some roads curve and make strange angles. Plus, we moved from a town of about 25,000 in the flatlands of Ohio, and Hiroshima was a city of a million people. We were dazed and overwhelmed. Walking now, Yamaoka-san hurried us across another street to the corner and headed up a side road, narrow enough to be one-way but buzzing with bikes, cars, and foot traffic going both ways. It was so cramped that a driver would have to pull over and wait for oncoming vehicles to swerve around and then could proceed. A parking garage was the first building after the corner complex. It fascinated me: cars pull in to the opening and the driver gets out—almost like an old drive-through car wash. Instead of being automatically pulled through a long hall, cars are hauled upward on a kind of elevator and disappear.

We walked quickly, trying to keep up with Yamaoka-san. If we knew what questions to ask, we could have communicated better because she understood much more English than she could produce. Mostly, as a result, we stayed silent. The hospital is on a corner, across the river from the A-bomb Dome, along a road that parallels the river. The city erected bronze markers at significant spots, some etched with photographs taken in the fall of 1945 to show the scene in the aftermath of the bomb. The marker at Shima Hospital has since been moved, so the experience now may be different, but on that day in 1993, I felt the ghostliness of Hiroshima. In the midst of an ordinary Japanese city-dweller's routine, on a street bustling with life and commerce, an amber marker the size of a large headstone stands draped with what I thought were flowers. As we came closer, I realized they were strings of multi-colored paper cranes. Someone had folded a thousand of them to place here, to remember the dead, to honor them, to offer them some peace. I had my first intimation of why Japanese novelist and Nobel Prize winner Kenzaburo Oe once observed: "All Hiroshima is one vast graveyard."[14]

The museum that we visited in 1993 reinforced this feeling that the whole city is a place of the dead. The Peace Memorial Museum was renovated—and completely re-imagined—while we were there, but what we witnessed that day with Yamaoka-san was the official story of Hiroshima for decades. The first display was the fire: a diorama with glowing red lights and human figures walking in tattered clothes, blackened and hair frizzed. They walked with arms in front of them, like zombies, hands dripping burned skin. Yamaoka-san, who lived through that day and witnessed such scenes, walked quickly through this part and waited in the next section. There, glass displays curved around the room, and its huge circle of the city in ruins mapped out before us. I became used to reading Hiroshima in concentric circles, as distance from the bomb signified levels of heat and blast exposure. Circles also showed the range of the fires that swept through the wooden buildings for miles and miles. The round topographic map of

Hiroshima after the bomb was gray and flattened to the ground; just a few concrete buildings remained.

The Peace Museum was a punch in the gut. Looking at an artifact meant feeling something of the experience of one person, a fellow human being. Once "artifact" became a "child's lunchbox," it meant imagining a mother packing her school-aged son a lunch, apologizing for not providing more food. But shortages were common after years and years and years of wartime rations. It meant picturing that same mother, frantic and possibly injured herself, searching the hot rubble for some sign of her son. It meant entering the personal world of the victim. Knowing that Yamaoka-san was just ahead of us made it all the more real, but it also meant I didn't want to delay, to slow her down enough to bring back memories. The knowledge she had was not imagination but experience. We ended up rushing through the museum, so that gave me only a jumble of images: the tricycle of a four-year-old boy who died that day, a piano with glass shards driven into it even though it was miles away, the block of sewing needles that were fused together, that lunchbox of ashes, a child's uniform…

To mark the loss of all these people, to remember them and to ease their anguished souls, there are monuments of all kinds in and around Peace Park. There are memorials for workers—the gas company, lumber company, coal company, and construction company—for when Pope John Paul II visited, for schools and teachers, for various individuals, and even for whole towns. Out of the more than sixty monument in this area alone, our first visit to Peace Park introduced me to some of my favorites.

To return to where the majority of memorials are from the hospital, we had to cross Motoyasu Bridge. On one side, rising up on a three-legged teardrop, a small child stands in the air, arms outstretched to hold an outline of a crane. On two sides of the support structure, two other children appear to be leaping, one foot on the ground and the other kicking out with the weight of their bodies lifting. Like the figure at the top, their arms too are over their heads in a perpetual dance. It amazes me how much motion is suggested in a fixed and sturdy sculpture. This is the Children's Peace Monument. Unveiled in 1958, it is sometimes called the Monument of Ten Thousand Cranes or just the Sadako Monument because it is so closely associated with Sadako Sasaki, the little girl whose story is told in children's books, videos, and paper crane instructions. At the time of the bomb, she was only two years old.

Because she was 1.5 kilometers away from the hypocenter, she was not apparently injured. She grew into an athlete, a runner. But when she was twelve, she grew sick—with "A-bomb Disease." In the eight months she lived after her diagnosis, she embarked on a project to fold a thousand paper cranes, which is said to provide for good health and a long life. She used whatever paper she had at hand, including the tiny sheets her pills were wrapped in. In some versions of the story, she never finishes the strand of one thousand. In others, her mother completes the string, while still others, she herself not only completes it but folds 1,300. Tiny samples of her cranes are on display at the new museum. Despite her hope and determination, Sadako died in October 1955 of leukemia, the cancer of the blood, the second wave to take the survivors. The first came for those acutely exposed to radiation; nearly 100,000 died between August and the end of December 1945.

While Yamaoka-san's burns make plain the incredible heat and blast of an atomic bomb, Sadako's story dramatically reveals another horrible aspect: not only did it kill school kids mobilized as labor that day and the weeks afterwards, it killed children miles away and years after the war was over.

Sadako's death caused a great surge of grief. Maybe it was because it came after the shock of the war was over, and so new layers of grief can be expressed. Or perhaps the sorrow was more intense because Sadako was only twelve. In any case, her death spurred many people to action. Her classmates organized an effort to raise money for a memorial, and the movement swelled. School children stood on street corners all over Japan collecting money. Already drained from pouring resources into more than fifteen years of war, the nation was still rebuilding after over 200 cities were firebombed during the war's relentless air raids. Still, the nuclear tests in the Pacific Ocean of the 1950s reminded the Japanese that the war may be over, but the Nuclear Age went on. One hydrogen bomb caused ash and other radioactive fallout to drift onto a Japanese fishing boat in 1954. The nation was also intensely aware of the cost of nuclear weapons. The Children's Peace Monument ended up being funded from more than 3,000 schools all across Japan as well as donation from overseas.

From that first day, I had the feeling that this lovely, sad, moving sculpture captured so many of the realities and meanings of the atomic bomb. When you look up at the monument, it seems that the folded paper bird is drawing the girl up into flight, but sometimes her outstretched arms make me think she is being crucified. These weapons cannot discriminate between combatant and noncombatant (not that firebombing can). It wages war long after the nations have stopped (not that landmines in a rice field turn themselves off, either). The images of the soaring child at the top and the boy and girl gracing the sides are not just heartbreaking, though; the monument is also hopeful. It is the result of the efforts of children to mark the death of their friend, and the way that effort built and included so many others is encouraging. People can be moved to action. Individual efforts can become movements.

Even today school kids around the world read the book about Sadako by Eleanor Coerr, and they can fold cranes in long strings and ship them to Hiroshima. When we were there in the 1990s, the low wall that surrounded the monument was usually draped with these offerings; now there are presentation cases made of Plexiglas with hooks to hang the offerings. Boxes would arrive at the World Friendship Center periodically filled with colorful origami, and Beth and I would ride our bikes to Peace Park to deposit them at the Children's Peace Memorial. We would take photographs of the colorful strings and write a brief letter letting the senders know that their cranes were gathered with gifts from all over Japan, New Zealand, England, the US, and countless other countries. Hope continues to ripple out, the tide going out from Hiroshima and flowing back to it. Directly under the monument a black granite block has words carved into it: "This is our cry. This is our prayer. For building peace in this world."

Another site in the Park also evokes many emotions while standing on the earth in that particular place. While Sadako's monument is right on the road and very close to other "major" memorials, the Peace Bell is a bit more isolated. The grove of trees around it gives it a feeling of privacy, and since it tends to be shaded, there is a relief here from the heat of summer. Lotus flowers in a narrow water garden greet a visitor as you approach and climb the stairs to stand in the small open air enclosure. Unlike our typical bell-shape, bells in Japan are long and narrow; rather than a clapper dangling within the metal bowl, Japanese bells have a striker on the outside, so the bell is a hollow metal space. Embossed on the bell's outer surface is a map of the world. If you look closely, as Yamaoka-san urged us to do, you see there are no national boundaries, just land and sea in their physical unity. The concrete structure that covers it is arched and rounded, standing on four supports. It is said to symbolize the universe. The striker is a log suspended to hang perpendicular to the bell. I drew it back using the rope, and though it flowed easily in its suspended range, I could sense the size and heft of it. The wood strikes a spot on the bell with the classic classroom model of an atom, electrons in their simple orbit around a nucleus. The symbolism is simple and direct: we are one world, and there is no room for nuclear weapons here. Low and resonant, the sound reverberates long after being struck, and I felt waves going out in all directions. Whenever I heard the bell, no matter where I was in the park, it brought a calm, inviting me to send out my own prayer for peace.

Over the course of the two and a half years we were directors of the World Friendship Center, Peace Park was the site of numerous events. I went many times with our Interpreters Class, helping Japanese volunteers practice live spoken translation about the monuments for guests from overseas. I came to learn a great deal more, and I coded that information with particular memorials, like the Monument for Mobilized students. It always reminded me of Yamaoka-san and the other *hibakusha*, those who were affected by the bomb, we were privileged to work with. And we both adopted more favorite monuments, ones that evoke all kinds of feelings. Peace Park is also the site of cherry blossom festivals, where city dwellers turn out to picnic under the flowering trees, drink beer, and enjoy the fine spring weather.

We returned again and again to the Merciful Goddess of Peace (Kannon), a statue of the Bodhisattva of Compassion. She stands tall over a town that is gone. She stands tall over a Peace Lantern that is dark. And now, she stands over the Monument for the Korean Victims, people conquered in war and forced into exile, to work in Japan as slave labor. Above all this ruinous history, all this human cruelty, stands the placid Bodhisattva. As we got to be familiar with the city, riding our bikes everywhere, we'd take a detour into Peace Park to visit her and to orient our intentions. We would stand in prayer before her, vowing to do what we could to be people of compassion and peace.

1995 in the "City of Peace": Spirit of Boredom or Hope[1]

I grew up near Philadelphia, the city where the US Constitution was drafted, where the Liberty Bell is displayed, where Betsy Ross is said to have sewn her famous flag. We once had a team called the Philadelphia Freedom, a football game called the Liberty Bowl, and little plastic Benjamin Franklin dolls. New residents to Philly begin to become cynical of the ideas themselves, holding the world around them up against "freedom" or "brotherly love" and snickering at the discrepancy. Soon the sport of cynicism becomes tiresome, too.

The same is true in Hiroshima. We live in a city with its Peace Park, Peace Boulevard, Peace Pagoda, even an Atom Pachinko Parlor and *Gembaku* (A-bomb) Ramen shop. Ian Buruma wrote that the "civic religion" of Hiroshima is "nothing less than world peace. It is a message hammered home so relentlessly...that in the words of the Italian

---

[1] Written in the spring of 1995 while as Resident Co-director at the World Friendship Center for the English language magazine *Hiroshima Signpost*. I have not revised it.

journalist Tiziano Terzani, 'even the doves are bored with peace.'"[15]

I came to Japan as a volunteer to work for that now-dismissed-as-saccharine ideal of World Peace. Seeing news photos of blade-wielding villagers in Rwanda, the wizened faces of teenaged (or middle-aged) soldiers in Bosnia behind rocket launchers, or the women in Russia pressing the authorities for information about their husbands or sons, the idea of peace itself seems quaint. What can one person do from Hiroshima?

In 1993, my spouse and I became directors of World Friendship Center, which was started nearly thirty years ago by a Quaker named Barbara Reynolds. We had read a notice that she had died, and the report said she'd been named an honorary citizen of Hiroshima, the first woman so honored. As we learned more, I was impressed by the strength of her conviction; equally, I was inspired that an individual does have power in this electronic age of anonymity.

In the 1950s—a time not open to social protest in the United States—Barbara Reynolds and her family sailed into the forbidden waters around Bikini Island to protest a nuclear weapon test. In 1962, she took two *hibakusha*, or survivors of the atomic bombings, on the first World Peace Pilgrimage to the US so people could hear directly from the witnesses themselves what nuclear weapons really do. Then in 1964, she organized the World Peace Studies Mission, which took twenty-five *hibakusha* to all of the nuclear powers at that time, including the Soviet Union.

The story of the *hibakusha*—and all victims of war—depends on the listener's sympathy for the appeal for peace to mean anything. Yet, there is something in us that can justify even the most extreme human behavior. Even the Nazis could "justify" their treatment of the Jews and others. What about Nanking? Pearl Harbor? But Barbara continued to appeal to the best in people, that capacity for love in each person which not only enables us to hear another's suffering but to be moved to act with compassion.

After the World Peace Studies Mission, Barbara started World Friendship Center because she understood that unless people have a chance to sit down and really meet others as human beings, there can be no friendship, no cross-cultural exchanges, and certainly no world peace. I think the reason the Center continues to exists—despite chronic financial troubles, changeover in directors, and only a fledgling sense of volunteerism in Japan—is because its way to world peace is not politically motivated. It's far more challenging.

In her Statement of Purpose from 1967—a time of feverish political activity in both the United States and Japan—she wrote, "Founded with the conviction that Hiroshima has international significance, the Friendship Center is based upon the need to build peace from within." This change in the individual is necessary "to raise the standard of loving throughout the world," and this work continues to be important.

1995—with its many war anniversaries—may bore the peace doves to death, and it may only raise the volume of cynical laughter. I'm learning, however, that nothing can be built out of boredom and cynicism. The World Friendship Center is trying to focus on hope, that elusive quality which often is as anemic as "peace" in the Peace Cigarette sense. But there is a hope that is founded on a realistic view of the situation as well as an evaluation of what can be done with the tools at hand, and this resilient, active hope sets out to build something of value. And this brings people together.

Barbara Reynolds passed away in 1990. In the first event in this spirit of hope, WFC remembered this remarkable woman with an afternoon piano recital on Saturday February 11. When we were searching for a fitting way to mark the fifth anniversary of Barbara's passing, Tanimichi Sugita offered his interpretations of Beethoven. Mr. Sugita has written that Beethoven sought to become an "instrument of the Voice of God," to bring solace and joy to the human race through the beauty of music.

What does this have to do with a world where the Japanese Government refuses to acknowledge the barbarity of its wartime policies, such as taking young women from their villages and forcing them into sexual servitude, until there is documented evidence? How does hearing a few tunes counter the images of the most highly praised photographs of our time: a vulture near a crumpled, starving child in the Sudan and the scar-crossed face and head of a man in Rwanda?

Beethoven thought, according to Mr. Sugita, the musical art was a creative, constructive effort which was imbued with great faith in humanity. I think this was also the spirit that Barbara Reynolds possessed. Regardless of what the Smithsonian Museum shows about Hiroshima in its proposed exhibit, each of us can "build peace from within," and we must use what we have at hand—family, school, work, community groups, and, of course, political structures.

Mr. Sugita has devoted his life to realizing the principle of "One World" through the universality of music, and he only plays in public for charity. In its very wordlessness, music can convey directly those emotions that elude words.

In our time, perhaps, it is difficult to have "great faith in humanity," especially as we remember the atrocities humanity committed fifty years ago. It's far easier to "investigate," i.e. take the heroes down a notch. It's safer to wait for the dirt—"the real story"—to come out because we don't seem to like living with saints. Mother Teresa admits the reason she began seeking her radical path of service was not pure altruism, but penance. She's said she realized her calling when she understood that she had a Hitler within her. This is where hope is far more powerful than anything glib advertisers can come up with—knowing our own potential for depravity can motivate cynicism, despair and escapism, or it can motivate greater goodness, deeper honesty, and more simple kindness.

World Friendship Center's way of marking the fiftieth anniversary of the atomic bomb will be A Celebration of Hope. We're inviting anyone over sixteen—anywhere—to send artwork the size of a postcard to Hiroshima on the theme, "Out of the Mud Blooms the Lotus," and we're inviting children under sixteen to send A4-sized art responding to the theme "One World—One Family—We

Shall Live Together." We're committed to displaying everything we can.

In the first ten days of June at the Fujin Kaikan (Women's Center) in Takanobashi, A Celebration of Hope will consist of art displays, symposia, informal discussions, and presentations. Along with hearing the submitted messages from around the world, we'll feature four photographers' work and host a poetry reading to mark the publication of John Bradley's impressive anthology, *Atomic Ghost: Poets Respond to the Nuclear Age.*

The keystone exhibit will highlight work by people who have experienced the extremity of war. One artist's story exemplifies the spirit of the festival. Claudia Bernardi fled Argentina's so-called "dirty war" in which the repressive government clamped down on its own people. Many people "disappeared," never to be heard from again. In her life in the US, Ms. Bernardi works with other refugees, most of whom are not artists, to bring some healing, perhaps to bring some "solace and joy to the human race."

She must be imbued with some "faith in humanity" because she continues to face those dark times. For the past ten years, Ms. Bernardi has accompanied her sister on anthropological digs in South and Central America. But they are not searching for lost civilizations; they are exhuming mass graves trying to identify the victims. As she said, despite many of these governments' policy of granting amnesty allowing murderers to get away with their crimes, she feels this work is emotionally satisfying because the families of the dead know what became of their loved one. Art for her is the other side of the coin from the anthropology. The creative impulse counters brutality, she said.

Living in Hiroshima, especially this year, can leave us feeling far from the real work of peace. All those hollow words, the official posturing, the windy editorials. Yet, there are people really seeking to live those high-minded words—freedom, love, compassion, peace—and their brave example makes humanity itself more worth our faith.

At the Crossroads: In Hiroshima at the Fiftieth Anniversary

The slogan for the first Peace Restoration Festival in 1946 was, "World peace begins from Hiroshima." The deliberate bombing of a civilian population with a nuclear weapon—regardless of the wretchedness of the context—showed that war itself had become too brutal, too capricious, and too inhuman to be allowed to continue. All humanity lost something that day; survivor-poet Sankichi Toge recognizes that loss when he cries out, "Give me back myself./ Give back the human race."[16] On August 6, 1995, thousands marked the fiftieth anniversary of that city's atomic bombing. And I was one of them.

Beth and I moved to Hiroshima and the World Friendship Center in late August 1993 and stayed until December of 1995. Over its thirty years as a guest house and community peace witness, World Friendship Center has welcomed many at this crossroads of history, both as volunteers and as guests from all over the world.

For the fiftieth, there were so many details to attend to, however, that we forgot to reserve seats at the Peace

Memorial Ceremony for ourselves. Actually, we didn't mind. Having experienced the previous year's ceremony—with its parade of politicians all saying predictable and insubstantial things, its moment of silence violated by amateur and professional shutter-bugs eager for a snapshot, and its conspicuous absence of the survivors themselves—we weren't upset by not having a seat. We'd been working toward the fiftieth for more than a year, and by the time it came, both Beth and I were in a hurry to see it go. So we guided our guests to Peace Park, got them situated in their seats, and began walking around the ceremony.

We were by the Motoyasu River, which divides the A-Bomb Dome from the rest of Peace Park, when suddenly the air became heavy with the sound of bells. That particularly solemn, hollow sound came from three directions simultaneously. On both banks of the river, everybody halted. The whirring of cicadas intensified the early-morning heat. 8:15—the moment "Little Boy" exploded over Hiroshima. In that stillness, tears welled up, bitter and swollen. Fifty years ago, Robert Lewis, the co-pilot of the *Enola Gay* said, "My God, what have we done?"[17] Inside me that prayer-plea felt just as urgent, as insistent.

Then, movement resumed, voices rising again from the podium at the ceremony. We drifted over to the Die-in at the Dome where, every year, hundreds of people fall and lie dead on the ground at the sound of those bells—children trying to keep still, a row of people in wheelchairs. That moment of stark stillness, that moment of death. It was a visual echo of the silence after the flash and before the waves of air and noise that were strong enough to knock the stone railings off Miyuki Bridge about a mile and a half away (and about two blocks from where we lived).

On our way out of the park, we ran into a photographer for *Stars & Stripes.* We'd met him in June down in Nagasaki when the military newspaper was preparing its retrospective article. We observed the writer's interview with a survivor, or *hibakusha (he-bahk-shah)*, then later we all met again in Hiroshima as we all took the same train. We were pleasantly surprised that Mark had taken time in the museum and seemed personally involved in the experience (unlike the journalist he traveled with); however, we expected he'd be gone, like most journalists, once the assignment was over.

"You came back," I said.

"I felt like I had to," he said.

He told us he'd been to Kobe after the terrible earthquake in January 1995. He witnessed the resulting fires in January and saw firsthand a city in ruins. Then, he said, hearing the *hibakushas'* accounts for days and days caused their images to blur with Kobe's flattened ruins, brewing nightmares in his sleep. He *had to* come back, he said again. Once you learn a fuller story of Nagasaki and Hiroshima, there is a certain imperative; each of us comes to ask "My God, what have we done?" One of the fundamental ways to gain this fuller story is to listen to the witnesses themselves.

On August 6, World Friendship Center asked two men to "tell their experience." In Japanese this is called *kataribe* (ka-ta-ree-bay), which is related to "storytelling," or *shogen* (show-ghen), which is more like "giving testimony." Both Hiromu Morishita and Hitoshi Takayama, like thousands of survivors, didn't talk about what they experienced of the atomic bomb for years before bearing witness. In 1968, Mr. Takayama attended a meeting where people claimed the "the voice of Hiroshima was slowly disappearing." When he finally spoke out, he created a book—in English—with survivors' accounts, photographs, and reflections by people around the world. In 1995, he was preparing a third edition of *Hiroshima: In Memoriam and Today.*

In that book Mr. Takayama writes that when he realized the knowledge was fading because of the silence of survivors, he "felt this bitterly in my heart." Here is his reflection:

> *I felt that I must continue to pray and work hard for the cause of peace. Though I am only one humble man, I knew that I had to try to make some contribution, however small, to the cause of peace. I know that the path to peace is a rough one, but I also know as a witness of the A-bomb that all humanity must never again experience such misery and suffering. We must keep telling the truth about that experience to people of good conscience. It is our responsibility to our God and to our fellow men [and women]. The horrible truth about war must be known, and Hiroshima is one of its hardest truths.*[18]

"The horrible truth about war" and phrases like it are often-used in Hiroshima because there is a basic conviction that if people really knew what war is and what the atomic bomb really did (and could do in exponentially larger terms even now), we would shrink away from choosing it as a way of dealing with conflict. This sense of Hiroshima having more meaning for the future than the past is what motivated teachers like Mr. Morishita to develop peace education around the same time that Mr. Takayama undertook his book. Their deep, personal responsibility felt like an urgency which pressed some *hibakusha* toward action, beginning with telling the facts of what happened to them as individuals.

Teachers learned that three percent of students couldn't answer the question, "When did the atomic bomb fall on Hiroshima?" While three percent seems small, it was far too many young people for the *hibakusha*. In addition to ignorance, the survey revealed common feelings that persist today. Students wrote such things as, "Atomic bomb affairs don't appeal to me, because I've no experience." Who can't relate to this comment: "I'm too busy with daily affairs to know how to bring about peace." In his essay in *Hiroshima: In Memoriam and Today*, Mr. Morishita responds:

> *Should that misery be forgotten? Shouldn't we foster a will toward peace among young people, so that they may not repeat the same error again? If we had a nuclear war again, even those inexperienced youth wouldn't escape it. There is no guarantee that these young people would survive it. Therefore they also have a responsibility to prevent war.*[19]

As Mark, the photographer from *Stars & Stripes*, shows, the truth of the survivors' experience can be passed on. The responsibility for making peace, including preventing war—for making "some contribution, however small, to the cause of peace"—can be fostered, as I saw from my own life which took me to Japan as a volunteer and there witnessed many other examples. While living in Hiroshima we became friends with Paul Quayle, a photographer from England. Somehow, he too felt this "will toward peace," which took him to India in the footsteps of Gandhi and then to Japan. He's been "taking snaps" in Hiroshima for more than six years, and the fruit of his labors is a remarkable book, *Hiroshima Calling*. Beth and I, Paul, and countless others have heard the *hibakusha*, and their message has fostered a sense of responsibility. But it takes all kinds of people waking up to the fact that they must try to make whatever small contribution they can. Teachers, writers, photographers, volunteers. One guest we met was a quiet British physicist who felt she had to make a kind of pilgrimage to Hiroshima. Her personal journey as a scientist crossed the path of history in Hiroshima.

If there is one lesson I've come away with from my time in Hiroshima it's this: politics and history are murky and painful. It was debilitating to deal with every day. And so the personal aspect of peace work is essential—almost regardless of the results. I must do what I can, if only to practice my own humanity. Meeting people and hearing their stories, not their titles or affiliations, helps us all to recognize our common humanity. We are all the same this way. The survivors who tell their experience appeal to that common ground, warning us that their past experience may be our future. So, on August 6, fifty years after the first inhabited city was destroyed by a nuclear weapon, in addition to the Hiroshima survivors, we asked two US veterans to bear witness to their experience at World Friendship Center.

Anthony Guarisco is a small man who looks at you with an intensity. In conversation, he moves with a stiffness, as if there were something wooden about him. He cannot move his neck to one side, so he shifts his eyes as much as possible. Then, if that doesn't work, he turns his entire torso. I'd written to his group, Association of Atomic Veterans, because of the shocking revelations in recent years.

In November of 1993, just after our arrival in the City of Peace, the *Albuquerque Tribune* reported that the US government experimented on hundreds of live human subjects using radiation. The English language newspapers in Japan followed the story closely. Some were given doses one hundred times the federal limit on internal radiation for nuclear workers at the time.[20] Some were injected with plutonium, the most lethal substance known.[21] Then, in a flurry of disclosures between 1993 and 1995, we learned that the Department of Defense, the Department of Energy, and the Atomic Energy Agency (now called Nuclear Regulatory Agency) all performed such tests—inmates had their reproductive organs bombarded with radiation, others were given hundreds of X-rays, intellectually disabled boys who thought they were taking part in a science club were fed radioactive milk, and many others. These tests continued, according to Energy Secretary Hazel O'Leary, into the time of these news reports.[22]

This spirit of experimentation completes the link to the atomic bombs. Some in Hiroshima still harbor resentment over the team of doctors sent by the US Government. Called the Atomic Bomb Casualty Commission, or ABCC, these researchers entered a city where more than 90 percent of its medical personnel were killed or injured, where most hospitals and clinics had only Red Cross medicines, and where knowledge of radiation was extremely limited. In comes a team of experts from the United States which the Occupation asks (demands? orders?) survivors of the atomic bomb to go see. The doctors examine, measure, and document. Do they diagnose? Prescribe medicines? Provide any answers to the mysterious ailments the survivors were facing? No. ABCC never treated the victims; it was merely gathering information.

Now when people claim that atomic bombs were merely experiments, I know that there is more than a grain of truth to it. If the US government was willing to perform experiments on its own citizens in secret, I am absolutely certain it would do it to "the enemy" regardless of the outcome of the war. The revelations about radiation experiments on human beings made me seek out the testimony of the Atomic Veterans, those servicemen who witnessed nuclear weapons' tests.

I was able to meet Anthony because he was attending the Conference Against A- and H- Bombs here in Hiroshima. On the fiftieth, he and Bill Bires told a gathering at the World Friendship Center about the other atomic explosions and *hibakusha*. Anthony was in the Pacific after World War II and witnessed the first bombs used in peacetime, a series of tests called Operation Crossroads. Being on a ship just a few miles away, he could clearly see the power of this weapon: an enormous battleship was blasted out of the water only to land, cracking in half.

But he could also witness, firsthand, the radiation. Sick for months then always more sluggish than ever in his life, Anthony Guarisco became an atomic bomb survivor—a *hibakusha*, which literally means "one who received the bomb." And the US Government denies his ailments are caused by his exposure. The same for Bill Bires who witnessed blasts in the Nevada desert in the early 1950s. Carole Gallagher's book *American Ground Zero* is indescribably heartbreaking because it pairs such personal testimony with portraits of people and places. She labored for ten years on that project.

Meeting the atomic veterans broke down the idea that all veterans were of the same mind. Japan in general and Hiroshima in particular followed the wrangling in the US over the Smithsonian's proposed then revised exhibition marking the end of WWII, which included the *Enola Gay*, the plane that dropped the bomb. The media coverage of the fury over the display made "veterans" seem like a single mass. Here were two men—representing hundreds, thousands more—whose combat experience and subsequent military service led them to think that the truth brought honor, not war. Like the *hibakusha*, their experience of the atomic bomb leads them to work for peace.

August brought us another forceful witness of this process. Robert Oliver called us up out of the blue and said he was in Hiroshima for the fiftieth, so we invited him to all our events over those hot August days. Robert had been in the Air National Guard, but slowly the truth became real to him about his job. First, he came upon a used copy of *Unforgettable Fire*, the collection of drawings by *hibakusha* made in 1970—twenty-five years after "that day." The images showed him what was happening on the ground under the belly of the *Enola Gay*. That book and an off-hand comment by one of his officers (something to the effect that "our job is to destroy things and to kill people") convinced Robert that he could not in good conscience serve in the military any further. A bold step. I wouldn't think conscientious objectors *in the military* are welcomed or respected.

In addition to our own event with the two Japanese *hibakusha* and two American *hibakusha* veterans, the WFC was full as a guest house. We hosted a delegation from World Friendship Center's American Committee (who all stayed with Japanese friends associated with the Center) as well as the Joanna Macy's Atomic Mirror Pilgrimage (who stayed with us at the Center). Busy understates our days and nights. And August in Hiroshima is humid and oppressively hot. Finally, the evening cooled down, and we held *toro-nagashi*. This beautiful ritual floats lantern down the river. Individuals light a small candle inside brightly-colored paper boxes and set them adrift on the Motoyasu River, under the A-Bomb Dome. With the special Noh drama on a boat mid-stream and the hordes of media people and equipment for the fiftieth, the intensity of personal expression and communion we felt so intensely the previous year was lost. It was like a show. It *was* a show.

Then, it seemed, everyone left. Next stop, Nagasaki. We decided against the trip south because Beth struggled with Lyme's disease the whole time we were volunteers, and the medication was just beginning to make some progress—a whole other story! We also had special events to mark World Friendship Center's thirtieth anniversary in these days as well, but again, another story. It's enough to say that we were guarding her against the heat, stress, and long hours of going down to Nagasaki.

As a result, Beth and I got a break, a chance to think about all these events and ideas. Peace and justice work seems to start with taking personal responsibility for "history," "politics," "the world," or "the future." Each one of us is urged to this in our own way, and we all name our obligation differently.

Most take a necessary step, once they realize the state of things: they issue a resounding refusal to participate in dehumanizing forces—within ourselves and our societies. Like Robert Oliver refusing to participate in the military. Over and over again, people's stories show that if you listen to the truth and act on it, making whatever contribution you can even if it means ridicule or worse, your life takes on a wholeness. One action might even invite the next, leading life into a realm of purpose and meaning you never guessed.

However, it's become clear to me that people must do more than protest. Issuing a profound "no" to the evil and unthinking cruelty of violence is essential, but ideas are not stamped out by denunciation. They must be displaced by something more viable, more full, and more true. The issue of nuclear weapons, for example, is huge, and it's entangled in politics—and international politics at that—and people are more and more disgusted with politics (both in Japan and the US). People's contribution can seem minuscule in the face of this. Certainly, we felt this. In our first months in

Hiroshima, we were wondering why we quit our jobs and moved across half the world. For peace? Washing guests' sheets? Writing up reports no one will read? Yet, the last nuclear tests by the government of France in the spring and early summer of 1995, like a lightning rod, focused the energy of millions around the world. People boycotted products, sailed into the Pacific, wrote letters, marched at embassies, and held prayer services. Everyone could participate, and no contribution was too small.

Still, how can we go beyond protest? Wisdom comes from a guest from India we hosted in 1994. Because he teaches Gandhian studies, we asked Mr. Jeyapragasam to speak one night. He called his presentation "Six Possible Futures." In it he said something I'll never forget: to begin making the future we most desire, we must take non-killing seriously. We need to behave in ways that bring comfort to those who suffer, and we need to begin doing what needs to be done to preserve humanity and life in general. It is essential to draw people to the positive, to call out the best in people.

Another chance meeting at World Friendship Center might illustrate what I mean. After the heat, hectic pace, and over-extension of the August 6 events, and while the attention turned toward Nagasaki, a French man called from Kyoto asking if we would accept some roses. France's announcement to resume their nuclear tests surrounded the August events with a dark shadow. It seemed another sign that the testimony and plea from Nagasaki and Hiroshima had not been heard.

Yet, here was a French person in Japan to mark the fiftieth anniversary of the atomic bombings who had come to present 1,000 silk roses and copies of a book he'd written. The lovely editions in French, Spanish, and English, *The Princess and the Birds*, were about Sadako, the little girl who died of leukemia ten years after the bomb.[23] Pierre Marchand had arranged to meet other international groups as well as a film crew from France to make a dignified presentation. Because of a mix-up, he was unable to. Now he had his parcels, but it was too late.

He had read about World Friendship Center in Paul's *Hiroshima Calling*, so he called and asked for some information. We sent him a brochure so he'd know that the Center was celebrating its thirtieth anniversary this year and that its founder, Barbara Reynolds, was the first woman to be named an honorary citizen of Hiroshima. And we told him we'd love to accept his roses.

Pierre was very pleased. As it turns out, he'd met Barbara in Paris, maybe thirty years ago, when she was on a peace pilgrimage with several survivors. There were other connections, other friendships that could only be known by meeting face-to-face. He further realized that a project he thought was ending with his coming to Hiroshima was just beginning: guests and friends of World Friendship Center can take a rose to the Peace Park and offer it. So, even now, one can take a symbolic action. He also encourages anyone who is moved by the story of Sadako to find some way of helping the children-victims of war, because kids still suffer from adult violence—look at Cambodia, anywhere in the former Yugoslavia, Iraq, Monrovia, Rwanda. (And since then, Syria, Iraq, the Sudan, Somalia…) Sadako's story is being relived even now, and each of us can contribute something to help if we have a will toward peace.

The anniversaries are now the far-less dramatic fifty-third, fifty-fourth, fifty-fifth...,seventy-fifth, seventy-sixth.... but the survivors are still in Hiroshima and Nagasaki bearing witness to their experience. We can still listen to them, for a few years anyway. It was a profound experience to meet and get to know Mr. Morishita and translate some of his poems, to become friends with other *hibakusha*. When she started the Center, Barbara Reynolds wrote, "World Friendship Center is based upon the belief that an individual can and must do something to create peace, and a faith that there is an ultimate power of truth and love that can help each of us to develop a center of peace within ourselves which will be highly contagious." It's as if I've "caught" something from these people and it encourages me to strive for more.

The value of World Friendship Center, which stands at the crossroads in Hiroshima, is in the power of the individuals who visit. Pilgrims of all sorts come, some with their own pain or their own project, some without knowledge or passion for such far off events, and they stay overnight. By having breakfast together or talking in a small group of others, by reading books or watching a video together, people experience that deep, common thread that links us. For more than thirty years, World Friendship Center has been a place of hospitality in Hiroshima, a city where they say peace begins. But we know that peace begins in the folds of the human heart and in the imagination which is a factory of possibilities.

Memories of the Future: The Poetry of Sadako Kurihara and Hiromu Morishita

As an invocation, I'd like to begin with a poem by Hiromu Morishita.

> *Hiroshima*
> *Watch dutifully*
> *with your eyes.*
>
> *Here, something happened that shouldn't have.*
> *Here now, something irreparable continues.*
>
> *Here tomorrow, signs of everyone's destruction*
> *may appear.*
>
> *Don't watch with one eye.*
>
> *Don't watch with your arm or with your head.*

With the heart of one who endures despair.[24]

Writers of atrocity, and I will focus on the atrocity of the atomic bombing of Hiroshima, overcome the powerful urge of silence; they, in the words of Minako Goto, are "reopening the grave" which they have "tried to cover for good." She says, "To reach into what lies at the base of consciousness, to retrieve it and turn it into words, is painfully difficult to endure."[25] Because their endeavor is so arduous, they appeal to their readers, as Morishita does in this poem. They request that we offer our "cooperation in a special relationship" as John Whittier Treat puts it in his excellent study *Writing Ground Zero*.[26] This cooperation requires that we listen with "the heart of one who endures despair." Mediated by the imagination, this special relationship has two hallmarks: compassion and what Treat calls an "ethical restraint, a sort of respectful restraint from naively 'understanding' what we read."[27]

Why this special relationship among author, reader, and subject? Perhaps the reasons are obvious to anyone interested in this topic enough to take up this essay, but allow me to sketch them out briefly because they are aspects that define their experience.

To simplify the matter, several forces compound to make "the project of telling"[28] so difficult. First is the magnitude of the event. While contemporary nuclear weapons use "Hiroshima" as a unit of measure, what happened in that city on August 6, 1945 and afterwards was unprecedented. The instant the bomb exploded a few hundred feet above the city, a ball of fire expanded sixty to one hundred yards across reaching temperatures of 54,000 degrees Fahrenheit, on the ground it is estimated that it was 10,000 degrees. For comparison, iron melts at around 2,800 degrees. These heat rays rolled out over the region ahead of blast-force winds that leveled all wooden buildings in a 1.2 mile radius. People in Miyoshi—a city more than thirty-five miles away—report seeing the flash, hearing the explosion, and feeling the concussion. Then the fires. They raged for days, smoldering long after.

Feel the exactitude of documentation? The scientific precision? The technological wonder? As our attention turns in these directions, we face away from the human dimension. It is imaginative literature that returns us to that level.

Unseen, of course, was the radiation, a whole new component to any weapon, one which kept emerging mysteriously in new manifestations: first as acute sickness and messy death in the months as summer turned to autumn and winter, then in the years that followed as leukemia and later still as solid cancers.[29] Another contrast to conventional bombing is how the weapon arrived. Instead of huge aerial raids where planes passed over in waves, their thrumming in the air a warning, the atomic bombs in many ways came—literally—out of the blue. A single bomber. A single bomb. The explosion's suddenness and simultaneity were dumbfounding. It seemed everywhere in the city at the same time, but each individual experienced it as a direct hit on his or her neighborhood.

And this marks the other aspect of this event's hugeness: the scale of human suffering. The number of dead the witnesses saw, the monstrous burns and bloating bodies of those still alive, their insistent and unanswerable appeals for help from all sides, the rapid-moving fires that so many writers could only compare to Buddhist hell paintings. Since the weapon had never been used before, it made no sense and it fit no pattern of warfare, let alone other ordinary human experience.

Writing about the scale of the event creates anxiety about the writer's ability to convey the experience because of the complexities of both the experience and its emotional impact. Hiroshima poet Koichi Tokuno said that he had "doubts over whether...the reality of that day....can ever be communicated by literature to third persons...No matter how much one writes, one is left with the feeling there is more to say."[30] In a similar vein, Sankichi Toge, one of the most famous Hiroshima A-bomb poets, wrote in 1951, "The bigger the event, the less we are able to recognize that, no matter how many people wail their laments, we will never come to terms with our truest feelings."[31] As we see in other attempts to write atrocity, language itself becomes suspect. Hiroko Takenishi asked "What words can we now use, and to what ends? Even: what *are* words?"[32] The truth of the event is betrayed by the language, as Shiro Ozaki wrote, "One has so many things to say, but speaking always feels like a lie."[33]

And yet, in and through these problems of expression, writers did indeed put words to paper. Paradoxically, it was that magnitude that also urged them on. Sadako Kurihara, writing in 1985, explains it this way: "People who have witnessed such tragedy must tell of it. That is the responsibility, the duty that survivors owe to those who died."[34] For her, "the atomic landscape…does not allow me to rest."[35]

Because we still live in this atomic landscape, locating ourselves in relation to Hiroshima informs our current experience. Treat creates a helpful taxonomy of atomic bomb writers that is both chronological and conceptual. The first generation's work attempts to "convey the unconveyable"[36] of what happened and how it felt. These writers suffered through doubt to record their experience, transforming it into literature in all its forms. They also had to contend with the US Occupation and its censorship, which restricted mention of nuclear weapons. The second generation could build on their work to document the ravaging experience and so could "treat the bombings as a social or individual inner problem often touching on broader political or social issues."[37] The contemporary generation turns more philosophical, to explore "culture reeling under the impact of twentieth-century violence."[38] The two writers I am focusing on belong to the first generation by birth but deserve wider attention because they also entertain the concerns of all three.

In the same way that the Peace Museum in Hiroshima collected artifacts from sewing needles fused together to a piano daggered by glass shards, from a child's lunchbox to the famous watch stopped at 8:15, Hiromu Morishita's poem "Fossil of Fire" focuses on a single object to glean from it some semblance of meaning.

Fossil of Fire

This is alas
human karma
sticking and clinging to each other.
Reddish-brown roof tiles burnt and melted. Black soil.
The kneaded folds
nearly bury human bones.
Pure white pain
as if just discovered.
Lump of bone. Powdered bone.
Human collage
kneaded into melted soil
and pasted with ceramic fragments.

The white cavity
gaping in weathered time
forms a fossil and permanently retains
the human tragedy which entered the human skull
and was burnt into its memory.[39]

    This image-based meditation embodies the immediacy and distance that mark this poet's work. While Sankichi Toge, Tamiki Hara, and Sadako Kurihara all composed poems documenting the horrors they witnessed that day, Morishita was only a mile from the hypocenter, and most of his classmates and teachers with him were killed. He was fourteen. He says, "All these sorrows came to me all at once."[40] The physical distance from the flash of those other poets—as well as their difference in age—provided them with emotional distance while his proximity forced him to live for survival first. Only later could he reflect on August 6 formally, as in this poem. Here, he is philosophical about "human karma" and "weathered time," but he also creates a symbol, not out of the "natural object," as Ezra Pound exhorted, but out of a strange "collage." He meditates on how the material nearly obliterates the human, and yet the memory, the story and its testimony, endures as fossils endure. Returning to the human scale is essential because, as Kurihara observes, both the Holocaust and atomic bombings resulted from a dehumanizing logic; she says, "Mankind stopped being mankind and completely became a machine."[41]

Like Kurihara, Morishita's sense of duty compels him, as a man and as an artist. He says, "thinking of this sudden change in fate at the moment of the bombing, as if we were thrown into a smelting furnace...I strongly felt that we who survived the atomic bombing should do something for those suffering so much, and should appeal to people everywhere to understand the disaster that befell Hiroshima so that it might not ever be repeated."[42]

Like Kurihara, he has been an outspoken advocate. He joined a world peace mission in the early 1960s, organized by Barbara Reynolds, was president of a national teacher organization to help educate about the atomic bomb, and is currently the chairman of the World Friendship Center, a community peace organization jointly run by American volunteers and a Japanese board of trustees. My spouse and I served there for two and a half years where I met and worked with Mr. Morishita. I was fortunate to also meet

Kurihara before she died; she was a much more political activist than Morishita (or I). I recall fondly that I was introduced to her on the street near Peace Park, where she was wearing a sandwich board, gathering signatures on petitions against nuclear power. She was already into her eighties at the time.

Although she published a substantial body of work, it appeared in mostly regional and local venues. Nevertheless, she is famous for two poems. The contrast between the two works shows the evolution of atomic bomb literature generally, as Treat laid out in his three generations.

Until recently, Kurihara was best known in Japan for "Let Us Be Midwives!" published in *Black Eggs*, her 1946 collection. American censors deleted stanzas and whole poems from the book before publication, and because of an earlier run in with Occupation officials, she herself cut additional materials out. The whole of the 1942 composition "What is War" was scribbled out, except for the title. It ends "At home they are good fathers, good brothers, good sons, / but in the hell of battle, / they lose all humanity / and rampage like wild beasts."[43] She could speak of these two worlds because she was no stranger to political intrusion: her husband, who was conscripted in 1940 and sent to China, came home and spoke freely of the Japanese brutalities in Shanghai and was arrested the very next day. Historian Richard Minear, Kurihara's translator, says that it was an "act of courage even to commit" some of her poems to paper during the war.[44] Her poem "Let Us Be Midwives!" was allowed in *Black* Eggs and is the one she is most known for within Japan. It reflects her vision of a culture based on humanistic values, not power and economic oppression. Because of its remarkable optimism, it became a hopeful, rallying cry for survivors, peace groups, and others.

Let Us Be Midwives!

—An untold story of the atomic bombing
Night in the basement of a concrete structure now in ruins.
Victims of the atomic bomb
jammed the room;
it was dark—not even a single candle.
The smell of fresh blood, the stench of death,
*   the closeness of sweaty people, the moans.*
From out of all that, lo and behold, a voice:
"The baby's coming!"
In that hellish basement, at that very moment,
a young woman had gone into labor."
In the dark, without a single match, what to do?
People forgot their own pains, worried about her.
And then: "I'm a midwife. I'll help with the birth."
The speaker, seriously injured herself,
*   had been moaning only moments before.*
And so new life was born in the dark of that pit of hell.
And so the midwife died before dawn, still bathed in blood.
Let us be midwives!
Let us be midwives!
Even if we lay down our own lives to do so.[45]

—September 1945

Even in poetry written this soon after the cataclysm, she is bending her poem to achieve her vision. First, she took liberties with the facts: the midwife survived and lived until she was sixty-five, but more importantly the poet's staunch will to live rises to what her translator called "the structure of thought."[46] In her own introduction to the 1946 edition of *Black Eggs* Kurihara dismissed poetry of mere feeling, so prized in Japanese sensibilities, in favor of the "unity of ideas," for "behind the emotions of human life lie the ideas that are the essential pillar of human life."[47] And for her, this structural idea was primarily a "longing for a society not based on power" but "freedom and love and a peaceful society."[48] Resisting Japanese Imperial culture prepared her to unravel the subsequent nuclear culture and continue to envision one built on other values. She is also resisting the Japanese literary tradition of misty suggestion, broad implication from precise imagery, resulting in her poetics built of statement and repetition, suited to the slogan and tending toward the didactic. Nonetheless, her vision is deeply human. She wrote in 1972 that "Experience has to rise to the level of antinuclear ideas, and ideas must descend to the depths of experience where hatreds eddy; without mutual verification, both will harden, and it will be impossible to carry forward a living movement."[49] This "living movement" is of course political and involves petitions and marches, treaties and elections, but it also involves the revolution of the heart to soften hatreds both personal and socially constructed.

Her other famous poem, "When We Say 'Hiroshima,'" which she is known for most *outside of Japan*, deals with perceptions of World War II, initially an Asian war, its aggressions and atrocities. It confronts the hatred that people in Korea, China, the US, and many other nations harbor because of Imperial Army behavior during the war. To take on such themes also requires courage. It necessitates feeling from the other's position. One brave *hibakusha* told me as we stood near the Peace Park monument to Korean victims, many of whom were rounded up and shipped off to Japan as forced labor, "We must remember that for many Asians August 6 means a day of liberation."

Consider this: Urged by the hoarse pleas of the dying, the haunting memories of family members vomiting blood and an eerie black foam as they died, and all the other perplexing, haunting scenes, both Morishita and Kurihara wrote poems to express these images as a warning to all of us because "Here tomorrow, signs of everyone's destruction / may appear." Unlike Holocaust survivors, such testimony was not met with outright denial but justification. Arguments about just desserts. And this becomes another layer in what urges writers to silence: personal experience tangles into political strategy and historic interpretation, national cause and call for reparation. Kurihara's poem takes these arguments on directly.

When We Say "Hiroshima"!

When we say "Hiroshima,"
do people answer, gently,
"Ah, Hiroshima"?
Say "Hiroshima," and hear "Pearl Harbor."
Say "Hiroshima," and hear "Rape of Nanking."

Say "Hiroshima," and hear of women and children in Manila
thrown into trenches, doused with gasoline,
and burned alive.
Say "Hiroshima,"
and hear echoes of blood and fire.

Say "Hiroshima,"
and we don't hear, gently,
"Ah, Hiroshima."
In chorus, Asia's dead and her voiceless masses
spit out the anger
of all those we made victims.
That we may say "Hiroshima,"
and hear in reply, gently,
"Ah, Hiroshima."
we must in fact lay down
the arms we were supposed to lay down.
We must get rid of all foreign bases.
Until that day Hiroshima
will be a city of cruelty and bitter bad faith.
And we will be pariahs
burning with remnant radioactivity.

That we may say "Hiroshima"
and hear in reply, gently,
"Ah, Hiroshima."
we first must
wash the blood
off our own hands.[50]

To many readers, it may seem easy to confront Japan's war history this plainly and clearly, but it too has a cost. Periodically, some nationalist leader in Japan calls the Rape of Nanking a fabrication. In fact, the Mayor of Nagasaki—a "politician with impeccable conservative credentials," as Norma Field puts it in her astounding book *In the Realm of a Dying Emperor*—was nearly assassinated in 1990 by right-wingers for saying that "the emperor does bear responsibility for the war" but was allowed to become the new Constitution's symbol instead.[51] Kurihara herself received threatening phone calls for statements and poems along the same lines. Wherever religion and nationalism converge, there is a mania that can kill.

So why risk all this? Why face the perennial failure of language to adequately deal with reality? For these poets dealing with these subjects, why re-open the grave and entertain their ghosts? Why subject oneself to the censorship and self-censorship of political authorities to remind people of things they don't want to think about? Why open oneself to accusations of profiting from one's pain or writing what cannot be considered "real literature" anyway because of its themes? Why get tangled up in such complex and difficult issues?

Galway Kinnell, speaking in July 1983 at a gathering of writers in Hiroshima, admitted that by its fundamental nature poetry of nuclear age is complex: "the subject is very difficult, inherently very difficult. If a poem is to be useful, it has to give hope, but if it is to be realistic, it has to cause despair. Despair is built into the subject."[52]

Walter Benjamin's angel of history, the guiding image for Carolyn Forche's 1994 collection, faces the past which is "one single catastrophe which keeps piling wreckage" at his feet as a storm from Paradise "propels him into the future." While the bombings of Hiroshima and Nagasaki came at the end of World War II, they were also the birth wails of the Nuclear Age and our current Age of Terror. With every warning about weapons of mass destruction, I remember that Kurihara said: "Hiroshima is the futurescape."[53] In an age of despair over the environmental situations as well as the political wars on terror, our hope is threatened. Are we, the readers and writers of the twenty-first century, willing to address ourselves to these same questions and engage in "useful literature"? As poets of witness continue to remind us, these events are neither settled nor gone. Not the Holocaust, not the atomic bombing of populated cities, not atrocity, and not its censorship.

It is Imagination, that elusive intelligence, which helps those of us who didn't have to experience such extremity firsthand to remember the future. Imagination is necessary, therefore, not only to listen to their testimony but to understand our own role in history, our force in culture, and our duty both to the dead and to the living. And so by facing the past and reading poetry like Sadako Kurihara's and Hiromu Morishita's, we learn the power and limits of Imagination, that critical and compassionate faculty, and return to the scale of human beings.

The Sculpture of Real Feelings: The Poetry of Akiko Yosano

Standing in the sway and whine of the streetcar, the metal pole was firm support in the motion of reading there. My friend, John Bradley, had sent me the Shambhala pocket edition of Whitman's great work, "Song of Myself." And as I stood on the *densha* in Hiroshima, the first city to experience nuclear war, I was startled to receive Whitman's opening lines:

> *I celebrate myself,*
> *And what I assume you shall assume,*
> *For every atom belonging to me as good belongs to you.*[54]

Over and over again, while living in Japan, those words and the sympathies behind them leapt out of the past and from my distant homeland to live and move in me, as my spouse and I were working as volunteers. How do we assume the subjective and distinctive feelings of another, and by "assume" I mean both making assumptions about and taking on their experience, sharing their load? How can anyone assume such mutuality? Such heart-travel seems challenging enough for anyone to do for their own parents, people of different generations, and yet with so much in common. Or for a student to do with a classmate sitting just a few rows over, especially if they have conflict. Is it even possible for a person of one nation to assume the experience of another?

And yet, even though we were Americans living in Japan, and even though we were born long after the end of World War II, we endeavored to inform others of the atrocities of that era. We were trying to cultivate exactly such mutuality. And as people working for peace, our efforts seemed not to change a world where a doomsday cult can poison the train tunnels of Tokyo with sarin gas, where blade-wielding neighbors can slaughter each other in Rwanda, and where nuclear weapons remain in silos, on jets, and in the oceans crisscrossing on submarines. It takes more than intelligence to enter into the experience of those generations before or nations away who experienced war, to understand the motives of the perpetrators, and to learn from the resilience of the survivors. The unity of assumptions Whitman speaks of with such confidence was one of our abiding practices. And it is a practice, an effort. The prevailing winds in culture blow toward othering, fueled by fear in the run-up to conflict and then by pain in the aftermath. It takes effort to call to mind that everyone is a "myself."

In our work as peace volunteers, most often these "others" were victims of war, atomic and otherwise, so Whitman's declaration was comforting as we faced the challenge of such imaginative and sympathetic travel. But his words were also challenging as we felt the comfort of our complacencies, our desire to turn away and numb down. Perhaps that is why, standing with my arm looped around the metal pole on the Hiroshima *densha*, reading "Song of Myself," that one word, "atom," was an electric charge. It zinged me. How contemporary. How true to science and to imagination. I felt that charge of mutuality in the compassion we all felt for the survivors as we understood to some degree their suffering. But it didn't stop there. Those who survived atomic destruction often lived to warn us that we face the threat of what they experienced, and in their brave telling, they were counting on this commonality, which goes down below language and culture, history and religion, to the shared elements of the earth, the atoms. The word also activated an awareness that we are all "bomb-affected," not only imaginatively or potentially, but literally: the radioactive elements spewed into the atmosphere by hundreds of nuclear detonations through the late 1940s through 1963, when the Partial Test Ban Treaty drove the tests underground, are in our bodies. And so, those who are aware of this mutuality struggle to live with the knowledge that humans clutch the means to end our world.

In this context, I first heard of the Japanese poet Akiko Yosano (1878-1942), a writer initially associated with Japan's women's movement. Then, after returning to the US, I read her work in more detail, feeling a similar time-traveling experience I had with Whitman. This time, though, my heart traveled west to the Far East. Imaginatively, I arrived back to a Japanese city, among women. Most of those with whom we'd organized peace and cross-cultural events with in our two and a half years at the World Friendship Center, and certainly those we taught regularly in our conversational English classes, were women. They did not balk at calling themselves "housewives." Many looked with envy at the freedom and strength of American (and other Western) women. Yosano's poem, "Mountain Moving Day," is the first in Sam Hamill and Keiko Matsui Gibson's collection, *River of Stars* in the section of "Modern-style Poems." Perhaps her most famous piece, it is a tribute to these same qualities in Japanese women:

> *Mountains were just sleeping for a while.*
> *Earlier they had moved, burning with fire.*[55]

Japan's landscape is defined by its mountainous and volcanic character, so this image reflects not only the land but also its people. Expanding on the structure of tanka, the poem seems to be about geography, until the crucial pivot to the final couplet. Then the surprise-awareness brings the previous images into sharper focus:

> *All the sleeping women move*
> *now that they awaken.*[56]

From the perspective of an American beyond the hinge of the next millennia, these words may feel almost quaint, but having lived in Japan (if only for a short time), I sense their power, their challenge, and their contemporaneousness—the same vital experience I had with Whitman while in Asia. They represent the latent power of women, and the metaphor challenges the role of women.

Sam Hamill and Keiko Matsui Gibson do a fine job giving a context to her work. Yosano's love life was scandalous in the early 1900s, and I think would be even now, but her challenge to the Emperor system was an even greater revolt. One linchpin in the chain of many causes on both sides of the Pacific that led to what we call World War II, the Emperor system is a political, religious, and social network of loyalties that even now suffers little open protest. An excellent investigation of this is Norma Field's book *In the Realm of a Dying Emperor: Japan at Century's End*. Field profiles four individuals who openly defy the system for different reasons, and the strong reaction they provoke, including death threats from the radical right.

Yosano entered this fray during the Japan-Russo War of 1904. Hamill and Matsui Gibson say, "She was the first poet in Japanese history to publicly and openly criticize the emperor, an act which so infuriated the populace that her house was stoned."[57] It was not only the direct defiance, but doing so in the context of war, I think which irked people so much. Every people closes ranks when an enemy is invoked, but when hostilities erupt, it becomes even more constricting. That tightening noose of group think was evident in the waves of attack-then-relent against Iraq in both the Gulf War of the 1990s and the reprised war there just years later. In her widely viewed TED Talk, "What It's Like to be Muslim in America," Dalia Mogahed summarized research into this dynamic. She says, "when we're afraid, at least three things happen. We become more accepting of authoritarianism, conformity and prejudice."[58]

To resist the tide of conformity, Yosano's poem, "You Shall Not Be Killed, Brother!" mourns her younger sibling in the "besieging army at Port Arthur."[59] The barb of social commentary is propelled by her personal grief:

> *Did your parents raise you*
> *for twenty-four years*
> *to kill and to die?*[60]

Using questions and appeals to him to think about others, Ms. Yosano frames an argument in feeling and the nets of relationships that are so human, and so Japanese. She even extends this level of feeling to the Emperor himself.

> *The honorable Emperor would not personally*
> *engage in the war.*
> *Since the Emperor's heart is so merciful,*
> *how could he possibly ask*
> *others to shed blood*
> *and die like beasts*
> *and believe dying is honor?* [61]

The danger of all social groupings is that they define an "us" and exclude a "them." On its own, this is not dangerous. However, when sympathy is limited to the in-group, it can actually motivate all manner of atrocity against the other. Limiting in-group empathy not only blinds us to the suffering of the other, but it can justify causing that pain. By personalizing the Emperor, who stands behind the order, Yosano crosses the boundary. Who is dying like beasts? Rhetorically, it is her brother and all "our" sons, brothers, and fathers, but her moral imagination includes all who kill and all who die. All the while, she questions responsibility. What is "honor" in these contexts? This poem joins the powerful flow of argument as Wilfred Owen's "Dulce et decorum est" does.

Not all her poems are so openly social, but they all emerge from this depth of passion, this love that is deeply personal but not contained by convention and custom. They range from sensuous (and angry and envious) love poems, sad farewells, self-affirming gestures, as well as these political/social pieces. What unifies them is the way she honors and gives outer form to her inner world. Jane Hirshfield, in her book *Nine Gates: Entering the Mind of Poetry*, distinguishes the Japanese pursuit of refinement of perception to the Western, particularly Modernist, drive to innovate novel means of expression:

> *In classical Japanese literature, the highest value was not on the creation of the new, but the ability to compress within brief written expression the greatest possible resonance of emotion and perception. Individuality of feeling mattered immensely, but individually of expression would have been found bizarre by these writers.*[62]

Through the variety of Yosano's poems, from the tight five-line *tanka* to the looser free verse poems, she sought "a poetry that requires the author to look directly into the heart to reveal the true emotional complexity found there," as Hamill and Matsui Gibson write in their introduction.[63]

It is this complexity of the human heart, rendered honestly, that feels so contemporary in her poems. For such a fleeting thing, the lyric poem endures because honest representations of personal experience resonates with our own. The actual message—the incidents and relationships—does not need to be consistent, but we sense this resonance in the layered richness of individual human experience, rendered in lines that express it directly, truly. In this lyric truth, we can travel from the seemingly sealed confines of our own circumstances and struggles to realize that we really do share, at an atomic level, something significant. Gregory Orr has written clearly and forcefully about this in his study *Poetry As Survival*. Noting the universality of this kind of writing, he says, "lyric poetry is written down or composed in every culture on the planet at this moment, which means something like one thousand different cultures and three thousand languages. All cultures on the globe have a conception of the personal lyric."[64]

Individuality feels like an infinity of unique forms, like snowflakes, and yet, even with the wide diversity of subjective experience within very different social and historical situations, there can be universality. Mutuality comes from our humanity, not circumstances, and, paradoxically, "humanity" is an essential dynamic in each life and one we share. We all experience death, each in our own way to be sure. And hopefully we all have also felt the elation of connecting authentically with another person. Who has not felt disorienting energy of anger over the injustices of the world and the cruelty of our race? Who is spared the collapsing that results from grief, the isolating lethargy of despair? Who has not delighted in some delicate beauty of nature, felt in its random offering a gift? Falling in love, the pain of break ups, and the balm of friendship—these are common experiences, but their felt sense remains unique. This interaction between the outer and our inner response is essential to poetry, and both sides of that equation can be baffling. Orr says that "we are creatures whose volatile inner lives are both mysterious to us and beyond our control. How do we respond to the strangeness and unpredictability of our own emotional being? One important answer to this question is the personal lyric, the "I" poem dramatizing inner and outer experience."[65]

We can sense interplay of inner and outer worlds when reading Yosano's tanka. In one love poem, she writes,

> *Concentrated so*
> *completely on each other*
> *I can't tell us apart:*
> *you, the white bush clover,*
> *from me, the soft white lily.*[66]

The last metaphors demonstrate sexual union and the blurring of identity, how two bodies joined can feel like one body, how two persons joined can feel like one. Such intensity of passionate union shifts our understanding of ourselves. In a later poem, she finds herself returning to a waterway where she and her lover had visited.

> *Both he and I*
> *were just barely 19*
> *when we saw our faces*
> *reflected in the waters*
> *of this gently flowing stream.*[67]

This *tanka* demonstrates Hirshfield's observation about a brief poem containing and evoking "the greatest possible resonance of emotion and perception." On one level it is a deft memory, the image of a couple gazing at each other's face floating on the surface of the water is recalled by the now-older speaker, seemingly alone. And so the poem resonates both with the young lover's delight and with the older speaker's nostalgia. However, the ambiguity of "this gently flowing stream" suggests another level of resonance. Time, with its stream of change, brings loss as well as gain, death as well as life, and this speaker feels the power of that current. Though gentle, it is relentless. It is difficult not to read such a layered poem and not sense the changes in one's own life. As I travel into her experience, I return to my own, and the journey may only take a few moments, but I return changed.

Empathetic travel—in poetry especially, but in good listening, too—allows us not only to meet another and find there familiarity but also to encounter ourselves. Likewise, if we go deeply into our own experience, we can connect to others. The Zen master, Dogen declares that Buddhists "study the self in order to forget the self." What seems like Zen wordplay is actually a statement of shared humanity. It is what Whitman said in "Song of Myself" when he asserts: "Do I contradict myself?/ Well then I contradict myself. / I contain multitudes." Both are pointing to the paradox that demonstrates how if we explore our own subjectivities we can realize a powerful mutuality.

At their essence, Yosano's poems embody a passionate love, even in the loss and anger, the injustice and violence.

It is this love that makes her poetry stand up to time, crossing cultures, even language. Yosano puts a primacy on this aspect, saying, "Poetry is the sculpture of real feelings."[68] This formal manifestation is demonstrated by this *tanka*:

> *In return for all*
> *the sins and crimes of men,*
> *the gods created me*
> *with glistening long black hair*
> *and pale, inviting skin.*[69]

Her inner turmoil about the chaos in the world and her own self-identity within that external reality are formalized into this balanced utterance. She is not merely praising her physical beauty—although affirming that from within and not as beheld by another is invaluable—she is upholding her own dignity as a divinely made creature. What answers the world's "sins and crimes'? Beauty is the response. While at the World Friendship Center, I heard many "sins and crimes." It was Hiroshima at the fiftieth anniversary of the end of World War II, and so all the stories of atrocities came out. And they all were stories of individuals—women corralled by Japanese soldiers as sex slaves; doctors doing biological and medical experiments on POWs in Harbin, China by Unit 734; soldiers and sailors in the wretched combat scenes all over the Pacific region; and the life-long suffering of atomic bomb survivors. Just hearing them made me want to turn away, to seek distraction, and to shut down. What is the role of lyric poetry, then?

Love and beauty open us and allow us to experience our lives and to feel the experience of another from within.

Wilfred Owen penned his motto from the trenches of World War I: "Above all I am not concerned with Poetry. My subject is War, and the pity of War. The Poetry is in the pity."[70] He might have leaned heavily on pity because of the anguish of his experience and to answer the ruthless limitation of empathy in service of the justifications of war. But the mutuality I am discussing is vaster than this. "Love allows us gently, respectfully and intimately to slip into the life of another person or animal or even the earth itself and know it from the inside," says Arthur Zajonc, who is Emeritus Professor of Physics at Amherst College. "In this way, love can become a way of moral knowing that is as reliable as scientific thought."[71] The travel of feeling, going out into another's experience and returning to inform our own, is the real art. As Yosano's and Whitman's poems demonstrate, the compassion and love inside any individual person is far more than sentiment; it is salvation, and when practiced and nourished in our nets of relationship, it is the basis of any moral reciprocity.

Beyond the Fishbowl

Lessons in Totalitarianism: Seeking the Path of Love-acted-out

During the day, the glass-walled lounge in the Commons at Penn State was always warm and quiet; people read or slept on the soft chairs. That night, and most times I went to the meetings, the Fishbowl—as everyone called it—was nearly filled with Christians standing in small clusters, talking intently. It was a Campus Crusade for Christ meeting.

These people encouraged me to read the Bible for myself and to take what it says seriously. There were many parts I knew well from weekly Mass and periodically serving daily Mass as an altar boy, but there were passages before and after those familiar readings I never knew about, and whole books in the Bible I'd never cracked. It was good to read a whole letter of Paul's to get the context of a passage I thought I understood. And it was good to gather together in someone's dorm room to talk about God, about Bible-values, about living what it said. It brought an experience to the words I'd heard about "where two or three are gathered in my name, there I am in their midst."

I continued to attend Mass and enjoyed the enrichment of increased study and devotion. I invited my born-again roommate who'd gotten me to go to Campus Crusade to my Catholic ritual; he found a lot of it "not Biblical." He liked parts, too, but only went that once. After nearly five months of intimate spiritual discussions, that night in the HUB Fishbowl, I was posed questions I'd been asked before; I was challenged in a way that made it my last Campus Crusade for Christ meeting. One man I remember well but not clearly: tall, neatly dressed in a sport-shirt, blonde-haired. His tidy, informal attire hint to me now that he may have been part of the leadership team.

Why do you call priests, "Father," when in Matthew 23:9 Jesus says, "And call no one on earth your father, for you have one Father, the one in heaven" (NRVS)? Why do you pray to saints when Jesus is our perfect High Priest and mediator with the Father? Where in the Bible does it say the pope is infallible?

These questions—along with ones about Mary, the Sacrament of Reconciliation (Confession), and other Roman Catholic dogma—were not put to me in a seeking spirit but in a spirit of correction. It was time, I was told, to purify my faith. "Why," asked the blonde man sincerely, "do you still go to a service that kills Jesus again and again? His blood was shed once, and the sacrifice on Calvary was enough. Don't you think it's a little presumptuous of man to try to improve on what God has done?"

Convinced of their truth, backed by Holy Scripture, and using the depths of their sincerity and concern for my soul, these people were undermining the authority—the

Roman Catholic Church—that had instructed me in what was True. And, what was most troubling, they were doing it with an ultimate Authority of their own. It was a standoff. More confounding, though, was how in some ways, we both invoked the same Authority to support different points. I was taught from childhood that salvation is achieved in the Catholic Church because under the mantle of the Church, which Jesus founded, I could receive the sacraments, especially the Eucharist, the actual trans-substantiated Body of Christ. Catholics take the passages referring to the Last Supper quite literally: where Jesus said, "This is my body," he changed the *matter* of the bread. "Do this in remembrance of me" is a command to continue this miracle. But those at Campus Crusade for Christ were taking other passages from the Holy Book to cast my beliefs in question.

Both of us couldn't be entirely correct. One or both was in error and had to change to more closely follow Christ.

I never went back to Campus Crusade, not because I thought I was right but because I felt judged. I was willing to listen and consider the truth of their position. I tried to understand. I wanted to learn. I'm not claiming sainthood—by no means. All I'm saying is: in a search for Truth and spiritual authenticity, I was being asked to renounce. I was being asked to disclaim not only elements of belief but my claim on the source of those beliefs. I know those who agree with Crusade doctrine would feel justified in putting someone at such a crossroads, but it struck me as presumption.

So, for the next two years after stopping my participation with Campus Crusade, I was deeply involved with the

Catholic campus ministry. Fundamentalism, the return to the foundation through a literal interpretation and understanding of the Bible, was always a lively issue. Many Catholics at Penn State and countless other schools had experiences like mine in the Fishbowl. Fundamentalism challenges what and how we construct Jesus' message. I used to say the heart of the issue was the literal reading of Scripture, but that's not the whole story because Catholics take certain sections very literally as I pointed out earlier, or the ability to forgive sins that Jesus bestowed on the apostles in John 20: 22-3. No, literalness is not the true issue.

If such word-by-word holy truth were the root concern, who could follow such Biblical mandates as Paul's exhortation in Romans 13:

> *Let every person be subject to the governing authorities; for there is no authority except from God, and those authorities that exist have been instituted by God. Therefore whoever resists authority resists what God has appointed, and those who resist will incur judgment. For rulers are not a terror to good behavior, only to bad. Do you wish to have no fear of the authority? Then do what is good, and you will receive its approval; for it is God's servant for your good.*[72]

In light of history's many murderous governments, particularly of the twentieth century, can we still believe that God institutes and "ordains" (in the King James Version) each and every civil government? Rationalizations become necessary to transform such passages into a livable ethic in the face of our human story. Perhaps, one might say,

God supports the *principle* of government, without which our lives together would be chaos, but not actual individual governments. Clearly, Paul's speaking of civil authority correcting injustices, so if one lives justly and honestly, then one has nothing to fear from any just government. But that's not what the passage says or implies. The command "be subject to the governing authorities" is unequivocal; in the New International Version, it's more compelling: "All of you must be willing to obey completely those who rule over you."

Perhaps, this is all too general with too many dimensions, depending on the nation in question and the era. How about the specific question of one person owning another?

> *Let all who are under the yoke of slavery regard their masters as worthy of all honor, so that the name of God and the teaching may not be blasphemed. Those who have believing masters must not be disrespectful to them on the ground that they are members of the church; rather they must serve them all the more, since those who benefit by their service are believers and beloved. Teach and urge these duties.*[73]

How can I be judged by a book that defends slavery (though some translations soften this support by using "servants" or those "forced to serve as slaves" (NIV) and surrenders to Nazis or submits to the Taliban or ISIS?

When we speak of totalitarianism, visions of Stalin's Soviet Union or Hitler's Third Reich or Saddam Hussein's Iraq or any ISIS controlled region march quickly to mind.

When compared to such brutal horrors, our petty judgments about a line or two of a sacred text seem harmless, trivial even. However, such a measure compares the wrong way. Our goal isn't "relative innocence" in contrast to the darkness of evil.

The central issue concerning fundamentalism is not one of literalness but of absolutes, a kind of totalism, not regarding God but regarding other people. If I believe—a matter of faith—I have an indubitable Authority, whether it's the Bible or the Roman Catholic Church, then I don't need to listen to anyone but that Authority and maybe other people who follow it. And, if the stakes are high enough, as they are with eternal life or eternal suffering, then I am not only entitled but encouraged—even commanded—to inform others of the errors of their ways. Here is where conviction blends into fanaticism so often associated with Muslims and the Middle East, with terrorists and violence. Absoluteness is very easy to find in others, but another experience helped locate the center of totalism in myself, which also shaped my spiritual journey.

At Penn State many denominations of Christianity, as well as other faiths, had campus ministries in what was then called the Eisenhower Building. I spent much time in the small chapel where the Eucharist is housed for devotion, and also at the Catholic campus ministry offices on the second floor. Downstairs, in the basement, was an Islamic prayer room. Muslims removed their shoes before disappearing from my vision as well as my imagination. They weren't even Christian, I thought, so why should I deal with them? It wasn't quite so callous or deliberate an attitude, but I never "bothered" with them.

One evening my born-again roommate and I got to talking with a Muslim student. Of course, we talked on and on about God, but I left early for some reason; I was confused. Part of me couldn't take him very seriously because I knew that Jesus was God's Son and had come to earth to redeem us by his blood. I believed humans are fallen creatures who need God's mercy, and the only road to forgiveness is sacrifice; Jesus' death on the cross was the supreme and perfect sacrifice—He was the innocent victim, the scapegoat for our sins. Despite my differences with Campus Crusade for Christ, my roommate and I shared this belief.

This man, a devout man who had studied his tradition deeply, did not believe that Jesus was God's Son, and had Authority for his faith, the Koran. When we got back to the room, my friend imitated him, "The Koran," he said pointing to the ceiling, "it is of God."

The Bible is "of God."

Can both books be *The* Word of God? Who is right? How do we know?

If the Muslim is wrong, will he be barred from eternal reward for denying the Christ despite his piety, devotion, and disciplined prayer? If the Muslim is right, well then...

And once we consider this, we must think of the millions of devout Hindus and Buddhists who consider our life as humans only as one sojourn in a countless cycle of appearances. These believers have a different sense of time, of the soul, as well as of God. Do they laugh when Christians say that we believe that a human sacrifice was needed by God to pay the debt people owed for sin, or when Christians say that Mary remained a virgin, conceiving Jesus by the Holy Spirit with no man involved? Do they dismiss them as "fables" or "myths"? (I'll never forget in a course on Hinduism and Buddhism, Dr. Charles Prebish recounted the conception and birth of the Buddha, then answered the snickers in class by saying that it was only as "absurd" as a virgin birth.)

From these two experiences—one where I was judged and my beliefs discounted, even repudiated, and the other where I judged and repudiated another's—I learned that there is danger in becoming so absolute in my beliefs that I cannot see the faith and truth in another. If I hold so absolutely to a list of essentially unprovable things that I fail to love—the behavior that enacts and enlivens those beliefs—then I myself deny those beliefs. I began to feel this censure in my other behaviors and in my reading as well.

Here is a story from Rev. Anthony de Mello's collection of disciple/Master encounters, called *One Minute Wisdom*, named because each potent story only takes about sixty seconds to read.

> *To the disciples' embarrassment the Master once told a bishop that religious people have a natural bent for cruelty.*
>
> *"Why?" demanded the disciples after the bishop had gone.*
>
> *"Because they all too easily sacrifice persons for the advancement of a purpose," said the Master.*[74]

Seeing my own capacity for cruel sacrifice of people to the purpose of "conversion" or "communion," I saw how those beliefs were diminished by my own behavior. The experience of feeling judged and misunderstood convinced me that no one deserves that sensation. I dedicated myself to trying to understand people who seem different and to trying to see situations and people through the eyes of the victims.

In the fullest description of the afterlife that Jesus gives in the Gospels in Matthew 25, he separates people, not according to what they believe or even in whom but according to their love-acted-out in care for the hungry and thirsty poor, the sick, prisoners, and homeless. These righteous ones always ask, "When did we see you like that?" not recognizing the Holy One in their midst. Jesus answers them by distributing his own identity: "Just as you did it to one of the least of least who are members of my family, you did it to me."[75]

Through encounters with community organizers in West Virginia and Kentucky on behalf of coal miners and the rural poor, with homeless advocates in Philadelphia and Springfield, Massachusetts, with activists working to realign our military policies and spending with values of justice and equality, and volunteering at a peace center in Hiroshima, I have come to question many of the beliefs I held so strongly.

Witnessing people living radical love and my own small efforts in that same direction led me to a conviction that when we touch the heart of the Divine, we experience the unity of all things and a love that bursts the wine skins. This unconditional regard reaches beyond economic class, occupation, race, gender, national boundary, even religion—maybe especially religion. When we touch this love, we are stirred to aid the suffering, right injustice, and cultivate this compassion in others.

My conviction and the witness of others eventually led me to Quakerism, particularly a book called *Quiet Rebels*. The consistent, humble expression of love for prisoners, slaves, war-victims, Native Americans, and the confident insightful awareness of women's equality felt like a lock had clicked open or a seed planted long ago had instantly germinated and sprouted. Such a small group has had a tremendous influence! I sought them out and their silent worship, which I first experienced after leaving Campus Crusade for Christ and after that I began doing a little meditation. The hour of seeking together was refreshing, invigorating, and challenging all in one gesture.

Two articles of faith that resonated within me have become my guide in matters of orthodoxy and authority. First is the unity of the Spirit, not bound by creed or any other human category. Second is that communion with this Spirit bears fruit.

From a very early age, I have been seeking God; at my Catholic high school, I took the unusual step of signing up for more religion courses than were required, including World Religions. I always imagined there are others who grew up with the training, passion, and conviction that I did, only in completely other beliefs. When I read what William Penn wrote in 1693, I feel like a hollow bell struck—it still rings true: "The humble, meek, merciful, just, and devout souls are everywhere of one religion; and when death has taken off the mask they will know each other though the divers liveries they wear here makes them strangers."[76]

When I start from a faith in the unity of the Spirit, my interaction with others becomes a search for truth and purity, not error and heresy. It also raises my own humility by recognizing that I cannot contain the whole and continuous Truth. This humble search then opens me to a wider community. John Woolman wrote,

> *There is a principle which is pure, placed in the human mind, which in different places and ages hath had different names. It is, however, pure and proceeds from God. It is deep and inward, confined to no forms of religion nor excluded from any, where the heart stands in perfect sincerity. In whomsoever this takes root and grows, of what nation soever, they become brethren.*[77]

In silence and open dialogue with others, this Truth can be known or, at least, glimpsed. This is part of the purpose of prayer and meditation. I have always felt this. George Fox, the Society of Friends' founder, wrote that we should "take heed, dear Friends, to the promptings of love and truth in your hearts, which are the leadings of God."[78] The silent meetings for worship, waiting and testing such leadings, brings me to the Authority which enlivens all churches and creeds, which writes holy books, which helps understand them, and which ultimately helps us live them.

Rather than Church teachings alone, the Bible alone, or any other authority, the Spirit who gives rise to them will teach us our path. We must seek, listen, wait. Then obey.

In questions of morality, I rely on a standard Quaker story. William Penn, wealthy aristocrat, sought out Fox because he was in a dilemma over his new conviction that Christians cannot be soldiers. Aristocrats always wore swords. When Penn asked him about it, Fox trusted the man's conscience and the work of the Spirit to enable him to do what is right. "Wear thy sword as long as thou canst," he said.[79]

Now I try to rely on the promptings of love and truth, on a community of seekers, and on the exercise of those promptings—all these bear fruit. Jesus often said you can judge people's faith by the fruit they bear. This standard was given to me by a Christian Brother spiritual director when I was seeking through fundamentalism. He quoted from Galatians: "the fruit of the Spirit is love, joy, peace, patience, kindness, generosity, faithfulness, gentleness, and self-control. There is no law against such things."[80] Whenever action manifests these, the Spirit is at work. Whenever there is hatred, envy, quarrels, anger, sexual impropriety, self-indulgence, Spirit is needed. I am often surprised to read how many of these signs relate to violence, fighting, and conflict rather than sex, another reason I respond so deeply to Quakerism's traditional testimony against war and for nonviolent conflict resolution.

Putting this middle way into language strips all the anguish out of it. For example, in our years at the World Friendship Center, we found ourselves working with a whole range of people like artists, political activists, Christians and Buddhists because we approached the idea of "peacemaking" very broadly. In Japan, many Buddhists' spiritual practice animates them mostly at a ritual level, and typically only around funeral arrangements, much like "Christmas and Easter" Christian churchgoers in the West. Therefore, it was certainly easier to recognize Woolman's idea of a "pure principle" in the Buddhist priest we met who wasn't interested in only being a funeral director. He raised money and awareness for people in need, to express Buddhist compassion. When the three of us spoke of compassion as an active force, we sensed our kindredness, despite obvious differences in language (which made expressing such complex ideas difficult), nationality, culture, and religion.

However, crossing boundaries like this causes me to feel like a contrary man, not fitting into any established group and not advocating clearly or forcefully for any cause. Some of the hardest expressions of seeking to align with the "promptings of love and truth" come when in the company of our "brethren." I felt the pain of this once when in Washington, DC, with thousands of other citizens voicing our opposition to yet another Iraq War. I remember the warmth and comradery I felt surfacing from the subway and seeing streams of people converging on the National Mall. All stripes of people were in communion, with a common purpose: there were Peace and Justice Catholics, labor unionists, busloads of Mennonites, whole congregations of Methodists (it seemed), and Buddhists chanting for peace. When the march rounded toward the Naval Yard, though, I could feel people's "natural bent for cruelty" come out. A chant went up and was launched against whatever service members could hear: "Ho-ho, hey hey! How many babies did you kill today?" Instantly, I felt exiled, a stranger in a strange land. I have always sought out the conviction of

Veterans for Peace and other people who've worn the uniform but came to refuse. These are my brethren. I knew that some of them could be in the Navy right at that moment, listening to such meanness, and their hearts would be hardened. That is not the fruit of the Spirit.

Likewise, when in gathered stillness with fellow Quakers, and one of us begins praying to Jesus, those with a more universalist spirituality tense up. When our Meeting decided whether or not to share our building with a Queer Church (which manages to be Biblically literalist as well), it took many rounds and great effort to listen through wording to what each heart was expressing. We didn't come to unity on the issue of renting the building, mostly because of practical reasons (insurance, ADA compliance, and the building inspection that revealed structural flaws). But those of us who hunkered down and met often for dialogue felt the bonds of community strengthened through that process. We sought to hear the sincerity behind their quoted scriptures and our reluctance to rent. For some, the long, painted nails and drag outfits, the speech patterns and gestures were just too much. The strain of these conversations sent one Quaker away forever; listening to the promptings of love and truth is difficult.

In an everyday example, I served on a work committee with representatives from all levels of the institution, but the president was a hard man to collaborate with. Essentially a narcissist, he always reflected others' points of view refracted through his own or, worse, consulted others simply so that he could say he had consulted. Those meetings caused me to knot inside and to carry on ranting rebuttals in my mind even hours or days later. I lost sleep contending with this person. A breakthrough came when I recalled the wise mantra of another Quaker I'd met years earlier who had a similar work dynamic. She said that all the while she was listening, she'd intone to herself: "What is the loving response? What is the loving response?" I knew I'd made progress when I was able to laugh at one point during a meeting and say simply, "That's not true, as far as I know. The minutes say different." And there was no sea of boiling acid in my stomach. I didn't want this man to "be shown up" or to "get his." At that moment, anyway. Instead, I felt stable in the truth as I knew it, and so I could express it without anger or resentment. Maybe someday, I'll be able to do so with a modicum of love too.

Rather than relying on an existing authority, one I must apply to new situations, I prefer leaving the question open. The answer to "Which authority?" becomes static, fixed. Even when pressed, the Divine wouldn't give a name but I Am Who Am, or I Am Who I Am, which is a whisper to listen for. It keeps me on alert to the unrepeatable braiding of forces moving to form each situation, and it keeps me lively to ways love can be expressed in it.

I have certainly come far from the long nights in Penn State dorm rooms interpreting a verse or two of the Bible. I have come to believe that I must practice love far more than preach it (or preach anything else for that matter). I have come to the conviction that we must enlarge our hearts by opening them to the Spirit, and we will learn what response is needed. Our hearts grow true by drawing close to elemental things—silence, water, soil, wind, rock; our hearts grow wise by learning to recognize our neighbor not only in those nearby but also in people who live far from us in custom and belief, even to those whom we deem enemies; our hearts grow peaceful by treating them with all the dignity and respect and compassion we can muster. By this path, whatever effect it has on others, I will be made more human and so more holy.

The Secret History of Our "Enemies"

Decades ago, when I first read *All Quiet on the Western Front*, I copied out this sentence: "A word of command has made these silent figures our enemies; a word of command might transform them into our friends." Then, years later, in the mid-1990s, when I was a volunteer at the World Friendship Center in Hiroshima, I saw for myself just how easily such a shift can be; a survey reported a remarkable percentage of Japanese born after WWII ended thought the US and Japan were allies during the war. Given our postwar solidarity with Germany, Japan, and Italy as part of the European Union, it certainly does seem true that enemies tearing at each other's throats could become friends. How does that happen?

Any process of human transformation begins in the imagination, and one great tool of the imagination is literature. With *All Quiet*, I remember the anguish of the emotionally terrible content being conveyed in pleasing language, an experience I have had with only a few other books (Toni Morrison's *Beloved*, for example). Balancing such conflicting emotions simultaneously requires courage, to stay with the experience even as one part of the self recoils and may want to flee. Karen Armstrong, the scholar of religion, in her book *Twelve Steps to a Compassionate Life* declares that art can also contribute to

> *expanding our sympathies. Plays, films and novels all enable us to enter imaginatively into other lives and make an empathetic identification with people whose experience are entirely different from our own. They can give us moments of compassionate ekstasis [a "stepping out" of habitual understandings], and we should resolve, during this step, to allow art to unsettle us and make us question ingrained preconceptions.*[81]

I also remember Paul's despair after the intensity of trench warfare. I copied out this passage, too, because I could identify even though I had not experienced anything like what he'd witnessed in WWI: "How senseless is everything that can ever be written, done, or thought, when such things are possible."[82]

Having traveled with him through the extremes of boredom and intensity of trench warfare, I also sensed a futility to blockbuster films and the dating drama most of my friends were caught up in. This same sentiment was echoed after WWII and the death camps by Theodor Adorno when he said, even more tersely, "To write poetry after Auschwitz is barbaric." Adorno later clarified this statement, taken out of context in a densely philosophical essay, saying that his position could support his statement at one end of the argument, given the import of the Holocaust, but he could also support "Hegel's statement in his *Aesthetics* that as long as there is an awareness of suffering among human beings there must also be art as the objective form of that awareness."[83]

The practice of art here is exactly that: to be aware of the suffering and the powerful forces that command and organize it, but also to situate it in values that are likewise powerful enough to transform the experience for those who suffer it and perhaps the structures that perpetuate it as well. In Remarque's novel, Paul reflects in a similar way, saying,

> *I am young, I am twenty years old; yet I know nothing of life but despair, death, fear, and fatuous superficiality cast over an abyss of sorrow. I see how peoples are set against one another, and in silence, unknowingly, foolishly, obediently, innocently slay one another. I see that the keenest brains of the world invent weapons and words to make it more refined and enduring.*

For many soldiers, medics, and others who encounter warfare directly, these lessons are imprinted through experience. However, for many of us, fortunately, we are able to learn some of this through a moral imagination engaged in literature, in words that are not trying to refine warfare. It's important that a war generation—as most are—practice sympathy for those who suffer.

The pointlessness of trench warfare's bloody stalemate seems all we recall of World War I. Aside from Wilfred Owen's poetry of pity, no other book captures its idleness, confusion, and animal ferocity as well as *All Quiet on the Western Front*. It's still stunning to me that Remarque's book is on high school reading lists, even *required* in some places, because it exposes the brutality rather than the nobility of war. Even more shocking is that it does so through the experience of "the enemy."

We are yet to allow an Afghan or Iraqi narrative such a place in our American consciousness. Heather Raffo's play *Nine Parts of Desire*, comes the closest. The drama depicts nine Iraqi women's stories, and is made even more intimate because it is often performed by a single actor playing all the parts. By witnessing one person embody the voice and experience of such a variety of people, it encourages audience members to likewise allow the arbitrary boundaries between self and other to soften, even disappear if the transference is full enough. As a second generation Iraqi-American, Raffo's voice is potent. I do hope that the play finds a prominent place in our literary imagination and history. Further, I hope for the Afghan novel or Iraqi story that will tell the story in a way that the common, human experience will break through our official version of ourselves as enemies in these conflicts.

However, given the amount of time that's passed, you'd think there'd be an *All Quiet* for us from Korea. I know of none in the popular culture or school curriculum. For Vietnam, our literary experience is well represented by memoirs, novels, and poems by a wide range of US citizens who went to Asia and were transformed. However, where are the Vietnamese stories of that shared suffering in American culture? Oliver Stone's film version, *Heaven and Earth*, of Le Ly Hayslip's memoirs is the most mainstream example, as he takes the journey of a Vietnamese woman who gets caught between both Communist and

South Vietnamese fighters before tangling with Americans. She eventually marries a US soldier who takes her to the States where she is subjected to his violent disintegration. So, the movie is a kind of American story viewed through the back of the mirror rather than a direct reflection of what war was like for our "enemies." Le Ly Hayslip's books are certainly more directly Vietnamese, but unfortunately they don't show up on anyone's high school reading lists, and in a video culture, they will remain eclipsed by the film version.

All this makes John Balaban's translations from the Vietnamese even more important. Balaban registered as a conscientious objector during Vietnam but volunteered to work as a field representative for the International Voluntary Services, which treated children wounded in the war; he tells the whole story in his memoir *Remembering Heaven's Face*. In "The Invisible Powers," a presentation given at the US Air Force Academy in 2009, Balaban gives this thumbnail description of his work:

> *The children that we brought to major US teaching hospitals were riddled by bullets, slashed by cluster bomb flechettes, blinded and deafened by tossed grenades, had their lips and jaws shot away, their spines severed. Others had their limbs blown off, including one 12-year-old boy left with only an arm after a road mine blast. Another boy had his chin glued to his chest by napalm.*[84]

Just like many combat veterans, he has awful memories of his experience and suffered from PTSD. We need literature to break into the conversation about warfare to deliver some of the on-the-ground experiences. We need these details to be personal, as they are lived, and not interpreted by the refinements of those who commanded it in the first place or those who justify it afterwards. However, imagination cannot stop there. For peace to be imagined, we need more than the horrors of war. For transformation to be possible, we need to experience other human beings as persons. Even Balaban says his experience needed to be broader than these awful memories. He says, "the memory of such suffering would have been my sole, unadulterated sense of Vietnam hadn't my job often taken me into the countryside" where he'd talk with parents about their children's care.[85] In the countryside, he encountered the poetry of Vietnam, and through his translations readers can, too.

In 2000, Balaban published *Spring Essence: The Poetry of Hô Xu Xuan Huong*, and his collection of folk songs, *Ca Dao Viet Nam*, was reprinted in 2003. Both help readers of English taste the long history and culture of a place whose image has been confined to relatively recent events and reflected through the limiting lens of "our" war. Such translations not only expand our historical understanding, they enable our cultural imagination to gain depth and nuance.

The original edition of *Ca Dao Viet Nam*, published by Blue Unicorn in 1974, was the first appearance of these folk songs in any Western language. In the new version, they are supplemented by a fine introduction and a moving account of how Balaban gathered songs over a nine-month period while the war raged around him. Most of the forty-nine pieces in *Ca Dao Viet Nam* are under ten lines long, and Balaban creates poems in English that are sparse and musical without ever denigrating into article-skipping phrasing or forcing English rhyme or meter patterns onto the originals. *Ca dao* (pronounced "ka zow" or "ka yow") are not Chinese-style poems in Vietnamese, but as Balaban reports, they are native to Vietnam and probably were sung as far back as a thousand years ago with even deeper roots.

What do these songs express? Moments of tranquility, the anguish of being far from home, putting a child to sleep, "Whisky Lovers," the roll of the seasons, and, of course, love—longing for it and pained by it. They are the same experiences of Japanese *tanka* and *haiku*, of the old English ballads, of literature around the world. It is our human heritage.

Balaban arranges his own poetry collections artfully so individual poems work together for a larger experience, and this is also true in these books. For example, he intensifies the loneliness of "The Homesick Bride" who says, "I pick up my bowl. I put it down,"[86] by following it with "The Outpost Soldier" who first describes the landscape of his exile then ends with "I've lived in the forest for three years."[87] The intensity of being in one place while longing for another is an exile's experience. These could be torn from any immigrant's letters coming to the US from any part of the world, or they could be notes in a diary of a settler of the North American prairies. Or they could be Syrians in the refugee camps all over the Mediterranean. By choosing songs so emblematically lyrical, Balaban zooms in on the emotional depth of the experience, and it is there that humans find common ground.

"The Body is Pain," for me, stands for the whole book, as well as for the potential of this book to humanize the "other."

> At the outpost now for three years,
> by day, on guard. My nights the mandarin plans.
> Clearing bamboo, slashing wood stands.
> The body is pain. I can't complain.
> My food is bamboo shoots and plums.
> My fuel and friends are the bamboo.
> In the well, one fish swims alone and free.[88]

The daily grind of army work is so tightly delivered, as is the self-motivating pep talk. The longing in the final lines moves in so many directions that I am stunned by the compression: frustrated with the monotony of bamboo, being homesick and friend-sick, envying the fish trapped in a well for its seeming autonomy. Except for details from a specific landscape, it could have been a Roman soldier on the borders of the empire, an American stationed somewhere in the Mekong delta, or one of Saddam's Iraqi soldiers during the long agony of war with Iran.

Along with this collection of folk songs, Balaban has given the English speaking world *Spring Essence*, the Nôm poems of Hô Xuân Huong, a woman writing roughly around the time Jane Austen was penning her novels. A monumental book, *Spring Essence* marked the first translation into English of this eighteenth century woman's poems. Michael Wiegers, now Executive Editor at Copper Canyon, called them "wickedly funny, incisive; and at times shocking poems."[89] When *Booklist* hailed the collection,

Donna Seaman noted that the author lived in an "era of political turmoil, war, famine, and corruption (not unlike twentieth century Vietnam),"[90] and I would add not unlike many places in our epoch of global terrorism and covert or proxy warfare. Hô Xuân Huong eschewed the Chinese script of the literati for the all-but-lost Nom script, which is printed (for the first time as type) along with modern Vietnamese versions and Balaban's English. Balaban compares her choice to Dante's choice to write in Italian and Chaucer's decision to use English.

Although much of what we know about her biography comes from the poems, we do know that as a woman, a widow, a concubine, Hô Xuân Huong was marginalized. In these ways, she is more like the Chinese poet Li Quingzhao than Jane Austin. But as an educated and highly intelligent person, "she survived," Balaban states in the introduction, "because of her exquisite cleverness at poetry."[91] Her formal precision is matched by a doubling of meaning, often sexual, breaking the Confucianist taboos of the time—and ruffling feathers even today. The reviewer for *Publishers Weekly* said that "such contrivances can make for entertaining reading" but without being able to read the dexterity of the originals, they "won't bear repeated perusals."[92] Amusement is not the only purpose or effect of double entendre; whatever breaks a barrier questions the barrier itself. For example, in one of her poems, Sappho addresses virginity. Willis Barnstone translates it like this: "Virginity, virginity, where have you gone, leaving me abandoned? / No longer will I come to you. No longer will I come."[93] Not only the individual speaker's longing for what cannot return, the poem questions what is the cultural and personal "value" of virginity for a woman of the seventh century BCE. If it's marriage, then longing for her virginity indicates that the speaker is confronting the culturally defined sense that a wife should be happy with her lot. The loss of virginity for girls and young women invite us to consider how willingly the speaker was initiated into sex. The barrier or taboo is doubled, then. Even today, men will stigmatize women who are the victims of sexual assault. Even without that shadow cast upon the speaker's situation, the poem leads us to ask: Is sex as a topic off limits for writers of that era? If so, just taking it on is a boldness that we may miss in our age of exhibitionism. Even more, as a literary text of our time, Barnstone's pun in virginity's reply puts the enjoyment of sex alongside the loss of "innocence," breaking the barrier of romanticism we build around virginity and the simplified notions of women's sexuality. The poem makes these points because they are embedded in the multiple meanings, even in a translation that cannot convey all the layers of association.

Furthermore, Philip Gambone, writing in *The New York Times Book Review* saw that Hô Xuân Huong's use of *double entendre* did more than entertain: they were "trenchant indictments of the plight of women and the arrogance, hypocrisy, and corruption of men."[94] For example, one of these brief poems makes its point at many levels at once. "Teasing Chiêu-Hô" targets one of the most learned men of her time, says Balaban, and engages him in literary banter, a feat that seems remarkable on its own. Here is the poem in its entirety:

Is the master drunk? Is the master awake?
Why flirt with the moon in the middle of the day?

Perhaps there's something I ought to say:
Don't stick your hand in the tiger's cage.[95]

Not only does the poem dismiss the master and the prospect of making romance, it likens involvement to the dangers of a crazed but wild animal. Playful in tone, trenchant in content.

Likewise, her poem "Tran Quoc Temple" seems a pastoral at first. She observes, "Weeds sprout outside the royal chapel," as she visits the oldest temple in Hanoi, some 1,400 years old. Her nostalgia turns to critique as the couplets progress:

I ache thinking of this county's past.

No incense swirls the Lotus Seat
Curling across the king's robes

Rising and falling wave upon wave.
A bell tolls. The past fades further.

Old heroes, old deeds, where are they?
One sees only this flock of shaved heads. [96]

She is not only saying that the past is no longer being tended to, but that the heroism of these previous days are gone, replaced by sheep-like monks. How contemporary this point feels. In cultures where the current state of affairs is dire, the backward glance often seems to indict contemporary leaders. Nostalgia like this is reserved for the powerful, those who have lost—or fear losing—their privilege. However, it is important to underscore that because the marginalized are often silenced, these poems gain power because of their perspective, not just their message. These poems demonstrate a fearlessness and intelligence that is remarkable for their time and culture, but are also needed by our time.

We now have a generation, since 2001, who have grown up inside the War on Terror, and feel it spreading. Terror is the weapon we inflict on ourselves in response to real or perceived dangers. Fear fuels the need to protect ourselves. It shuts down circuits that foster openness to experience, which is a hallmark of creative thinking. It shuts down trust and patience in favor of quicker decisions and hasty action.

Literature can nourish our empathetic imagination, the facility that enables us to envision and be moved by lives far from our experience, those different in custom, religious belief, range of economic choices, and political commitment. In his address at the Air Force Academy, Balaban says that Vietnamese culture prized the demands of poetry, and that even now, it has value. "Precision in the use of words is the talent which lends all other professions and skills their usefulness." But he points out that this capacity is more than utilitarian; he says it "brings to its practitioners and their societies a more enriched sense of self and an inevitable moral expansion."[97]

Reading the literature of societies that we considered or still consider "enemies" requires that we identify, to some extent, with others, and this capacity to empathize is even more crucial now than ever. We need it to build a new future. After the conflicts, it is empathy that helps the survivors to cope and allows noncombatants to help them integrate back into their home societies. It also is the essential component to transforming former enemies into allies.

The writer Roman Krznaric envisions just such a possibility. He says, "The 21st century should become the Age of Empathy, when we discover ourselves not simply through self-reflection, but by becoming interested in the lives of others. We need empathy to create a new kind of revolution. Not an old-fashioned revolution built on new laws, institutions, or policies, but a radical revolution in human relationships."[98] While empathy does cement personal relationships, such relationships are more difficult the more removed we are from one another in culture, religion, language, etc. Even our media interactions, which seem to connect us, actually remove us, calcifying established positions and impressions of the "other." Poetry, especially the intimacy of lyric poetry, has the power to close that gap. Sam Hamill, the poet and translator, has also noted how poetry, and particularly poetry from other languages, can enlarge us individually and socially. In his book *The Poet's Work: The Other Side of Poetry*, Hamill writes, "The translated poem begins an expanding process that sometimes leads to new languages, new cultures, whole systems of awareness."[99]

In his selection and his translation, Balaban has created reading experiences that expand and transport. For some remarkable moments, one wanders a land far from home, traveling on a human voice. In addition, *Ca Dao Viet Nam* and *Spring Essence* help us know our fellow human beings, ones we are still struggling not to call our enemies. We need books like these, like *All Quiet on the Western Front*, especially in a time of war and afterwards, to regain our humanity. Longfellow wrote, "If we could read the secret history of our "enemies" we would find in each man [and woman]'s life sorrow and suffering enough to disarm all hostility."

Imagining Creation: A Poet's View of Evolution[2]

A priest, an evolutionary biologist, a rabbi, and a poet all walk into a bar...and the bartender says, "What is this, some kind of joke?!"

My father, a salesman and then manager for IBM, gave all kinds of public presentations, and he always said it was smart to begin with something to loosen things up—mostly the speaker, I think. Or in this case, the writer. He had a joke for every occasions—a parish meeting, the Kentucky Derby, business lunch. It was amazing how creatively he could take the strands of any conversation and knot them together in a related story to make everyone laugh. My father died in 1991. Lung cancer. Two brothers and their one cousin, my godfather, Uncle Phil—all four died of cancer. Each year in June, I mark his passing, but in 2009 we also marked the 200th anniversary of the birth of Charles Darwin and the 150th anniversary of *The Origin of Species*. So much remembering is tinged by death. For all the biological research into cancer, we still don't know what causes our cells to hyper-divide or the ways to prevent it, let alone sure-fire

---

2   A version of this essay was originally presented on February 15, 2009 at the First Baptist Church in Painted Post, NY.

cures. There is so much more to discover. It reminds me of Robert Frost's profound two-line poem:

> *We dance round in a ring and suppose*
> *But the Secret sits in the middle and knows.*[100]

Whenever I approach the topic of evolution, both in light of these memorials and in light of our era's debates pitting religion against science (and vice versa), I try reading up on the whole evolution vs. Intelligent Design controversy. However, all that rational and overheated argumentation—talk that mostly goes past each other—leaves me dispirited and sad. I lose sight of the Secret.

And so I turn to poetry. Here's one by our contemporary, Stephen Dunn, about his daughter going to Vacation Bible School:

At The Smithville Methodist Church

It was supposed to be Arts & Crafts for a week,
but when she came home
with the "Jesus Saves" button, we knew what art
was up, what ancient craft.

She liked her little friends. She liked the songs
they sang when they weren't
twisting and folding paper into dolls.
What could be so bad?

Jesus had been a good man, and putting faith
in good men was what

*we had to do to stay this side of cynicism,
that other sadness.*

*OK, we said, One week. But when she came home
singing "Jesus loves me,
the Bible tells me so," it was time to talk.
Could we say Jesus*

*doesn't love you? Could I tell her the Bible
is a great book certain people use
to make you feel bad? We sent her back
without a word.*

*It had been so long since we believed, so long
since we needed Jesus
as our nemesis and friend, that we thought he was
sufficiently dead,*

*that our children would think of him like Lincoln
or Thomas Jefferson.
Soon it became clear to us: you can't teach disbelief
to a child,*

*only wonderful stories, and we hadn't a story
nearly as good.
On parents' night there were the Arts & Crafts
all spread out*

like appetizers. Then we took our seats

in the church
and the children sang a song about the Ark,
and Hallelujah

and one in which they had to jump up and down
for Jesus.
I can't remember ever feeling so uncertain
about what's comic, what's serious.

Evolution is magical but devoid of heroes.
You can't say to your child
"Evolution loves you." The story stinks
of extinction and nothing

exciting happens for centuries. I didn't have
a wonderful story for my child
and she was beaming. All the way home in the car
she sang the songs,

occasionally standing up for Jesus.
There was nothing to do
but drive, ride it out, sing along
in silence. [101]

    This poem reveals the typical antagonism toward a certain *kind* of religion, one that is itself antagonistic toward the discoveries of science. Most of the ardent atheists' denunciations of religion, likewise, categorize only part of the religious current, and the Creationists don't speak for any of the churches that host Evolution Weekend events, for example (search the web for "Clergy Letter Project"). The debate is a more tangled knot than most of the headlines and news reports allow for. And yet, I'm not equipped to unravel it. I admit: like many who rely on school-house lessons in biology, I am ignorant of a great deal about evolution, of natural selection, and of the fossil record. Likewise, and again like many, even those who occupy pews all over the nation, I'm no expert in the history and cultural forces of Biblical history, in the linguistic difficulties of translation of that complex anthology, let alone in the doctrines of various Christian traditions.

But, also like most people, I don't let such facts get in the way of my deeply held convictions!

I am convinced that science and religion are simply two different ways of *coming to know* rather than merely collections of facts. Reciting a creed doesn't mean having faith any more than knowing what a mitochondria is makes me a scientist; we must actively engage in the process because beyond their teachings, beyond the body of knowledge is a dynamic engagement with the unknown, with the yet-to-be-discovered, the unsolved. Like Jacob and Esau, Religion and Science are twins, each with its own personality, but belonging to the same family.

Dunn's poem illuminates our need for a good tale, a harmonizing narrative that makes sense of the scattered facts of our lives and our world.

The Bible's rich with complex stories. Consider the one about how Jacob tricked Laban, his father-in-law, twice-over. As we examine this story, it's important to note that a great many Biblical concepts, such as of multiple wives, of slavery, of the afterlife, and so much more have all evolved since these texts were written. Because this tale is not read out from the Lectionaries on Sundays, even many church-goers are not familiar with it, so I'll summarize it.

Trapped in indentured servitude (to win the hand of first one then the other of Laban's daughters), Jacob finally got the wily Laban to let him go by agreeing to only take the less valuable mottled and black lambs and goats. Jacob proves just as wily: he then bred the remaining pure white flocks in front of "fresh rods of poplar and almond and plane," which he peeled to expose the pale soft-wood. What's not explained in the Scriptures is that Jacob knew that whatever parents are gazing at during conception will determine the coloration of the next generation. The dark and light pattern of the wood created "pied" offspring, all of which walked back with Jacob to Palestine.[102]

We now know that more than striped rods influence what color sheep will be. But this story reveals the long human tradition of husbandry, the knowledge and skill required for caring for cows, goats, fowl, and other animals. For thousands of years, human beings have been breeding animals and cross-breeding plants to create more desirable offspring. This is how we have now have Labradoodles, a cross between the Labrador Retriever and the Poodle. This story shows that even in the Bible, people have participated in the selection process of evolution, but now we understand with more precision about chromosomes and genes.

As most who follow the evolution/creationism debate, most arguments against evolution are based on a literalist reading of the Bible, which is far too limited. But most scientific assertions also use the Bible to show how unreliable a source it is, which is also too limited.

A towering figure in the Quaker tradition, Howard Brinton, offers another approach. He lays these two approaches out first, as a potential progression. Rather than using what he calls an "uncritical acceptance of every statement,"[103] he establishes the second stage, which can occur when one exposes Biblical stories to "scientific facts and historical research,"[104] sometimes resulting in skepticism and sometimes a complete rejection of the Bible. This may account for many rationalist attitudes about religion, which is essentially the same kind of literalism being used *against* the Bible. However, sometimes, a person may creatively synthesize "this critical attitude […] with an understanding of the deeper meanings inherent in the words."[105] We can exercise our knowledge and rational analysis, along with an openness to the Secret in the middle of the ring. Rather than literal, historical truth, which contemporary human beings arrive at in ways unknown to those who "knew" that mating sheep that see black and white shapes will produce mottled offspring, we seek mythological truth, symbolic truth. Brinton says,

> *At this stage we are not so much concerned with historical validity or rational consistency with our scientific or philosophic outlook as we are with the inner significance of history, myth, and symbol. Symbol is a language of religion....*[106]

We seek this "inner significance" through metaphor. Because print's black squiggles on paper only make sense in the person who learns the symbol system, language itself is metaphoric. There's a gap between each word and what it signifies that can only be crossed by an imaginative understanding to get the correspondence between the word "Labradoodle" and the panting animal pawing at the door in the dark of morning. And, in poetry, there is the largest leaps of all: words create images and concepts, pointing metaphorically to meanings that cannot be spoken of directly. For example, here's a short psalm that presents a simile that does exactly this kind of pointing:

Psalm 131

> *YHWH, my heart has no lofty ambitions;*
> *my eyes do not look too high;*
> *I do not occupy myself with affairs*
> *too great and too marvelous for me.*
> *But I have calmed and quieted my soul,*
> *like a child in its mother's arms;*
> *as content as a child that has been weaned.*[107]

This image of loving care and tender quietude represents the very heart of the spiritual affirmation. It says that the universe is our field of love-in-action. The image draws us into the circle where the Secret sits. But in terms of the "truth," on a strictly literal level, it is clear that I am not a child, and we all know that God is not a mother, right? And yet. I am, yes. And, yes, God is. It's not a matter of either/or.

It's both/neither.

In the land of paradox, the most important faculty is Imagination. Where I am both a child and neither weaned nor calm. And God is both a mother and neither mother nor father. We live in an ongoing story where the Bible is both symbolically true and historically wrong, where evolution can be both an Intelligent Design and neither the whole answer nor a substitute for the Divine. This frustrates the literalist believers and the strict rationalists, but I find that both groups of people are frustrated by poetry, generally. So we may be able to move beyond their frustration, too.

As far as I can tell, there is another critical question to ponder—beyond the literalist reading of the Bible and people's general ignorance of the evidence for evolution as a fact as well as a scientific theory. The question is a matter of purpose. Is the known universe sacred expression, manifesting Divine will in time? Or is it a random, accidental matrix of interactions. Why would a benevolent Being create a world in which the lovely gazelle bounding across the savanna is then ripped apart alive?

Stephen Dunn is right: the world does stink of extinction.

Such questions return us to the Book of Job. Good, patient Job wanted to know why we suffer. What's the purpose for losing his wife and children, his farm and livestock, and on top of it all was struck with an awful illness? A metaphor, perhaps, for anyone who grieves for their beloved dead, for those facing foreclosure or layoffs, for those who are sick and poor and look to heaven for an answer, "Why me, Lord?"

Job's friends came to comfort him, laying out all the traditional explanations for human misery—punishment for his sins, his lack of faith, punishment for his ancestors' sins, his own pride, and did I mention punishment for sin? Punishment. The story of Job shows us that beyond these logical, mechanistic stories about what people call "God's Will" is a deeper truth, one that can only be found in direct engagement, personal encounter. The answer Job gets does not answer his question at all. Instead, he experiences the presence of the Divine. In essence, God says, "I am who I am, I will be who I will be," or as the Scriptures say elsewhere, "I will be merciful to those I will be merciful to."[108] Or "I create weal and woe, goodness and evil."[109] The Divine Paradox does not fit our rational, literal configurations; it moves in the unknown, in middle of the ring we haven't even entered yet.

We must, in the words of the poet Rainer Maria Rilke,

> *have patience with everything that remains unsolved in your heart. Try to love the questions themselves, ... Do not now look for the answers. They cannot be given to you because you could not live them. At present you need to live the questions.*[110]

It is questions, not unquestioned statements, that give our lives energy and purpose, and that is the common ground between science and religion, between art and science. Not answers, not a set of facts to memorize or creeds to assent to, but the lively unknown to live in. We wrestle with all that is unsolved, as Jacob did, all through the dark night, all our lives, and the Unknown will bless us. And wound us. And rename us.

Centering down in the Mystery is what keeps us humble and that helps us stay in communion with one other. It locates us on this side of cynicism by enlivening our curiosity, activating our intelligence, and exercising our imagination. The passage into Mystery leaves us beaming.

Lewis Thomas, the writer and physician and former President of the Memorial Sloan-Kettering Cancer Center, agrees when he says that:

> *What we have been learning in our time is that we really do not understand this place or how it works, and we comprehend our own selves least of all. And the more we learn, the more we are—or ought to be—dumbfounded.*[111]

From the flies that suddenly fill the air with buzzing during a strange January thaw to the spruce trees that become even more elegant when coated with snow, from the fossilized trilobites curled into shale to the next generation of flu virus, the variation of life and the conditions that support it form a vast intricate unity, which is the Great Mystery, and it swirls within us as well as around us. If science ever discovers a cure for cancer, it won't solve the question of how we can live a life of love, how we can treat our present-day Samaritans with compassion, or how we can forgive and forgive and forgive 7 X 70 times.

That's why we need both the facts *and* a wonderful story, we need both the truths of evolution *and* the meanings of contemplation. This unity is the music we sing along to, in silence. The closest we come to this direct encounter is awe. Argument rarely brings me to the brink of wonder. Of amazement. Of gratitude. And so, I join Gerard Manly Hopkins when he declared that "The world is charged with the grandeur of God." In his poem "Pied Beauty," he exclaims, "Glory be to God for dappled things."[112] Glory be to God, says the poet, for "All things counter, original, spare, strange."[113] We might add: rain, snow; clouds, sunshine; youth and age; sickness and health. Glory be to God for all things: for life and for death. For Spirit and matter. For mystical prayer and the scientific method.

A Writer, Not Writing

Except for a sneeze muffled into the crook of an arm, a sigh here or there, an occasional cough, or the sandy shuffle of someone shifting weight on their cushion, there are very few sounds. We are nearly a hundred people. Most sit on the floor, but some are upright in single rows of chairs along the sides or the very back of the room. The great hall is quiet enough that I can hear the heating system kick on and start to thrum. I feel its cycles, the swaying rhythm of any motor, but it feels ship-sized under us.

I'm being paid not to do my job.

As a community college teacher of composition, literature, and creative writing, I was granted a sabbatical leave from classroom duties to pursue my writing. I've been composing poems, revising and collecting work into book manuscripts, and crafting book reviews. That side of my work is the primary research of my discipline; a colleague in biology spent part of her sabbatical doing lab work at Cornell. For me, I'm also reading biological and social science research into creativity and interviewing painters, potters, and performers about their process.

But for one week, I'm not even doing that.

Here retreatants are invited into Noble Silence: we are not to speak, read, or write. We're invited to offer each other relief even from the social negotiations of eye contact and non-verbal communications. Normally, when I pack for a trip, I spend more time considering what books I'll take than what outfits I'll need. *Okay*, I thought, *I'll leave the books, but no writing? For a full week?* That was harder to relinquish. I had slipped my poetry notebook and daily journal into the suitcase with my clothes. Only on the morning we left did I (with my spouse's encouragement/urging) reconsider.

On retreat, there isn't much to "do."

The focus for our seven days is an ancient Buddhist teaching on the Four Ways of Establishing Mindfulness, which is the basis of the whole mindfulness movement; in fact, Jon Kabat-Zinn got the idea for his Mindfulness-Based Stress Reduction program while at this same retreat center. On my cushion for the morning session, I'm working with one of the first ideas about the difference between attention and mindfulness. Eyes closed, I'm listening. Usually, we "listen for" something, trying to tune in so that some single relevant detail in the soundscape stands out, or we "listen to" a particular focus, like someone talking, but our mind wanders. Here, I'm opening the field of perception, allowing sounds to enter.

I notice a rough rustle as someone adjusts their posture, the canvas or thick cotton of the zabuton rubs against the cushion's fabric. Then back into quiet. A high, thin whistle sounds off to my right. I notice how immediately the internal engine of inquiry starts up with the initial noise: "What is that? A person whistling?" Then the internal chatterbox begins its commentary: "Why would someone whistle in the middle of a meditation session? Do they not know that's inappropriate? I guess some people could be inexperienced meditators here? I thought they all teach MBSR."

I almost open my eyes to take in my fellow meditators, but then I recall my intention to be listening. And I begin again. The winter wind sound has broadened and lowered into what we call a "howl." ("Why do we call it that?" Just listen. Begin again, again.)

◆ ◆ ◆

Our teachers make it clear that "mindfulness"—the buzzword for our hyper-stimulated and over-extended era—is not the same as "attentiveness," but it's a good place to start. Western psychology has identified voluntary and involuntary attention. Most of the time, we follow our attention involuntarily, which scans surroundings and inner experience seeking novelty so we can respond quickly to threats and capitalize on opportunities. In a sense, then, we are tuned into what is new or different in our field of experience, and then that singular perception is automatically sorted for "relevance." Typically, we are not consciously aware of any actual goal of this sorting. It's the default operation. Such episodic attention naturally leaps from thing to thing, and only if interest is maintained do we linger there. Our teachers quipped that this capacity has been enormously helpful for survival, but not so much for happiness.

A great deal of research has been conducted lately about "mind wandering," which is "characterized by a decoupling of attention from an immediate task context toward unrelated concerns."[114] Daniel Gilbert, author of *Stumbling on Happiness*, said in an interview that "most of us think that it is fun to let our minds wander (which happens about half the time). But our data show that when the mind is wandering, people are less happy, not more. People are happiest when thinking about what they are doing and not something else. This is true even when commuting or washing up."[115] Mind-wandering also hampers tasks that require us to chain thoughts together for coherence, like reading.

Learning to sustain attention is a matter of training. And that's the word the Buddha used. Mind *training*. Our teachers also translate it as "cultivation," which has more gardening connotations. It's still work: consider how the effort to break up sod is different from sinking tiny carrot seeds in the ground. That variety is more appealing to me. (I can also recognize that this is purely analogy for me, not experience; my spouse is the gardener.) On the retreat, I can train with this myself. In fact, meals are good ground to break up.

In the dining room, two pairs of wooden tables are set end-to-end running down the middle of the room while five are set on their own near a bank of windows. Socially, it's an odd thing for me to take a place amid other diners and not greet them, or if one joins my table not to look up and at least nod to acknowledge their presence. And yet, our task is simple: eat your squash soup, eat your buttered bread. The food is delicious. The room rings with the sound of spoons on bowls, like a harbor, with masts clanging musically in the breeze. I resist the impulse to look up when I sense someone passing, recognizing it as simply involuntary attention tuning into new experience, and devote myself to my hearty meal.

Reducing the field of experience this much has an interesting effect. We all slow down. A full spoonful is too much. I load up a squash chunk, a translucent half-moon of onion, and some broth and, before gobbling it up, take a sniff: an earthy sweetness is mixed with an herbal tang. The mind wants to name it: "Is that thyme? Basil?" I put the whole spoonful in my mouth; it's too hot. I swallow. Fast, tasting nothing. Then, immediately and unbidden, a voice like a parent with a child, directs me, "Remember, blow first." The inner voices are legion, taking as many tones as a crowd at a hockey game. I hear from many of them over the course of the week, but that's another story. Right now, I notice how this parental relationship of one dimension of myself to another part separates my awareness from the simple experience of my meal. I return to my intention. I take up some black bread, enjoying the spongy texture of the heart of it, the crack of the crust, the density of the whole slice. I tear a piece. Dip it into the soup, watch how broth slides off butter but soaks into bread. Move it to my mouth, smelling the yeastiness. Okay, I love bread, so attending to this part of the meal is easy. I chew and smile. I swallow and smile.

But then suddenly, I'm aware that my spoon is already cued up, loaded and heading mouthward. While enjoying my bread, I was also—without intention or attention—curating my next bite, and it is a pretty exact little ritual to arrange a perfect taste experience by balancing the chunky bits with broth. All that was happening while I was blissing out on the black loaf. It's an involuntary habit—yet another that has come to my conscious knowing. I practice putting my spoon down. Just chewing. "Is that old man looking for a seat?" And not looking up when someone joins the table. Not chomping more of the oh-so-yummy bread until I swallow the soup. "Her slippers are tearing loose; they must be comfortable, though."

◆ ◆ ◆

The late John Daido Loori, a photographer and abbot of the Zen Mountain Monastery, described creativity as a process with several elements. The first and last aspects would be no surprise; he says "a sense of inspiration initiates the process of creation," and it is completed by "the act of expression itself."[116] In between are elements that reveal the essential and significant. He locates our responsiveness in the body, in what the Japanese call "the *hara*, a place within us that is still and grounded," and the interactive dynamic between inner and outer, individual and world, which is mediated by *chi*, "the energy contained both in us and in the subject. Out of chi emerges resonance, a feeling of recognition between the artist and subject."[117]

In his preface to *100 Poems from the Japanese*, the poet and translator Kenneth Rexroth said that "Japanese poetry does what poetry does everywhere: it intensifies and exalts experience."[118] It is exactly this intensification of experience that I respond to when reading good poems; it causes me to pause, lift my gaze from the book, and ponder. I love that resonance, that moment of suspension—not feeling any need to take in anything more at that moment and instead wanting to savor what has been given. Emily Dickinson compares such intensification to how the essential oil or attar is gathered from rose petals:

> *Essential Oils — are wrung*
> *The Attar from the Rose*
> *Be not expressed by Suns — alone*
> *It is the gift of Screws*[119]

I don't think we need to twist our experience to wring out all the juice, but attentiveness can't be so loose that days go by without noticing their distinctive flavors and scents. There needs to be some effort, some steadiness of concentration, to harvest our resonant moments. Significant experiences are not significant on their own but in conjunction with our own responsiveness.

◆ ◆ ◆

Buddhist psychology has a helpful concept, called *vedanā*, which Joseph Goldstein explains has a very specific meaning: "that quality of pleasantness, unpleasantness, or neutrality that arises with the contact of each moment's experience."[120] He says this "feeling tone" is helpful to be aware of because "it conditions our various reactions in the mind and actions in the world."[121] Our teachers told us this feeling tone co-arises with our perceptions. After about a half hour of sitting cross-legged, I sense pain in my right knee. Immediately, a cavalcade of internal sensations follow: I register the physical sensation, the feeling-tone rings out bold and clear: *unpleasant!* And then I want to stop that sensation (so the will is activated), and I begin strategizing (thoughts) how to adjust my posture.

Having done this for days and days, I can report that I can change position, but the cycle just begins again. Some new pain asserts itself. Or it's an itch. Or I'm too cool ("I need a blanket. I don't have one. Can I go back and get one or will that be too disruptive? Will someone think I don't know the protocol for meditation?") Our teachers pointed out how helpful it is to be aware of *vedanā's* role in our perception, particularly for clients who suffer from depression; they might be able to forestall the escalation of an ordinary rainy-day mood into deleterious mental proliferation like this, thus solidifying one's depressive self-identity and feeding the build-up toward disaster. (This is not to imply that depression is simply a matter of mindful awareness of one's *vedanā*. It was just one example, and the clinicians put it into the context of a full therapeutic situation and treatment.)

The Tibetan Buddhist teacher, Yongey Mingyur, worked with neuroscientists studying the brains of long-term meditators. His book, *The Joy of Living: Unlocking the Secret and Science of Happiness*, reports on both his Buddhist practice and his gleanings from Western science, which confirms this ancient discovery the Buddha made from his own contemplation. Mingyur says, "From a strictly neuroscientific standpoint any act of perception requires three essential elements"—a stimulus, a sensory organ, and "a set of neuronal circuits in the brain" that take signals in and comprehend them. He provides an example of seeing a banana. The light bounces back from the curved, yellowish tube into the optic nerve where the signal goes to the thalamus, which is like a central switchboard from old TV or movies ("How may I direct your call?") The signal's first stop is actually two stops. One signal goes to the limbic system, which Mingyur says is "chiefly responsible for processing emotional responses and sensations of pain and pleasure."[122] Simultaneously, the thalamus directs the info from the optic nerve to the neocortex, the "analytical region of the brain," which compares the sensation to patterns experienced before. These patterns are already codified into concepts and names, like "banana." It also activates associations we have with the concept/label.[123] This dual path explains why we might get a creepy gut feeling to someone we've never met. Or why we jump and squeal at the quick slither of a garden hose in our peripheral vision.

This feeling tone is automatic, co-arising with the sensory perception. It is conditioned by culture and personal experience, of course, but it's not an intellectual commitment. That is built later, and on top of it. These distinctions feel critical to me for two reasons. First, we can get to the root of some of the habitual reactions we have. What registers as pleasant, we tend to want more of or to want to continue. That's partly why I'm always curating my next bite of good food and why I overeat. Likewise, we can grow anxious that such good things will end or that someone will take them away. The opposite (but oddly similar) chain reaction happens with unpleasant *vedanā*—"this better stop soon, I gotta get out of here, you better quit that, what if this never ends," etc.

The second reason attending to *vedanā* is important is because of that vast middle section where sensations register as "neutral." We tend to ignore these. Or we quickly grow bored, and seek one of the other two, even unhealthy or harmful thoughts and experiences for the pleasant *vedanā* of diversion. But the boring, everyday, expected stuff of life is where a great many miracles are blooming, eclipsing, and replicating.

◆ ◆ ◆

Mihaly Csikszentmihalyi, the world-renowned researcher into human happiness and creativity, could have been on this retreat. His description for our typical ways of paying attention echo what our teachers were saying. "We pay attention when we must," he writes in *Creativity: The Psychology of Discovery and Invention*. But if we're "dressing, driving the car, staying awake at work," and there is

> no external force demanding that we concentrate, the mind begins to lose focus. It falls to the lowest energetic state, where the least amount of effort is required. When this happens, a sort of mental chaos takes over. Unpleasant thoughts flash into awareness, forgotten regrets resurface, and we become depressed. Then we turn on the TV set, read listlessly the advertisement supplement of the newspaper, have pointless conversation—anything to keep our thoughts on an even keel and avoid becoming frightened by what is happening in the mind.[124]

His prescription? For decades, Csikszentmihalyi interrupted people's daily lives to assess their engagement in whatever task they were performing and their level of satisfaction. The feeling of "flow," which is what many of the people who participated in his studies called that experience of total absorption, was intensely pleasing. But he found that this focused engagement was not the rare achievement of a particular personality; all kinds of people reported having periods of flow. It was also not restricted to particular activities; while some pursuits lend themselves more easily to flow, any task can facilitate the experience, if we know how to regulate our attention.

And so, to combat the downward spiral of mental chaos—and this might seem counterintuitive—Csikszentmihalyi prescribes that we put in more effort rather than seek rest and leisure: "Whether writing a poem or cleaning the house, running a scientific experiment or a race, the quality of experience tends to improve in proportion to the effort invested in it. When the demand of a task is *almost* beyond our skill and capabilities, we need to lean in, concentrate, and monitor our actions to be sure we're fulfilling what we set out to do.

Csikszentmihalyi explains it this way: "Having clear goals and expectations for whatever we do, paying attention to the consequences of our actions, adjusting skills to opportunities for action in the environment, concentrating on the task at hand without distractions—these are the simple rules that can make the difference between an unpleasant and an enjoyable experience."[125] He also suggests that people who want to become more creative start this process with simple stuff, "the most mundane activities," in fact. If we begin with something like figure painting when we haven't drawn for years, we may grow frustrated or bored by the gap between our current skill level and the challenge. Too much frustration or boredom? No flow.

I could see this in my "yogi job" on retreat—doing pots after the mid-day meal. Kitchen cleanup can be drudgery. Not hard, but messy, hot, and repetitious. Or, using these principles of flow, it can become a game where I strive to complete as many of the hard-baked casserole pans as possible before the next shift comes in. I survey the pile of bowls, soup pots, and baking pans for the hardest ones, get them soaking, then select the easiest stuff. I ferret out lids, do a quick and efficient soapy wipe, scrub the few that need it, and set them on the drying rack. Our put-away person can now take multiple items to the same area of the kitchen, making his yogi job easier. In this way, my forty-five minutes fly by, in part because my work is invested with meaning—to help out my teammates, the next crew, and the whole kitchen staff who are feeding the entire community—and partly because all my attention is focused on devoting more of my skill to doing a good job, as efficiently as I can.

In addition, Csikszentmihalyi's research reveals that this dynamic can become an on-going and upward cycle: the better we get at a task, the more challenge we need to seek to hit the flow sweet spot. It all begins with harnessing our own capacity for attentive awareness.

◆ ◆ ◆

Walking meditation used to be a chore for me, one I avoided if I could. I sensed my *vedanā* registering as soon as I saw the schedule posted: after breakfast and after lunch, forty-five minute sessions alternated between sitting and walking meditation. "Unpleasant." Not only did the slow movements seem artificial, I felt self-conscious (but social comparison is trap for another essay).

In an enclosed porch with massive potted plants and very creaky floorboards, four of us walked back and forth. Woods edged a snow-covered lawn outside the windows. The brilliant arc of white birches seemed both placid and active against the stillness of the forest. I enjoyed walking toward the windows. Walking back, toward the door and a blank wall, I realized I got bored. My mind wandered far more often heading that way.

Just as attending to the breath gets to be a little repetitious, walking meditation strips experience down to the basics, allowing me to observe my mind at work. My intention was to bring mindfulness to the body as it walks. First, notice the foot rising, then notice how it moves forward, then notice the heel and sole touching down. Our teachers were clear to expand our sense of "being mindful." It's not a rigid and determined focus of attention that stays in place no matter what. Instead, mindfulness is a friendly curiosity, an attentiveness made gentle by appreciation. And "appreciation" includes valuing and gratitude.

So, as I took my place at the far end of the room, a leafy plant beside me, I settled into an intention to see what I could notice. Make it a kind of game. At first, I didn't observe any sensations in my calf and shin areas. All dominant sensation was in the feet, knees, and thighs. It was odd. Why couldn't I sense a whole section of my leg? Rather than "think" about that, I just kept walking, playing the What's Happening Now? game. Session after session. The body in motion is a marvel. The trembling was one sign. Balance is a set of actions occurring in many different elements that constantly monitor and adjust to motion. Because I slowed down even more than I had been, I began to sense a whole host of micro-movements in the foot and leg that kept me in balance. Each step rippled muscular engagement up the leg and around the hips and into the lower back. No footstep is located in the foot alone.

Harvard psychologist Ellen Langer has pioneered research into mindfulness, but she is not interested in meditation, only the fresh approach to our experience where we recognize the distinctive elements of our situation and can freely choose. In several studies, she has documented how "drawing novel distinctions increases liking."[126] Whether it was music, food, or paintings, the more participants engaged with a subject and noticed new aspects each time, the more they enjoyed the thing itself.

Opening up that neutral zone in our *vedanā* helps us experience more of our own lives. As we do so, we are happier. I started looking forward to the walking meditation. I wanted to experiment to see if I could notice how breathing felt in my belly, back, and sides while also tuning in to how, step by step, bones in my legs and hips shifted. I wanted to see if I could sense how electrical pulses sent by the nerves initiated muscle action that made motion possible. I wanted to feel the changing rhythm of blood flow across the activity period. And through it all, I was amazed by the body's knowledge and skill that was operating below all conscious activity. This knowledge asserted itself whenever I'd lose my balance (usually when attention wandered), but the body knew what it was doing. I didn't catch myself. The body caught me.

◆ ◆ ◆

In an interview, Gary Snyder once reflected on the Japanese word for song. He said that the word they use, *bushi* or *fushi*, means "a whorl in the grain. It means in English what we call a knot, like a knot in a board…, like the grain flows along and then there's a turbulence that whorls, and that's what they call a song. It's an intensification of the flow at a certain point that creates a turbulence of its own which then as now sends out an energy of its own, but then the flow continues on."[127] I want to be well-tuned and sensitive enough to be aware of the whorls that form in the flow of my experience. I want to be sensitive enough to the turbulence to hear its song in its novel distinctions. These happen in a moment, then flow on. They are so easy to miss.

◆ ◆ ◆

Before the retreat, I knew my knees would ache. I knew my hips were not all that flexible. What I was not prepared for was the pain in my neck and shoulders. Had I not gotten excellent instruction in mindfulness, I would have been trapped by these expectations. Ellen Langer says that "most of us see what we expect to see without realizing that there is a choice."[128] She reports a great study where Dan Simons instructed participants to watch a videotape of a basketball game, counting the number of passes made by one team, but not the other. This led their minds to narrow down and focus on the passing, and so nearly half of the participants didn't even notice when the person in a gorilla suit walks across the court, even stopping to beat his chest. When she repeated the experiment, she gave half the participants the same instructions Simons had and the other half alternative ways to consider their upcoming experience. They were told that despite the fact that we use the same word for every "basketball game," each one is actually unique, so tally the ways this one is similar to and different from the last basketball game you saw. Most of this group notice the gorilla.[129]

I expected pain, but I learned how to exercise my choices in how to experience that pain. I was, in fact, surprised about how little it bothered me. Pain is pain, and there's no escape from that. Usually, in response to what's happening in my knees and hips, the *vedanā* is unpleasant, and that operates like the experiment's instruction to count how many times the players pass the ball. Before the retreat, my attention zoomed in on my knee pain. It blocked out all potential gorillas.

I was guided to receive these painful sensations into mindfulness, which not only was infused with appreciation for the body's intricacies and forgiveness for my out-of-shapeness, but also includes a looseness of judgment and a modicum of curiosity. This didn't let the pain trigger thoughts about how I should be going to the gym, doing yoga, or at least stretching every day, and then planning how I'd do so when I got back, budgeting the membership fee and arranging my schedule. There's an alternative to letting the sensations be a train door swinging open, and then climbing aboard for a linked series that lead to inevitable conclusions.

First, opening up my field of awareness to *vedanā's* neutral zone allows me to tune into sensations not registering as pain (unpleasant) or pleasure (there weren't many). When my neck throbbed—and after I adjusted my posture—I could check in on the shins (a drab area of few sensations, I've learned) or what's going on in the arches of the feet (another region of radio silence). As I registered no *vedanā*, the volume on the pain I had just sensed was also turned down. Sometimes, I could sense something, and that spark of curiosity would shower a pleasant *vedanā*. If my hands were in my lap, sometimes the pulse became perceptible, or if they were on my legs, I could sense their warmth. I could note whatever my involuntary attention was drawn to, but not be stuck there. I could actively and consciously—voluntarily—attend to other things, and it changed my experience of what was unpleasant.

Langer's research is also helpful here. She has designed a number of studies exploring how shifting one's perspective affects experience. She points out that social scientists have been looking into the Actor-Observer dynamic, where the person performing an action has one point of view while an observer has another. I might think of my behavior as "spontaneous," but an observer may call it "impulsive" or even "unpredictable."[130] In meditation (and in daily life), we can have both the experience and generate a label for it, because we can be both Actor and Observer. This is freeing because just changing the label changes our experience. Instead of calling the sensation "hip pain," I could attach the label "becoming more flexible."

Mental labels can be a trap, one we fashion for ourselves and then catch ourselves in. "Taking concepts too far simply solidifies our view of reality," says Joseph Goldstein, "and we get boxed in by mental constructs of our own making."[131] Not only do we think our way into the box, but the box is made of thinking. Letting experience be its own unique dynamic, without the prefrontal pattern and label allows a greater fluidity to reality and a greater freedom in our response to it.

Mindfulness enabled me to regard the throbbing ache in my shoulders as a sign that I've stopped attending to my posture. My head and upper back slumped as I sat, and I never noticed it. It took sitting for this many hours to reveal it. The pain earned a different mental label, and I had a different emotional reaction to that label, which triggered different thoughts. Watching this new train route, I was amazed at the mind's dexterity. And it made me glad. I expected to experience discomfort, even outright pain, which I did, but I was unprepared for just how much I liked it.

◆ ◆ ◆

Thoughts appear from whatever wings the stage of the mind has, do their dance, and hope to get us to pay attention to them, do their bidding. I liked this description of the unbidden mental activity. It allows me to lighten up, spend less energy sifting and weighing each thought for importance, and invites me to shift my loyalty away from the content of thought to the awareness that recognizes it.

We were instructed to watch the content of our mental activity and let it pass. We were given this analogy: imagine standing on a busy street corner. One bus after another will stop, open its doors, and the driver might even urge you to get on. Taxis. Bicycles even. You do not have to climb aboard your thoughts. We can simply allow awareness to be steady, note that another bus has arrived, but we can wave it on. We can note that the screen of the mind is now playing a movie, but we don't have to get popcorn, sit down, and watch the whole thing.

Much of the time, I employ these methods. Sometimes, the film was well into the second act before I noticed it was even playing, but I could return to my intention and start again. Each time we did this, we were told, the capacity to sustain our attention was strengthened.

However, I discovered that I enjoy my mind-wandering. In fact, because daydreaming and those other fuzzy associative states of mind are a writer's friend, are the friend of anyone trying to be more creative, I *wanted* to get on some busses. They might take me to new poems and new projects. Those resonant moments where the knots of experience revealed themselves are significant. And I've spent decades developing the discipline of carrying pen and paper with me so that I'm ready to write when I noticed them.

Would this meditation thing hamper my creative life?

On the retreat, I cannot resolve this question. Instead, I resist my impulse to write.

❖ ❖ ❖

While others are doing their after-breakfast yogi jobs, I step out the front doors of the retreat center into the clarity of single-digit weather. The just-days-from-full moon is a bright silver disk in the sky, still streaked with pastels. The sun has not crested the hill behind the center, so I head down to circle the pond, wind through the woods, and head up into the dawn. Having been practicing for days, I feel vibrant, alert and open—tender, even—to how beautiful the morning is.

At the pond, I stop at the outlet, listen to the changing voices in the water as it gurgles through a pipe that heads under the roadway.

Water voices.

Had I not been on retreat, I would have taken out my little blank daybook from my back pocket and started jotting things down. I definitely would have had a pen on me. Probably a fountain pen.

I sense a resonance between the outer world and my own body—it may have even started before that phrase because I stopped walking for some reason, not one I consciously weighed. But when that metaphor asserted itself in my mind, I knew, and I also noticed that I was moving into language creation, playing with phrases and ideas.

I have a confession to make: I do have my daybook on the retreat. But I resisted the temptation to carry it with me.

It's back in my room. Standing at the outlet of the frozen pond, I drop the phrase-making activity and all the images that attend it, turn toward the woods, and walk on.

◆ ◆ ◆

In the mid-1970s, Jerome L. Singer invented the term "positive-constructive daydreaming" to indicate that some kinds of mind-wandering is valuable, particularly in problem-solving. One reason is that much of our daydreaming is future oriented. Mooneyham and Schooler summarize the scant recent research on this aspect of mental activity, saying, "The future-directed orientation of mind-wandering, combined with the fact that spontaneous thoughts are often closely coupled with individuals' current concerns... suggests one possible function of mind-wandering: the anticipation and planning of personally relevant future goals, otherwise known as autobiographical planning."[132]

For creative people of all kinds, not just writers, the stage of problem-solving called incubation is critical. It's a fuzzy zone where the usual rational approaches to unlock a solution have gone nowhere. You just have to take a break. Or take a bath. Our word "eureka" comes from the ancient story of Archimedes solving the puzzle of how much gold was in the king's crown. After working over many different formulas to figure it out, he stepped into the bath. Seeing the water his body displaced running over the rim of the tub caused him to exclaim, "I've got it!" The Greek word is eureka.

Many scientific breakthroughs and product innovations have occurred in these "non-work zones," like when taking a walk, driving, or even sitting on the toilet. Shelley H. Carson, *Your Creative Brain* says that taking a shower may be just the kind of change of scenery that dislodges the mind from a fixed way of conceiving of a problem.[133]

◆ ◆ ◆

At one point in the week, our teachers invite us to consider our intentions for taking up contemplative practice. Since many use the mindfulness techniques as part of their clinical work, it's a good question to entertain. Do we want to reduce our stress, to experience stillness in our over-wrought lives? Is meditation and the accompanying shifts in attitude toward our experience enough of a pause that we're satisfied? Do we want this practice to promote well-being more generally? Now that we've experienced a stable calm, do we want to adjust our habits toward those that foster greater health and happiness? The mindfulness movement has demonstrated, experientially and experimentally, that these are fruits of these methods. So these intentions are not off the mark.

As the Buddha taught, and all three teachers pursued in various ways, our intention could be more fundamental and sweeping: do we seek awakening?

They were clear to demonstrate—and each day I experience it myself—developing sustained attentive concentration does facilitate bodily and interior calmness, but these are only the beginning of this cultivation. "When awareness is well established and mindfulness is happening by itself—what could be called *effortless effort*," says Joseph Goldstein, "then we can simply rest in the continuity of bare knowing."[134] He cites the Japanese Zen monk and poet, Ryokan: "Know your mind just as it is."[135]

In many places in his writings and talks, Thich Nhat Hanh describes the different functions, and perhaps stages of mediation as stopping, calming, and looking deeply. Periodically pausing to be mindful of our experience right in this moment helps promote the stability of attentiveness, and that can increase our appreciation of our experience. Then, once grounded in the flow of our current experience—and able to stay with it—we can begin to look deeply at destructive emotions, habits of perception, and ingrained ways of responding that are not skillful means to maintain healthy for ourselves or others.

I'm not interested in "using" meditation for my writing. I want to be free of unhelpful and petty compulsions so that I can be responsive to the distinctive dynamics of each situation. And I want to be able to answer the world's needs with my full presence and compassion. I want to wake up. I also believe that the more I am able to do all that, poems will also emerge, so there's my out.

◆ ◆ ◆

I haven't resolved the mind-wandering question and the artistic benefits of allowing my mind to de-couple from washing the dishes or driving a familiar stretch of road to incubate some impression or other. I have to take it on faith from others that meditation and writing are not mutually exclusive. Gary Snyder says that "the practice of sitting gives me unquestionably an ease of access to the territories of my mind—and a capacity for experience—for recalling and revisualizing things with almost living accuracy; I attribute that to a lot of practice with meditation; although, strictly speaking, that is not the best use of meditation."[136] He explains further that meditation helps dial down the self, where "the conscious mind temporarily relinquishes its self-importance,...of direct focus and decision-making and lets peripheral and lower and in some sense deeper aspects of the mind to manifest themselves."[137]

An important aspect of these deeper aspects of the mind is intuition. John Dado Loori links the two very directly:

> *One way that our spiritual power begins to manifest itself is through the emergence of the intuitive aspect of our consciousness. This is one of the reasons why Zen and creativity are so intimately linked. Creativity is also an expression of our intuitive aspect. Getting in touch with our intuition helps us to enter the flow of life, of a universe that is in a constant state of becoming.*[138]

Strange as it seems, a disciplined approach to mind-training may free this intuitive and spontaneous part of ourselves. These are not mutually exclusive or even in conflict. In fact, all aspects of consciousness are welcome.

Scott Barry Kaufman states the same thing, only in more scientific terms. He says that "the entire creative process...consists of many interacting cognitive processes (both conscious and unconscious) and emotions. Depending on the stage of the creative process, and what you're actually attempting to create, different brain regions are recruited to handle the task."[139]

Wholeness is my ultimate goal. I welcome cultivating the interaction of internal ways of knowing as well as the outer flow of the world in its process of becoming. And citing research from UC-Santa Barbara, Scott Barry Kaufman and Carolyn Gregoire say achieving this may be easier than I imagine. They say the "balance between external-directed focus and free-flowing inward attention may be our natural state."[140]

Laying It on the Wire

Laying it on the Wire: Delighting in Poetry's Form and Rhythm

Like that character in *Little Big Man* who walks backwards and speaks in riddling reverse, I'm a contrary man. In high school, instead of lining up against the walls with the other guys, I flailed on the dance floor. But somehow I didn't dance to the bass or drumbeat; instead, I tuned in to the lyrics and the guitar. How you can dance to that, I'm still not sure. When it comes to responding to form in poetry, I'm still the contrary one. Shaped by Denise Levertov's poetics, I am committed to the idea that verse can be free from meter but not free from form. As Charles Wright says, "Good free verse is free in the same way that good abstract art is abstract. Which is to say, not very."[141] And yet, after decades reading poetry and crafting it, I can't seem to hear meter. In my ear, it's always "MY mistress' eyes…" as the speaker distinguishes his love from all those falsely compared.

Imagine my relief, though, when Lewis Turco in his professorial *The New Book of Forms: A Handbook of Prosody* indicates ways that the system of metrics, like any poetics, is *a priori*, an abstraction prior to the language at hand. For example, he says that "English does not easily accommodate three unstressed syllables in a row; therefore, [...] the middle syllable is *promoted* to stressed status."[142] Why the middle one? Couldn't it depend on the rhetorical movement of the sentence, like in that Shakespeare sonnet? (Duh, that's "cadence," which "mainly refers to phrasing, which is foreign to foot-based scansion," according to T.V.F. Brogan, editor of *The New Princeton Encyclopedia of Poetry and Poetics: The Most Comprehensive Guide to World Poetry*—longest parenthetical title so far).[143] Then, shouldn't it be promoted according to the prevailing meter, the ear filling in the foot-tap? Turco says, "Whatever remains most constant is the poem's prosody"[144] and "scansion describes a norm, not an absolute."[145] Ultimately, I take heart in Prof. Turco's summation, which stresses the principle of counterpoint:

> *Variations in a line of English verse are important, for in normative accentual-syllabic verse, it is variation against the pattern, and not strict adherence to the pattern, that satisfies the ear. The poetaster (an unskilled versifier) memorizes a pattern and works with it, whereas the poet understands the pattern and works against it. Regularity of meter is uninteresting; counterpoint—rhythm against the normative beat—is interesting. On the other hand, too much variation is disconcerting and awkward.*[146]

You can see both systems at work on the dance floor, too. The robot guy who's got too much regularity going on and the "disconcerting and awkward" guy about to bloody somebody's nose. Counterpoint in poems, some argue, results from the spoken rhythm of a line that moves parallel and simultaneously to the regular metical line. For example, I hear Frost's sentences and voice inflections. In his famous woods poem, does the speaker know who owns most of the woods around here but is unsure of who owns *these* woods? Does he just *think* he knows? The speaker and situation bear on any spoken line, and of course, on its rhythm. However, if meter is only the "norm," then such inflections may not touch the patterns of stress and slack syllables. "Double audition" was what C.S. Lewis called these two rhythms.[147] In his *Princeton* entry, Brogan basically calls double audition hooey since we can only really hear one line at a time. Still, contrary rhythms reflect my experience. Singers tell me they can hear the bass line while they sing the melody, and of course piano players bring forth both the melody and basslines, one from each hand. Inference tells me that anyone who has pounded their steering wheel or dashboard while singing along to their car sound system gets the idea of double audition. More importantly, I relish the potential that we could hear variation against regularity or hear patterns in the disconcert.

Hearing doubly like this is exactly the zone of commonality that Alice Fulton named between so-called formal and so-called free verse. She says the regularity of meter is satisfying because "we can readily anticipate the rhythm of the lines to come. The pleasure lies in having our expectations fulfilled."[148] It's the same deep pleasure we have in every genre—the romantic comedy is pleasing in part because the cute couple actually do get together (if we like them and if we buy that the complications are overcome, and if, if, if). We want form to *nearly defy* our expectations. "Free verse," Fulton goes on, "is most compelling when most rhythmic: the poet must shape the irregular rhythms of language to underscore, contradict, or in some way reinforce the poem's content."[149] It's pleasing when we find meaning in the chaos; there may be no predictable pattern of rhyme but we like feeling a reason for the music.

The key to either approach is the tension, the suspense.

And it's not only in the form. The tension of expecting occurs in the phrasing and lines, of course, but also in the whole composition, even in the context of the composition. When a Russian émigré offered a piano concert, I was lucky to be one of seven people invited. She'd stopped performing and teaching music when she came to this country, but she was still a musician. Just rusty. The room's three-story wall of glass overlooked December woods in upstate New York. Elena approached her instrument formally, noted her nervousness—and how cold the room was—announced her playlist, centered into herself, and began playing. Bach. A piece I love, so I was pleased by even the first phrases. As the music built, I worried for her, hoping she could enact this gift she had begun creating. Oddly, I was concerned for the music, too. Would it allow her to not just play the notes but convey all that can get lost when translated from the page to the air?

The tension in form, whether a live performance or a fully revised poem, is essential. Theodore Roethke, who wrote masterfully in various forms, declared that "rhythm is the entire movement, the flow"[150] and that "rhythm depends on expecting."[151] The entire movement of that concert was not limited to the music Elena played but was shaped by the context and the player as well. The Bach was the Bach, but it can't remain fixed or abstract. Literally, it had to be influenced by the tall windows and the winter seeping into the music through the player's hands and the grand piano. But more delicately, the notes on the page always have to be warmed by the player's interpretation. Further, the way my emotions rose and fell with the music was influenced by my hope for Elena and my gratitude for this vast experience she was giving us.

Expecting is created by the content as well as the shape of the material. And somehow when we get exactly what we thought we would, it's not what we thought we'd get. If it's nothing like what we expected, we might not get anything either. In this way, I always remember hearing about Phillipe Petit's 1974 walk between the Twin Towers just as they were being completed (his book and the documentary are called *Man on Wire*). Once he stepped on his wire and was 110 stories above lower Manhattan, the walk had to be immediate—spontaneous—despite being meticulously planned and practiced. He spent more than six years mulling about the project and then eight months in New York working out the details. Still, that hour feels improvised, fresh in the present, in the suspensions. Petit makes it seem so. Watch his performance—walking back and forth eight times, kneeling down with that enormous pole jutting out. The rhythm of walking is created the moment he stepped off the South Tower, but the expecting builds each time we think he could fall, each time we think the dance will end. When that tension diminishes, he creates a whole new expectation: he goes to the middle of the span, and lies down. Face to the sky. Intention and spontaneity. Deliberation and freedom. Some say he spoke with gulls flying by. Contrary forces working together.

Applied to poetry, expectation can be created at the micro level as well as the macro level. In both, the poet writing so-called free verse has to haul the wire to the top of the building, shoot it across the span, ratchet it tight, and then do the dance. We have to create the expectations. Then, nearly defy them. Or, like a good joke, we need to sidle up to the central issue so people don't even realize it's central, but when the surprise comes, it feels inevitable. The spontaneity is planned. That's the craft. Ferlinghetti was exactly right: "the poet like an acrobat / climbs on rime / to a high wire of his own making."[152] Well, not right about poets being "he" all the time. And I'm not so sure about the "rime" part, either. But making our own wire, yes.

Just as the looseness of cadence counters the pattern of meter, a pattern within unmetered lines can create this tension. Stress and rhyme (usually restricted to end-rhyme) establish their pattern, but as Emerson says, "Another form of rhyme is iteration of phrase." Anaphora or other reiterations create eagerness for another round or a resistance to that expectation. In H.D.'s "Adonis," she uses all the techniques.

> *Each of us like you*
> *has died once,*
> *has passed through drift of wood-leaves,*

*cracked and bent
and tortured and unbent
in the winter-frost,
the burnt into gold points,
lighted afresh,
crisp amber, scales of gold-leaf,
gold turned and re-welded
in the sun;*

*each of us like you
has died once,
each of us has crossed an old wood-path
and found the winter-leaves
so golden in the sun-fire
that even the live wood-flowers
were dark.*

2.
*Not the gold on the temple-front
where you stand
is as gold as this,
not the gold that fastens your sandals,
nor thee gold reft
through your chiselled locks,
is as gold as this last year's leaf,
not all the gold hammered and wrought
and beaten
on your lover's face.
brow and bare breast
is as golden as this:*

> *each of us like you*
> *has died once,*
> *each of us like you*
> *stands apart, like you*
> *fit to be worshipped.*[153]

H.D. establishes the refrain of "each of us like you / has died once," then defies us at the start of part two, and so it's pleasing again when it returns in the fourth. Even the variation, the standing in the third stanza, returns in the final stanza. Do I even have to mention all that gold? It's like a long guitar solo which we enjoy at first, but then it draws our attention to itself—"*Again?*" we ask—and then it keeps going, and we admire the endurance. (It's a risky maneuver, though, because once aware of a recurrence, repetition can feel, well, repetitious.)

But there are smaller points of tension as well, more like the footfalls on the wire than the larger amazement of the performance. These draw us on, like the phrasal repetition "has died once / and has passed through" in the second and third line, and then the list of modifiers in lines three and four. Different phrases but the same grammatical pattern, and she employs it throughout, because each time we sense the iteration, we briefly wonder if it will continue, and we also notice each time that expectation is defied. Then in the ending, the deep formal and conceptual satisfaction happens because several versions of the repetition converge to emphasize our spiritual similarity with Adonis.

While meter, rhyme, and other iterations operate at the level of the phrase and line, the poetic form itself can assist a poet in establishing tension. For example, as soon as we read a title like "Little L.A. Villanelle," we know a little of what's coming. We anticipate the form's inherent recurrences. But the actual tension comes in, like when I was listening to Elena's Bach, as we wonder, *can this writer pull it off?* Will repetitions merely fulfill the form, or will it also fulfill the poem? The poet is already up on the wire. Carol Muske sets the scene in her villanelle's first line "I drove home that night in the rain,"[154] but it manages to also set the expectations because the emphasis is on "*that* night." The iambs reinforce it, which we feel when we consider that in desiccated southern California, a rain that overflows the "gutterless streets" would be a stand-out event. The meter is also inverted by this context so that "I drove *home that* night." In this way, though the words repeat as the poem progresses, cadence varies. In the next stanza, listening to a "cheap love song on the radio" the speaker notices the "maddening, humble gesture of the wipers" so that the refrain in the last line now emphasizes "in the rain." Such movement of meaning creates a counterpoint to the repetition because we get the words we expected, but we now get new implications. This is a function both of knowing what to anticipate by being familiar with the form and how Muske works at the micro level using voice and context.

The tension is created by pushing against the conventions of form. Moving one step beyond what Muske does in her villanelle, the form itself can be implied. For example, Robert Hayden's "Those Winter Sundays" is shaped like a sonnet and it moves within that shape like one, too, starting with the nearly iambic first two lines and down to the final couplet. But he starts with an inversion (SUNdays TOO), which by deftly emphasizing the little tiny adverb, signifies a whole lifestyle of faithful service. Also, the third line only has six syllables (which even I can hear is no way pentameter). It's a sonnet, but not. Among other features, its "variation against the pattern" make it compelling. In the same way, James Wright's "Lying in a Hammock at William Duffy's Farm in Pine Island, Minnesota" echoes a translation of a T'ang era Chinese poem. The description progresses from overhead to the speaker's right, as if off-hand, leisurely observing the "bronze butterfly, / Asleep on the black truck" through the cowbells and even the "droppings of last year's horses." [155] Lulled into an easy recline by these sensations and the golden tone they are rendered in, readers are startled, awoken as if from a nap, by that last line: "I have wasted my life." The poem owes much to the Western tradition as well as Eastern, even the sonnet. The ghost of form leads us to expect resolution, something connected to the previous pastoral scenes, but Wright reverses that expectation. Instead of the box clicking closed, it springs open. Wright's poem operates under a different metaphor. Poems like Muske's where the form is established before reading its contents, are like a football player catching a kickoff—the player is all but tackled before he wriggles free and sets off again, pursued by a single defender angling across the field. We marvel at the performance, knowing the goal and method of the form (or game). But Wright's poem is more like the form of a joke. It's resolution is like a punchline, but we can't forget the "punch" part; it should pack a wallop. Sudden. It both comes out of the blue, and yet it's all there somehow.

Some argue that this ghosting, like the double audition in individual lines, is the only way free verse is interesting. But expectations can arise without reference to these forms and instead, like H. D.'s poem, emerge from within one. Flowers on anniversaries or birthdays are expected, and that's one kind of delight in form, but flowers received "just because" have a whole other elation. The action is the same, but the experience is not. When the gesture emerges from the lived details of daily life, somehow it has more meaning. Poetry's formal delights operate similarly. It's worth watching how form emerges from within its distinctive content.

In all kinds of writing, the usual techniques of narrative provide ways to create tension. The suspense is in the relation of events to purpose, to the characters. Whether a film, short story, essay, or poem (in meter or not), stories have hundreds of ways to twine its threads and then tighten them. Maggie Anderson's "Long Story" is a remarkable example. It grounds the storyteller and setting from the first lines: "I need to tell you that I live in a small town / in West Virginia you would not know about."[156] The poem evokes a place like few I know, but it reflects on the idea of narrative, too. "History is one long story of what happened to us, / and its rhythms are local dialect and anecdote" the speaker points out before saying that "Anything that happens here has a lot of versions."[157] Around these guiding statements, the poem characterizes the people so that by the final stanza, we're oriented to the region and its ways. Our speaker is a good tour guide, repeating the stories she's heard from Uncle Craig and the kids. All this sets the stage for the final episode, which three of the kids "swore it was true." I won't ruin the ending, but I'll just say this: "they sealed up / forty miners in a fire."[158]

In a similar way that exorcising the ghost of form and meter can create pleasing suspension, prose poems and fabulist fiction slip the knot of storytelling structures to deliver other possibilities. It's as if writers are entertaining the ghost of narrative. For example (and keeping with the mining theme), Mark Nowak's *Coal Mountain Elementary* pairs newspaper accounts of Chinese mining disasters with eyewitness accounts of the Sago, West Virginia, explosion in 2006. These are set against elementary school teaching material, provided to school districts by mining companies. His fragmentary method, what one reviewer called a "striking, 'synthetic' compositional technique based on the 'sampling' or juxtaposition of counter-narratives,"[159] resists standard narrative structures by dodging the storyteller, sustained point of view, and suspenseful buildup of plot. And yet, it works. What draws us through the story isn't story's usual question of "what will happen next?" so much as "what's going on, exactly?" It cross-pollinates the musical method of sampling with the visual collage, and the hybrid blooms a new form. *Blue Front*, the tour de force collection by Martha Collins, employs similar juxtaposing of documents, but to even greater effect. Her story traces versions and details back to a lynching in Cairo, Illinois, which her father, as a boy, witnessed.

Collins and Nowak employ multiple points of view while Maggie Anderson limits herself to one who speaks for others. And the tensions created by speaker can propel a poem, whether narrative or lyric. Like a play, readers feel like they overhear a conversation or intercept a letter, and the intimacy itself sets up the tension. Soon the initial questions of "Who are these people, and how do they know each other?" give way to "what's at stake between them?" Averill Curdy's "To the voice of the retired warden of Huntsville Prison (Texas death chamber)" immediately torques both intellect and emotion by establishing this monologue right from the title. "Until wolf-light I will count my sheep" the poem opens, when "Night is already a thirsty county in Texas." Disturbed by the heat (and so much more, we immediately suspect), the speaker confronts "my genial, / My electric ghost."[160] You might expect a moralizing rant from such a set up, but the poet surprises with the interdependent nature of the relationship: "We are convicted / As we are also pardoned." [161] At first, this suggests that within the criminal justice system the methods are the same, but the metaphysics of guilt and redemption shadow of this statement as well. Having turned the monologue from what we anticipate once, the poem does it again when the speaker reflects on "What keeps me awake? Nothing / More than a fly's dysenteric violin." Clearly, there is more to this insomnia than an annoying bug in the room. Such a deflection is like Phillipe Petit kneeling down on the wire, a pause, an added twist to heighten tension since he's already walking a quarter of a mile in the air. The internal motives and passions of this speaker are rhythms of obsession and pain, confrontation and deflection. The final stanza is perfect; it resolves all the musical themes of the dialogue, the warden's work, and the sleeplessness, but it doesn't resolve any of the moral questions the poem raises. Listen how it fulfills some expectations and defies others:

> *What puts me to sleep*
>
> *Is your clement voice, saying*
> *The dark has no teeth. While men like you live*
>
> *In this world do I dream*
>
> *I am either safe or spared?*[162]

These many ways of drawing out a reader's expectations and then using them to foster the rhythm of a poem demonstrate what J. V. Cunningham said: "A poem is a convergency of forms."[163] And not all of those forms need to be on the page; they can be in the reader already. The question isn't either free or formal, but does the poem create its own tension and then how's it handle these expectations?

Poems employ the full range of approaches, so that it often feels like other modes of expression limit themselves. A George Oppen poem, so devoid of imagery, can border on philosophic essay, while a John Haines poem can feel painterly. Ai's dramatic monologues evoke whole lives as HD's feel like scripts.

Because of this variety, I remain in the middle, contrary to both sides, pulling for more meaningful repetition and tension in so-called free verse (Roethke: "Freedom has its tyrannies—even in verse"[164]) but desiring more elusiveness from work that delivers what the form leads me to expect. Rather than static structure, I'm more interested in the unfolding, in process. I agree with Charles Hartmann when he says, "We comprehend the poem only as a process, not as an object."[165] It's the high wire act: its delight and defiance—it's the moment between buildings that counts.

Walking in a Flame: The Affirmations of Lucien Stryk

In a time of readily-recognizable poetic "camps"— the fault lines and groupings are many and pervasive— to encounter a poet like Lucien Stryk for the first time, a reader may struggle to find the right pigeonhole to place his work into. However, to fully participate in his work, one needs to become acclimated to the imaginative landscape he creates rather than apply to him the characteristics of any given poetics.

From the outset, this poet is as clear as water but varied in content. In his collected poems, *And Still Birds Sing*, a healthy gathering of translations as well as original poems from eleven collections and new work, his early efforts are not fixed in a place or in a person. The selections from his first two books (published in the 1950s) have no first person speaker. Then the first few poems from *Notes for a Guidebook* (1965) are set in various places from Japan to Iran, establishing Stryk's embrace of the world's habitations and his work's rhythm of journeying off and returning to the American Midwest. And yet, there is stability rather than restlessness in the tone and persona, for as Stryk himself has written in 1983, "An artist, wherever he happens to be, is alone, rooted in place and time."[166]

Throughout his career, such variations can seem like lack of locus. In addition, the poems appear stiffly regular (mostly three-line stanzas). The formality of his lines requires acclimation because they often end so slackly (ending on articles or prepositions, for example) that they seem to be merely filling out a count; other times they end firmly enough to fulfill the line. Except for a few metered and end-rhymed pieces early on, Stryk's poems have a remarkable consistency over decades, a continuity varied by his translations. The delicacy to the lines themselves is one born of voice. The subtlety of Stryk's accentual line allows the slack-stress endings to create a disarming softness of tone. These elements of form continue throughout the poet's work, reinforcing the quiet, spoken voice rather than an arbitrary prosody enforced on the poems.

In his essay "Making Poems" Stryk relates how his poetics radically shifted as a result of a reprimand. The poet confesses in his book *Zen: Poems, Prayers, Sermons* that he "said some very stupid things about rock gardens" but finally the temple's monk, Tenzan Yasuda corrected him, saying that to "appreciate his garden fully, you must have almost as much insight as Sesshu himself. This, needless to say, very few possess. Ideally, one should sit in Zen for a long period before looking at the garden; then one might be able to look at it, as the old saying goes, 'with the navel.'"[167] This humbled Stryk, causing him to reconsider the purpose of art and his own methods. He says he took up a piece he'd been working on about the garden and kept at it for hours, "ridding it of 'filling,' breaking down rigidly regular stanzas, a welter of words, to a few 'image units' of around two and one-half lines, while keeping to a constant measure."[168] The stripped down diction and measured but flexibly voiced lines arranged into small stanzas remain the emblems of Stryk's poetry. The result, as the critic Ralph Mills, Jr. observers, are poems that

> *demonstrate their author's strict commitment to technical and formal resourcefulness, to making of a linguistic object that is firm, solid, trim, that avoids all excess or flabbiness. Diction and imagery are precise in a manner rendering them also highly evocative; movement, organization in any poem are sure*[169].

Concise, sure, solid. These are the words that over and over are used to characterize this poet's work. From this discovery, sprung from correction and humility, Lucien Stryk embodies what Coleridge said all true poets must do: they write from a principle within, not originating in anything without.

The poem "Web" (1997) shows Stryk at his finest. Here is the entire piece:

> *Stumped for words*
> *I watch*
> *the spider, nimble*
> *vagabond*
>
> *shuttle among twigs*

> *of the ever-*
> *green. Its patience*
> *mesmerizes.*
>
> *From my pen a thread*
> *criscrosses*
> *lines of silk into*
> *a geometric*
>
> *sphere, a fragile cup,*
> *to filter*
> *morning sun into*
> *my window,*
>
> *frescoing the wall.*[170]

Nothing extra, not in the words, lines, or overall conception. It has the feeling of haiku in the focused single image, the correspondence between inner and outer worlds, and the direct but fresh expression. The stanzas demonstrate Stryk's "image unit" but never feel static or forced. The poet pauses in his composition, finds his interest aroused by a spider, which is a "nimble vagabond," as it weaves a web in evergreen twigs, but soon the slow work of this creature "mesmerizes." There a transition occurs, as if in the space between the stanzas, and the writer and the spider are one; now the poet's pen is spinning "thread" and "lines of silk." Both poem and the web in the twigs catch the sunlight that makes its own artwork on the wall.

In Clark Strand's excellent introduction and guide to writing haiku, *Seeds from the Birch Tree*, he gives an example by Basho then comments that a "Japanese critic once said that a poem like this, which is plain but evocative, can be written only by a total amateur or a great master."[171] In a similar way, this could be said of "Web." In fact, the editors of the *Virginia Quarterly Review* call him "one of America's finest contemporary poets...[and] one of its most subtle presences."[172]

Lucien Stryk's mastery comes from years of being "stumped for words" and yet being "led to resonant / spots," as he put it in another poem.[173] These places of resonance are often the everyday observations, like the spider in "Web," but there is something more. Precise observation can be sterile or distancing as detailing can dismember. Observation needs to be combined with another quality, and in his poems that quality is a willingness to being led to a kind of absorption by the event, thing, or memory; to allow the observed that deep an identification requires the boundaries of the self to be permeable. In this process, description yields insight: "Its patience / mesmerizes." This surrender to being mesmerized warms the poems because the speaker is drawn into the observation; trusting this process of identification, the reader is likewise drawn in as well. Ralph Mills praises this quality this way:

> *These poems, so deeply personal in their basic sensibility, the lively affective responsiveness underlying their finished forms, still display, again and again, Stryk's amazing capacity for entering the being of another—human or animal, tree or house or painting, animate or*

> inanimate—and revealing that experience in the alloying texture of the poem....[174]

The critic Gary Eddy claims that the way a Zen practitioner "opens himself up to identify with an object" is by means of *zenki*, or inner formlessness. Inner formlessness requires that one's sense of self remain fluid, ready to change in response to outer influences and inner realizations, but it also invites curiosity about sensations and formations in the world. Empowered by *zenki*, the poet is able to connect with the world, and Eddy says, "the contact is direct, unpretentious, and hopefully egoless."[175] For Stryk, this is an essential quality for writers. He says, "Poems written about others are good poems only when the writer becomes the other. In other words, he [sic] can't be anything other than selfless if he is to make important art."[176]

There is a fine example of this process of absorption in "Friends" (from his 1989 collection *Of Ink and Paper Scraps*). While most of Stryk's poems employ a speaker that is clearly an aspect of the poet, in "Friends," there is no poet-writer visible, not even an I, just a voice speaking. In his usual triplets, "Friends" is a brief story of two men who enter Regent's Park "arm in arm."[177] The speaker relates how the men wander through the flowers, passing a waterfall and the ducks and swans of Bird Island. In the middle of the fifth stanza we get "The blind man glances / through his friend's eyes..." which transforms the intimacy of the whole scene and intensifies the joy they feel at the end when "a sparrow chances on the // blind one's outstretched hand."[178]

In addition to being carefully observed, this poem is a tender portrait of a relationship. This union between friends and between men and bird is widened to include us as the poet is mesmerized by this resonant moment. The ambiguities of sexuality, their ironies, are presented and not commented on; there is no need for such self-defining reflection. And such restraint is the sign of a master poet.

Each poem of his is a luminous moment, but in an era of conflicting poetic schools, readers may expect more urgency to larger claims. When considering Lucian Stryk's body of work, it's clear that individual works achieve a clarity and full resolution, but they don't appear to accumulate into "something larger." In fact, John Haines' line about "American poetry lacks ideas"[179] seems to apply to Stryk's work.

In his 1983 essay, "A Hole in the Bucket," Haines goes on to explain, "By 'idea' I mean, among other things, some kind of conviction about the world and the place of poetry in it. It is an insight, let's say, that makes of experience and perception a particular way of seeing: what we sometimes call the poet's '"vision."'"[180]

Without poems obviously wrestling with convictions of the place of poetry in the world, Stryk's finely-made poems can feel "occasional" or even random. The most overtly unified book is his 1986 collection *The Bells of Lombardy* springs from the poet's stay in Italy, so the resonant moments have a shared setting and concern, even in their diversity. His other collections, however, include many travels (Japan, England, Sweden, among others); reflect on music and art; refer to the poet's family and midwestern haunts; cast back into memory, its difficulties and pleasures;

and explore principles of Zen. From all this variety, a "vision" certainly does emerge; the poems demonstrate it rather than talk about it. What seemed an absence early on in one's encounter with this poet's work becomes another sign of Stryk's mastery.

In fact, that the vision is hard to glimpse would be high praise for this poet. "A man's poems should reveal the full range of his life and hide nothing except the art behind them," he has written on several occasions.[181] In "Making Poems" he asserts this credo: "I believe not only in the need to 'hide traces,' an invisible art, but as much in the wisdom of hiding sources."[182] Such humility is rare in all art, but is characteristic of Zen. What's the purpose of this kind of restraint? Stryk says that in Zen art, all the detail contributes; he observes that "foreground, background, each was part of the process, in poetry as in painting the spirit discovering itself among the things of this world."[183] This discovery is all in all. The art is attendant upon it, not the other way around. When Stryk reflected on the Zen art and poetry he was working with at the time of his rock garden reprimand, Stryk was translating not just any Japanese literature, but Zen poetry. In light of the monk telling him he needs to actually do *zazen* to "get" a Zen garden, he realized he was missing something in the poetry as well. He says,

> *my failing in poetry was the result, in great part of a grave misunderstanding concerning the very purpose of art. The Zen masters who had written the poems I was translating did not think of themselves as "poets" at all; rather, they were attempting to express in verse nothing*

> less than the Zen spirit—and the results were astonishing. The poems, without any pretension to "art," were among the finest I had ever read, intense, compact, rich in spirit.[184]

And so there is clearly "a particular way of seeing" put forward by this poet: the vision of Zen. The resulting poetry's role is "to enliven, inspire, transform."[185] And it is this purpose shaped by Stryk's long engagement with Zen that holds the key to questions of form, content, and overall vision. Ralph Mills links Stryk's hidden art with his "image unit" and so forges the union between purpose and method. Mills goes on to say, "That invisibility of art, that hidden technique, is characteristic of our poet's work and owes much, I feel, to his determination to formulate his poems in the stark, compressed lines and abbreviated stanzaic patterns he has chosen for himself." In so doing, the poet must struggle, but "The reader, on the other hand, discovers an art that seems nearly artless, imposing no elaborate screen of rhetoric or ornament, never attempting to sway him with verbal or symbolic exhibitions."[186]

Lucien Stryk is most known for is his translations of Japanese poetry and other Zen work for readers of English. Even in his own collected poems, he includes a suite of haiku by Issa, a selection of modern haiku, and a whole book by Shinkichi Takahashi (Stryk's two excellent collections of Basho translations are still in print). It seems to me a sign of great generosity and humility to include others' poems in one's collected works, and that loss of self is a mark of Zen.

Stryk has written that when his poem, "Awakening" (from the 1973 collection of the same name), came to him, "I felt I was giving body, shape, to impulses born of my meeting with Zen."[187] It is a seven-part offering to Hakuin, the Rinzai Zen master who, according to Stryk, "expressed more fully than any before or since, through art, painting as well as poetry, the transforming power of Zen discipline."[188] This poem, "Awakening," also sheds light on the poet's own subtle expression of this same vision. In his essay for *Singular Voices*, Stryk explicates the poem section by section, so I won't, but he also writes of Zen practice and how *satori* (enlightenment) differs from what many consider Zen-moments of insight or what James Joyce called epiphany: "the passing of the epiphanic moment (a return to reality rather like the street stepped back into after a luminous few hours in a theater) is invariably a come-down, whereas true satori is permanent in its effects: the world (that street) has been forever altered."[189]

One means of practicing this state of mind, says Stryk, is *zenkan*, or "meditation through close observation," which, as we've seen, is evidenced throughout his body of work. Even his translations model this way of Zen, as if the poet were trying to get inside such awareness by "english[ing] / sparrows, temple gardens, fish, // time, universe—"[190] In "Note on Translating Japanese Zen Poetry," Stryk says that "the translator should be, as much as possible, familiar with the details—objects faces, landscapes—found in the original poems."[191] He backs off that in a later essay but stands by the need for translators to be "infatuated, feeling his poet is giant among midgets. Only then will he rise to the awesome occasion of being his voice and, at that moment, become his equal."[192] That transformation to "being his voice" and becoming equals is the same process for translation as for other interactions with the world. Close consideration of things—including states of mind and feeling—is crucial to train the mind, and it results in clear, precise images in poems.

In "The Ordinary" from his 1984 *Collected Poems*, he makes grand philosophical comments, but always through images. Here it is in its entirety:

> *To love the ordinary—*
> *fifty feet of dandelions*
> *and burdock,*
>
> *and a small house perched*
> *on concrete under a dying*
> *Chinese elm.*
>
> *To be content with neighbor-*
> *banter over a crooked fence,*
> *days, nights, years.*
>
> *And not to regret—sun*
> *torching the willow-oak—*
> *some Elsewhere.*[193]

The poem names particular objects and conveys their value through adjectives. The dandelions take up exactly "fifty feet" (a lot size, perhaps, and so the whole yard?), the house is small, the tree is dying, and the fence is crooked. In the final stanza, the moment is redeemed by the interrupting gesture of the sun "torching the willow-oak," as if setting it all ablaze. The word "torching" suggests burning down the worthless thing, but the image also suggests a brilliance and passing because soon it will be transformed to ash and smoke, as we all are. Instead, we are here, amid neighbors who "banter," a playful term and not at all antagonistic, over the fence with actual trees and actual weeds, as opposed to the capitalized, idealized "Elsewhere." The objects are observed closely but so are the mindsets. Inner and outer worlds are reflected in this small poem.

When discussing this practice of close observation, Stryk quotes the eighth-century Chinese poet Beirei: "Oh my disciples, examine, examine. / What? Why this. This only."[194] In some ways, it doesn't matter what the object is, since careful examination fosters a sense of the world that is universal in particulars, and through those particulars to the moral and spiritual landscapes within us. Lucien Stryk's own work demonstrates this dynamic. His poem "Cherries" develops the speaker going through an entire bag of fruit; "One by one I lift them to / my mouth, slowly break / their skin…"[195] But this is no poem of delight. It is charged with moral clarity: it starts "Because I sit eating cherries / I did not pick / a girl goes bad under // the elevator tracks…" And later, he goes further: "Because I want the whole bag, // grasping, twenty five children / cry for food." In the end, he says, "My happiness, // bought cheap, must last forever."[196] Again, it is not only the outward behavior the poet observes but the inner desires, the mental structures. It is not the "gorging" only that is the cause but the "grasping."

This inherent relatedness, Buddhist cause-and-effect turning on an eternal wheel, is also reflected in a later section of "Awakening." The speaker is at the beach with his daughter mesmerized by shells. He writes, "I take them from her, / make, at her command, / the universe." They clasp hands and "watch till sundown / planets whirling in the sand."[197] Exact observation of the world gives way to a sudden recognition of how everything is intertwined, the oneness at the heart of shells and sand, father and daughter, time and eternity. And yet, at the heart of everything according to Zen is also emptiness, the lack of solid, discrete selves; instead there are processes, intention and act and ramification all in motion. While Stryk's poems do not directly explore this awareness, his translations of Shinkichi Takahashi do.

In "Destruction," Takahashi writes, "A paltry thing, the universe: / Here is all strength, here the greatest strength."[198] This is philosophic statement rather than image; Takahshi's figure for this is, of all things, a sparrow. "There's room enough / On the sparrow's eyelash for the whole."[199] In a sense, the sparrow's eyelash is the "this. Only this" the Chinese poet exhorted his disciples to examine; every particular thing is sufficient for the whole. Takahashi's way of exploring this oneness includes wildness of imagery that is in sharp contrast to Stryk's humble, precise observations and to the haiku translations Stryk is famous for. Takahahi's poems jam images together, sometimes with humorous results ("The sparrow came at her, bill like a sword, / And suddenly from her buttocks—the sun!"[200]) but also with surreal effects ("Suddenly a butterfly, / My eyeballs spots / On its wings, / Takes off, brilliant."[201]). Difficult because of such associative imagery, Takahashi's poems are also more deeply involved with Zen *koan* training, where a practitioner is given a question or puzzling statement to take with him or her into *zazen,* or sitting meditation. In his essay, "Death of a Zen Poet: Shinkichi Takahashi (1901-1987)," Stryk traces Takahashi's life and poetry from his early, reckless dada approach to art (and life, it seems) to the discipline of Zen practice. In this practice, logic and conventional reasoning do not "solve" the *koan* because *koan* practice is designed to break the mind of such limitations, opening one to the pure perception of things-as-they-are. Stryk says Takahashi's poems sometimes interpret this struggle and the difficulty of meditative observation. "He always cautioned, as he himself had been, against dualism, assuring that little by little one learns to know true seeing from false, that it was possible to reach the unconditioned. The world, he claimed, is always pure—we, with our dripping mind-stuff, foul it."[202]

In breaking through the attitudes and pre-judgmental constructions of the mind, Takahashi seems to be trying to open the reader to the essential emptiness of conditioned things, perceiving the fluid arising and dissolving nature of all experience. Stryk, on the other hand, seems to be presenting the purity of the world. These two methods converge, however, when Stryk considers the foulness of war.

"The Pit," "Return to Hiroshima," "Sniper," and "The Face" (among others) explore how war's inhumanity returns unbidden in memory. Sometimes it is just a glance, like in "The Face," a poem that describes a boy's face that is shown at the start of a documentary about World War II. Such images are designed to be introductory, leading into the story of the show itself, but the speaker's connection suspends the image in consciousness; this boy is "doomed" and his face is "sharply beautiful."[203] The speaker is caught up with this person through the screen and across time. The face is "a dark balloon," which is an image that begins by merely describing the action of how his face "floats in the screen," but it also suggests how fragile this person's existence is amid "a field of barbs, / the stench of gas." Now the darkness suggest the boy is Jewish and the gas the reason for his being "doomed." In the final stanza, Stryk continues the metaphor to suggest the responsibility we have in an interrelated universe: "Whoever holds the / string / will not let go."[204] On the one hand, those who hold the boy captive will not let him float to freedom and life, and on the other, we who now know cannot let go of this disturbing image and its implications for the individual and we mean to hang on, not forget.

Sometimes, memory itself seems to be the battlefield challenging us. "Return to Hiroshima," a three-part poem from different points of view, starts with the bombardier confronting "the cripple who had clopped...across his dreams / For fifteen years"[205] by visiting the first city to experience nuclear war. Susan Porterfield has accurately declared that this poem is about more than the event of August 6, 1945. "More specifically, it is about how humans have responded to that tragedy."[206] At the end of the first section, the Bombardier returns home thinking that his visit to Hiroshima has cleansed him of his guilt and resultant nightmares; instead, his sleep is as troubled as ever.

> *On waking*
> *He knew he had gone too late to the wrong*
>
> *Town, and that until his own legs numbed*
> *And eyes went dim with age, somewhere*
> *A fire would burn that no slow tears could quench.*[207]

While the Bombardier stews in his complicity, the Pilot in section two takes on the competing arguments for using the atomic bomb, revealing the moral superiority that supports both sides of the debate. His voice is defiant and confident. "All right," he says in the first line, "let them play with it, / Let them feel all hot and righteous…" He is willing to dismiss the critics of the bombing because he was there, and like those who count the number of victims in Hiroshima, "I too have counted corpses."[208] Porterfield analyzes this section with this insight, saying that the speaker

> accuses [those who condemn the bomb] of feeling a 'savage joy,' born from their assumption that in this matter they have the moral upper hand and thus that they are in some way better. Their 'joy' in thinking themselves morally superior is 'savage' because to make these kinds of distinctions, to separate people into us and them is, ironically, the basis for every act of barbarism committed among humans.[209]

This section grows more complex when the speaker personalizes the discussion, naming his slain friend, Tom Staines, and how he regrets that Staines couldn't "taste the / Exultation" they all felt, knowing they wouldn't have to die alone and anonymously "as fertilizer / for next spring's rice crop" in the planned invasion of the Japanese mainland. In the end, the speaker adds it all up: "take one away / From one, and you've got bloody nothing. // I too have counted the corpses."[210] Remarkably he comes to the same ending as the Bombardier: convinced by the gore and war's erosion of humanity, he is haunted by the dead. The tone is different, but the experience is the same.

This poem embodies the two principles of emptiness and purity. In death, the essential emptiness is most clearly evident. Everything—people, nations, arguments, angers, regrets—changes form; they are essentially devoid of distinct structures but instead swirl in a process of formulation and disintegration. And yet, the integrity of lives remains in memory, in loss, and in regret. The mental states that justify violence begin the divisions from the unity of humanity, which death always reveals. Porterfield points this out when she says, "Despite the divisions that this poem catalogues, those that split us into two camps or divide us internally, death binds us all and by so doing turns such speculative issues into red herrings."[211] It is the oneness that remains, pure and complete and beyond the individual.

The images Stryk creates are as sharp as his other poems, but the violence and destruction are akin to Takahashi's more metaphoric work. These extreme experiences are like a *koan*: senseless and absurd, they question all prior assumptions about how the world operates and why. In the end, it is by confronting death that true meaning and purpose can be discovered. As he says in "Buddhism and Modern Man" from *Encounter with Zen*,

> *Buddhism teaches us to understand that death is a natural part of life. It teaches us how to deal with our fears and to realize that death plays no more and no less a role in human existence than anything else. We should not, therefore, allow our fears to personify death into being the great adversary, because to do so is to grant it a status that it does not have.*[212]

The last poems in Lucien Stryk's *And Still Birds Sing* are like some of the "death poems" Stryk has translated from Chinese and Japanese Zen masters. Stryk's are not the often-cryptic final teachings of some masters, but his do have a conclusiveness which is also open to the always-generative emptiness. In "For Helen, on Her Birthday," Stryk describes a place where "a small mound that one / day will hold / a scrap of granite bearing / our poor name."[213] An elegy-in-advance, the poem also seeks the future by promising that there's no need for despair because "We will / have begun // another journey into the unknown..." The poem seals the promise as the long-time lovers will be "content"; they will be "holding tight / to each other."[214] A lovely poem that by its directness escapes sentimentality.

"Voyage," the final poem in the collection, is about "the year / on hold."[215] A health crisis (heart attack?) landed him in the hospital. In three sections, the poem's second part opens out beyond the personal or, more accurately, it opens through the personal experience as the patient reads the Sunday paper, staring "at faces of those / Auschwitz children"[216] and

> *the last photograph of Primo Levi,*

> *their fire-eyed witness, before*
> *he took his life,*
>
> > *slamming*
> *the door on a half a century's pain.*[217]

This inclusion of the Holocaust and Primo Levi, the survivor-poet/writer, sets the poem on edge: such an impure world, and yet the patient wants to live. In the face of such horrors, suicide (or at least allowing oneself to be taken from the world) seems appropriate. But the third section confronts this way of seeing. Returned to the hospital, or "botched up / once again," the patient is cared for.

> *My wife,*
>
> > *my dearest friend, stroked*
> > *the blue flower round*
> > *the IV in my arm, coaxed*
>
> > *darkness from my eyes.*

The love of others and the beauty of the natural world—continual moments of resonance in Lucien Stryk—make leaving difficult. His poems catalogue such moments, and this one ends on a note of confidence that is consistent with every line that comes before it: "I know for all it lacks // this world is still the only / place, and walking in a flame / of sunset I have things to do."[218] An understated, subtle affirmation seems fitting for this skillful, attentive poet. Readers can be grateful that Stryk continually sought words to equal the world, "the only place."

There are no gimmicks or axes to grind in the whole of this man's work, only a voice worthy of trust. His is "an art of revelation," says Susan Porterfield, one that synthesizes intellect and senses because "all faculties are engaged in realizing essence."[219] Here is a poet who lives and composes from a principle within him. His fidelity to his vision and to bringing it forth in a subtle range of poetry make him an example. After more than forty years practicing careful observation to the details of the world, to the shifts and motions of the mind, and to the vibrancy of language itself, Lucien Stryk is a master American poet.

Robert Hayden, American Master

Edward Hirsch, poet and critic, noted that Robert Hayden's *Collected Poems* is a slender volume, "And yet it has a profound and passionate scope. Every one of its poems is meticulously crafted."[220] Such comprehensive praise is rare, and so it is gratifying that this richly varied poet is no longer represented in anthologies by only a few set pieces, like "Those Winter Sundays," which is such a splendid poem that it deserves readers' recurring attention. Jay Parini's *The Wadsworth Anthology of Poetry* also includes the whole of "Middle Passage" and the deceptively simple "A Plague of Starlings," while Dana Gioia, David Mason, and Meg Schoerke not only include a healthy group of his work for their *Twentieth-Century American Poetry* but also selected his introduction to *Kaleidoscope: Poems by American Negro Poets* for their companion anthology of *Twentieth-Century American Poetics*.

This exposure for students and respect from editors is important because Robert Hayden is not just a poet's poet. His range and depth, in such a compact oeuvre, is remarkable. Over and over, readers remark on his craftsmanship and his embracing perspective, which sought the lessons of the past to engage in crafting the future. He was a poetic biographer, writing poems that contain the lives of Nat Turner, Frederick Douglass, Phyllis Wheatley, John Brown, and El-Hajj Malik El-Shabazz (Malcolm X). These lyrical, dramatic, deeply felt, and richly researched historical poems explore the story of America's shame, but his handling of these events and biographies achieve an articulation of human aspiration that inspire readers of all races and times. He was also a political poet confronting war and racism, mourning the loss of life and of human sympathies. When recording the histories that impinge upon our time, he did so, as Joseph A. Lipari put it, in a way that "combined an intimate knowledge of evil with an acute appreciation of the sublime."[221] He made use of modernist techniques of multi-voiced collage and fractured narrative in "Middle Passage" but surpassed previous examples by Pound and Eliot by his moral force and transpersonal vision. While he wrote of his own experience in an autobiographical way similar to the Confessionals, his restraint enabled him to discover the mythos, which allows readers to identify with the poem's content and so enlarge the poem with a fuller presence, an inclusive and transformative presence. And his religious work articulates the longings and teachings of his Baha'i faith, but while reaching for the numinous he avoids dogmatism.

In all these ways, Robert Hayden embodies the American soul and expresses it with such a radical independence that his body of work stands as an emblem of what poetry itself can achieve. In his tribute "Remembering Robert E. Hayden," Michael S. Harper said it best: "he was a national poet in the voicings he could capture in a phrase; he could also recall Wallace Stevens and take us into that hidden arena of transcendence…"[222] In his review of *Collected Poems*, Jim Elledge praised Hayden's combination of what his poetry strives for and how well-made they are: "Marked by wisdom, without being stodgy, Hayden's poetry is a blend of unrivaled craftsmanship with a sharp, unrestrained vision."[223]

Most students are introduced to Hayden through "Those Winter Sundays," which stands up for teachers as well. In his essay for *Touchstones: American Poets on a Favorite Poem*, David Huddle calculates that he's read this piece aloud approximately 240 times, and yet "it remains a poem I look forward to reading and discussing in my classroom."[224] He gives it the highest praise a reader can give when he says that "for hours and sometimes days after it visits my classroom, I'm hearing its lines in my mind's ear."[225]

Those Winter Sundays

Sundays too my father got up early
and put his clothes on in the blueblack cold,
then with cracked hands that ached
from labor in the weekday weather made
banked fires blaze. No one ever thanked him.

I'd wake and hear the cold splintering, breaking.
When the rooms were warm, he'd call,
and slowly I would rise and dress,
fearing the chronic angers of that house,

> *Speaking indifferently to him,*
> *who had driven out the cold*
> *and polished my good shoes as well.*
> *What did I know, what did I know*
> *of love's austere and lonely offices?*[226]

This poem stands as an emblem of Hayden's mastery of the lyric poem. It is a clear scene, presented with only the essential details. The economy of "too" in line one contains the father's lonely work all the other days as well. The fact that the man would only call after the house was comfortable shows that he's doing this Sunday duty for the others of the household, but polishing his son's shoes indicates his care for the boy in particular. Hayden's care with the language is most evident in the first stanza's description. The phrase "blueblack cold" creates the visual impression of pre-dawn light, but it also suggests a bruise, so that the cold is beaten up or is strong enough to beat one up. The condition of the man's hands likewise shows how Hayden's language begins with the image but goes beyond it to the feeling, this time with sound. The "cracked hands" echoes "-black" and prefigures "ached" which leads to "labor," so that all the key words are linked and reinforced by consonance and assonance. That long sentence with its interrupting phrase seems to ache along inside the lines before the sudden appearance of the fire. Then comes the clipped comment: "No one ever thanked him," shifting from description to statement, an admission. Cadence and music set up how this short declarative contrasts to establish the poem's true subject. Huddle names it when he says, "And what is the poem if not an elegantly fashioned, permanent expression of gratitude?"[227]

"Those Winter Sundays" also shows Hayden's other gifts as well. The emotion is clear, but not flat or simple. G.E. Murray noted that "Hayden's poetry has an indelible honesty and directness."[228] One way he achieves this indelible effect is his precise, resonant diction. The phrase "the chronic angers of that house" could be read as metaphoric description of the cold or as an emotional description of the relationships. Knowing Hayden's biography clarifies this, but in the poem the phrase remains a lovely ambiguity.

In an interview with Al Poulin, Jr., Hayden credits his foster father, William "Pa" Hayden, with his education, saying "when other boys would have to go out in the summers—winters, too, for that matter—and work, why he would help me to stay in school."[229] He continues that he regrets that his foster father "never lived to know that I cared that much."[230] This lack was not only because the boy-poet didn't express his appreciation but because the household was profoundly tense. Pa Hayden often contended with the poet's Aunt Roxie, an alcoholic who would wreak havoc. Their arguments frightened the boy and caused him to never really know what to expect from a day. In an interview from the 1970s with Dennis Gendron, Hayden said it pained him still—in his late fifties—to speak of some parts of his childhood. To illustrate the poet's restraint, here is a passage from that interview:

> *I got a few hidings like [the one depicted in "The Whipping"]. But my aunt objected strenuously, and I*

> *didn't get whipped that way too much. But I was often abused and often hurt physically because they were ignorant people. They didn't know how to handle children, and they were neurotic themselves. My foster mother was just as neurotic as they come; I know that now. I didn't know it then. She had some kind of nervous ailment. They called it neuralgia. She would have dreadful pains in her face, and she even had an operation. They tried to kill the nerves in her face and so on. But nothing helped. I know now that that was psychosomatic because the time came when she didn't have that anymore. The pain was just so terrible, and she would just.... Very often it would be brought on by some great anger outburst or something that upset her, and then she would blame it on me. it was terrible. That part I don't want to get into too much because it was painful; it really hurts me to even think of it. But they were cruel to me. And, without my knowing it, I guess I was cruel to them. I don't know. But I was a child. I was at their mercy. I really did get abused and hurt and so on. I saw dreadful things.*[231]

As he relates "the chronic angers of that house," he seems to be seeing all sides of it. He understands his foster mother's pain, but it disappeared over time, suggesting that her own responses brought on the nerve pain. On the one hand, he concedes that he may have been cruel to them, but then, on the other, holds them responsible since they were the adults and he "was at their mercy." As a person and as poet, Hayden was mature enough to explore a situation's complexities, to allow even conflicting emotions to co-exist. This results in a poem which, as an expression of gratitude, is not confused by mixed feelings; in fact, it is even more convincing and remarkable because of them.

In addition to outstanding lyric poems, like "Those Winter Sundays," which is autobiographical, Hayden's work takes on a historical sweep that includes multiple voices and perspectives, and the result is "Middle Passage." Hayden's synthesis of voices, allusions, and morality in a single vision of true humanity is the hallmark of "Middle Passage," the finest long poem of the century. A verbal collage made musical by Hayden's fine ear, its modernist techniques of multiple points of view and fragmented narrative consistently serve the overall conception rather than a vaulted aspiration for poetry itself.

The poem dramatizes the slave trade's commerce in "Black gold, black ivory, black seed,"[232] but it does so through the voices of traders. One speaker reflects wistfully on those journeys and longs for the sea, saying "I'd be trading still / but for the fevers melting down my bones."[233] Another ironically prays, "We pray that Thou wilt grant, O Lord, / safe passage to our vessels bringing / heathen souls unto Thy chastening."[234] The poem also includes the 1838 Amistad case, made famous in the 1997 film, but uses it as an epitome of the entire wretched system. The poem begins by listing ship names—*Jesús, Estrella, Esperanza, Mercy*—the religious culture of both the Old and New World making a pointed irony as there is no mercy or hope in this voyage for the Africans. Hayden's image of the ships journeying back and forth across the ocean weaves the cloth that tells the New World story. The third part of the poem begins:

> *Shuttles in the rocking loom of history,*
> *the dark ships move, the dark ships move,*
> *their bright ironical names*
> *like the jests of kindness on a murderer's mouth;*
> *plough through thrashing glister toward*
> *fata morgana's lucent melting shore,*
> *weave toward New World littorals that are*
> *mirage and myth and actual shore.*
>
> *Voyage through death,*
>   *voyage whose chartings are unlove.*[235]

America, with its bright hope of freedom and wealth, is an actual place where these Africans will arrive, but because American values have always been mythic in that they are beyond our achieving, they are mirages for those oppressed and impoverished here. The word "littorals" refers to the physical shoreline or, as metaphor, they are the tidal zones of history, of culture, and of the human heart. They are places where water and land shift, where voyage and arrival merge. This is the region where the American myth of freedom could be the firm principle on which social structures are constructed or merely a mirage, airy words mouthed from bandstands, while the actual world is fraught with enslavement and incarceration, and the law is on the side of the slaveowners. That a poem can reflect such subtle realities is a mark of high accomplishment.

"Middle Passage" is centrally witnessed through participants' log-notes, a deposition of a survivor, the retired trader, and the argument of the prosecuting attorney in the *Amistad* case. The haunted details of the voyage are related plainly, clearly, directly. When the ship *The Belle J* caught fire, the captain and crew were naked in the cabins with captured women, but when the conflagration grew beyond control, "the negros howling and their chains / entangled with the flames," crew members abandoned ship, leaving both "their shrieking negresses behind" and the captain too drunk to depart from his place with them.[236] Another case, told in clipped, ship's-log style describes how with three weeks still left in the journey, a plague, ophthalmia, strikes, first among the blacks "stowed spoon-fashion" so that more than 500 could be jammed aboard and then to the crew. "It spreads, the terrifying sickness spreads," the sailor writes.[237] These scenes are haunting for their imagery and the suffering they reflect.

The morality of the slave trade and of slavery generally may seem defined, but there are always levels of complicity. The slave trader implicates some African leaders "whose vanity / and greed turned wild black hides…to gold for us."[238] One reasons he loved this business was dealing with "nigger kings," especially one they called "King Anthracite" who would "honor us with drums and fest and conjo / and palm-oil-glistening wenches deft in love…" While Hayden doesn't shy from complicity in Africa, he also complicates things on this side of the ocean, too. While former-President John Quincy Adams did represent Cinquez, the uprising's leader, the poem presents his arguments in reverse, as it were, through the pleas of one of the two survivors.

The survivor calls for Cinquez and the others to be extradited to Havana for trial. He briefly relates how a storm delayed the *Amistad*, which enabled the slaves to rise up. Then he speaks of the sailors' deaths, saying "Our men went down / before the murderous Africans." Having called them "murderers," he later dehumanizes the Africans, calling them "apes" who "threw overboard the butchered bodies of / our men, true Christians all, like so much jetsam."²³⁹ He's made his case against the slaves, accusing them of heinous murder, and shows that the dead deserve justice because they were good men, "true Christians." By this point in the poem, the irony of that phrase is nearly painful. But before we get a chance to climb too high on our horse, he turns to criticize John Quincy Adams and the nation itself, "whose wealth [and] tree of liberty / are rooted in the labor of your slaves":

> *We find it paradoxical indeed*
> *that you whose wealth, whose tree of liberty*
> *are rooted in the labor of your slaves*
> *should suffer the august John Quincy Adams*
> *to speak with so much passion of the right*
> *of chattel slaves to kill their lawful masters*
> *and with his Roman rhetoric weave a hero's*
> *garland for Cinquez*²⁴⁰

The economic benefits of slavery, all free people's involvement in that windfall, widens the circle of guilt. Americans can be proud the case was heard and yet be shamed we grew rich on these people's unpaid labor. We can righteously condemn this speaker for his emotional arguments, but we remain indicted by his accusation that our very "tree of liberty" is tainted by the blood of the very people of this poem. Once again, Hayden presents the many emotional aspects of the situation and then, in the final lines, brings us to the present and the continual human longing:

> *The deep immortal human wish,*
> *the timeless will:*
>
> *Cinquez its deathless primaveral image,*
> *life that transfigures many lives.*
>
> *Voyage through death*
> *to life upon these shores.*[241]

It is a "human wish," not locked in history nor the province of any group, race, or nation. And so "these shores" refers to America, the actual locus where this history occurred, but as the poem culminates with a timeless longing for freedom, for dignity, "these shores" become a metaphysical place as well. It is the littorals of the human heart as well, the zone where individual conscience and social obligations flow into each other and boundaries blur. Hayden addresses this region most passionately and dramatically in his curtail sonnet "Frederick Douglass." In it, he uses long iterated phrasing to call upon a time when freedom is actual, then the eighth line brings in Douglass directly, but only in the final couplet does his true tribute become clear. In method, the poem enacts a timeline.

Frederick Douglass

> *When it is finally ours, this freedom, this liberty, this beautiful and terrible thing, needful to man as air,*

> usable as earth; when it belongs at last to all,
> when it is truly instinct, brain matter, diastole, systole,
> reflex action; when it is finally won; when it is more
> than the gaudy mumbo jumbo of politicians;
> this man, this Douglass, this former slave, this Negro
> beaten to his knees, exiled, visioning a world
> where none is lonely, none hunted, alien,
> this man, superb in love and logic, this man
> shall be remembered. Oh, not with statues' rhetoric,
> not with legends and poems and wreaths of bronze alone,
> but with the lives grown out of his life, the lives
> fleshing his dream of the beautiful needful thing.[242]

The critical word from the outset is "ours." Read as African Americans, as descendants of slaves and inheritors of slavery's assumptions and ramifications, freedom is an action, a habit of being, a force within them as people and as a people living "lives grown out of his life." This image echoes America's "tree of liberty" rooted in slavery but also transforms it. Hayden envisions a living system nourished by freedom and this one man's life. But, read as Americans, then when we—of all races—actualize this "beautiful needful thing," all will render tribute to Douglass, and so a rift shall be healed, a new unity achieved, where the lives we live grow from slavery's roots and also from this slave and his vision. As we are "fleshing" this dream, making it incarnate in our nervous systems, impulses, and reactions, we must ensure it "belongs to all." Hayden offers complementary, not competing, futures; the force and promise of his vision is communal as we internalize liberty, which is "beautiful and terrible" as it breaks concepts and social structures that seek to divide.

In his final book, Hayden offers a more reflective tone, so that "[American Journal]" is an entirely different work, one from the point of view of an alien sent to gather data on "this baffling / multi people," the Americans.[243] The language is softer, perspective more detached, and wisdom conveyed in humor. The speaker describes the variety of Americans: "i have easily passed for an american   in / bankers grey afro and dashiki long hair and jeans / hard hat yarmulke mini skirt."[244] Earlier he reports discussing the American dream with a man in a bar, but the conversation ends when he asks where the alien's from, saying "notice you got a funny accent pal."[245] Since people arrive in America from all over, we're not shy about pointing out such differences. In fact, it's an opportunity to share backgrounds. It's a commonality of our migrant, multi-ethnic life. But it can also be a threat when the new immigrant is faced with xenophobia. It can also be uncomfortable—even dangerous—for anyone trying to fit in and instead is called out. Either way, the alien has no legitimate answer for his bar mate. He comments to himself, "must be more careful item   learn to use okay / their pass word   okay."[246]

While exploring "charming savages   enlightened primitives,"[247] the poem is unique. Disarming and pointed equally. It criticizes through a fictive speaker whom we cannot condemn because of his genuine affection. He has to "confess i am curiously drawn   unmentionable   to / the americans."[248] He appreciates exactly those aspects we celebrate: our "variousness" and "ingenuity," but he also recognizes that "i doubt i could exist among them for / long however psychic demands too severe / much violence much that repels."[249] He presents that violence in a way that we accept and the critique remains implicit. For example, the report includes this scene of a demonstration:

> *crowds gathered in the streets today for some*
> *reason obscure to me   noise and violent motion*
> *repulsive physical contact   sentinels   pigs*
> *i heard them called   with flailing clubs   rage*
> *and bleeding and frenzy and screaming   machines*
> *wailing   unbearable decibels   I fled lest*
> *vibrations of the brutal scene do further harm*
> *to my metabolism already overtaxed* [250]

We almost laugh at this "soft" witness overwhelmed by what's become "normal" unrest in the streets, but then we should recognize that it is we who have grown too blasé about our brutality. We have ceased to realize the harm we cause ourselves. Once again, Hayden approaches indirectly and is able to activate several levels at once.

In the end, "[American Journal]" explores the concept of America itself, since we are bound by beliefs and the laws that express them. It is a poem about how America is "as much a problem in metaphysics as / it is a nation."[251] The metaphysical reality of enacting freedom means we must learn how we use liberty to construct a society where a human being is permitted to be a human being.

Robert Hayden is one of this nation's great poets, a craftsman of the language, a man of vision for both the individual and for humanity. While shunning a limiting definition of himself as a "Negro poet," he achieved a poetry that confronts racism and also reveals the possibility of living beyond race. It is the future that this poet, this man, sought, and it is the future that will honor him. Gary Zebrun says that "Hayden has earned a place in literary history as one of the few contemporary poets of major distinction—a knowledgeable, competent, and inspired craftsman—who illustrates what may be in store for our poetry descending from Dickinson, Whitman, Frost, and Williams."[252] As more readers access his work—his wisdom and compassion, his strength and originality—his lyrical creations will inspire and point the way to a grander humanity.

The Making of a Poem

I.

For me, it is not unlike a cold and cloudy day. Experience moves through me and I move through my experiences like the conditions of weather: the sky largely unnoticed, just there above us, the light flattened out and casting no shadows. But then, sometimes, when those conditions are aligned exactly enough, dewpoint and whatnot, the first few snowflakes begin to fall. It often starts with an image.

Picture a sleepless girl, lying on her back on the family's flat-roofed house staring at the night sky, its light-dust and depth of dark.

From the image, sometimes language emerges. I don't know if there is going to be a poem, and I certainly don't know if it's going to be good, but we must start somewhere, right? And I start with this combination: some few physical details and whatever phrases assert themselves.

It has been the work of a lifetime, sometimes more deliberately than others, to attune myself to these impressions that arise in me. Whether they arise from lived experiences, from artwork or reading, or as in this case from imagination, I can sense these assertions.

When I am busy or preoccupied, these conditions may align, and I do not notice them. I may notice and even begin manipulating phrasing inwardly. However, unless I honor this coming-together of impressions and the resulting arising of language, honor it with the discipline to actually write, little else happens. In fact, I grow grumpier the longer I live with the lid of routine screwed tight over this well of happening.

As I've attuned myself to my own internal weather, I have noticed that the images need to have some kind of clarity and specificity to them, not something generalized. For me, close-ups are better than vistas. That's where feeling is active, not the other way around. Rarely, but occasionally, I can start from strong emotion and let it propel its way toward what the body registers: images and rhythms. Also, unlike my apprentice days, I can also begin by playfully working with language, and out of the associations, thoughts, and shadows already operating in word-roots and syntax, emotion or story or imagery coalesces. No matter how it happens, there needs to be a fusion: feeling (the insubstantial impressions that the body registers) unites with the sensory (the body's knowledge of substantial impressions).

◆ ◆ ◆

The energy of her sleeplessness is not anxiety but excitement. The world is enormous but not threatening. Her solitude up on the roof is not lonely, but capacious and hospitable. The sky bends over her, an arch or billowing sheet that is floating, is always floating above her and towards her.

Now, see if you can do more than picture her: can you *be* her?

This is unusual for me, but I've been allowing it, even seeking it, practicing it more and more: can the one who speaks the words of a poem be someone else? A character, of sorts. Or: just another self, one I can know inwardly through empathy and imagination, if not through related lived experience.

Here I was imagining Mary, the mother of Jesus. In Luke's Gospel, the only one with this infancy narrative, we read in one verse that, "Mary set out and went with haste to a Judean town in the hill country…" and the next verse has her arrival, "where she entered the house of Zechariah and greeted Elizabeth."[253] I was interested in the in-between-ness of her travel. Having had the angel "overshadow" her and invite her to participate with God in a grand plan, she leaves her home. Between leaving her childhood home and the welcome of her relatives, Mary was not only moving through the land toward the hill country but moving into a whole new life for herself. She was giving birth to a new version of herself.

She's <u>remembering</u> those nights on the roof!

With a fictive speaker, I am more conscious of how the mind moves, what might startle it into insight or strong reaction. When the speaker is a dimension of myself, these layers are hidden from me until revision. But whoever is the speaker and whenever these concerns are workable, these too need to be embedded in the body of the poem's language. They are part of the overall sequence, the pacing of whatever reveals the poem will make, the rhythms, the line and stanza units, the linebreaks and stanza breaks.

Sometimes changes in formal aspects help me realize the speaker's internal state, and so revision can be a means of discovery about the heart-mind of the poem. Other times, the inner workings are already fairly clear; revision then becomes a means of allowing formal choices to reveal them.

What causes her to cast back to those nights? What in her current situation makes the past attractive? Or what now needs to be escaped to the refuge of memory? What's happening now that prompts a new understanding or at least a re-examining of what's gone before?

◆ ◆ ◆

In the earliest drafts, the Salt Sea (commonly referred to as the Dead Sea) was up front, prominent. To allow young Mary to speak of her landscape with authority, I felt I needed authentic detail. And so I did quick, impressionistic research. I grabbed my *Oxford Companion to the Bible* and the *Oxford Biblical Commentary*. The Commentary drew my attention to how she responds not to the predictions about her soon-to-be conceived son, but to the method. She does not inquire about his greatness or what it will mean that people will call him the "Son of the Most High" or how he will be given David's throne. Instead, she asks how she could conceive since she's a virgin. This reveals her concern in that moment. While this characterization interested me, and while it reoriented my attention to the story so that I noticed how it says Mary was "perplexed" by the angel's greeting but he reassures her to not be afraid, these details did not resonate the way others did.

When I browsed the language of the verses, one word rang out, like a hollow bowl being struck. In his answer to Mary's fairly practical question about how she'll conceive if she's a virgin, Gabriel says, "The Holy Spirit will come upon you and the power of the Most High will overshadow you…" (Luke 1:35). Reading the word "overshadow," immediately, I could picture an over-sweeping darkness, a cloth of shade waved over her like a cloak. I also sensed this was a rich Biblical image, one with intricate associations. The *Harper-Collins Study Bible*, with its New Revised Standard Version, directed me to the story of when Jesus was transfigured, and a cloud overshadowed the men on the mountain. Biblical theophanies often blend light with clouds, but I was mostly interested in the paradox of darkness. Rather than a revelation "dawning" on someone, a darkening can bring revelation.

Her childhood is ending. The curtain is falling on that phase of her life, and she can feel the change in her own body.

◆ ◆ ◆

Most poems (and stories, in writing or film) map a terrain. There is movement from one place to another, whether that travel is geographical or psychological. A decision, any decision, marks a change in location, even if that change is in the will. There is something pleasing when the decision or action is small, but the significance is outsized.

The question is whether that travel is reported on, having happened, or if it is enacted within the piece itself. In my apprentice days, a moving realization or discovery would become the basis of a poem. It would be about what happened, and so they would be written in the past tense because the action had already been completed, and it occurred in the writer, not in the writing.

For this poem, Mary is literally traveling; she is also passing from one form of life to another. And yet, she is in-between, also. She is suspended between home and her relatives' house but also between the news of what her life will become and the actual unfolding of that news. As a person, Mary is no longer a child but not yet a fully grown woman, but she is pregnant. How does she feel about these movements, these forms of stasis?

She would not travel alone, not in those days. And according to the maps in the Biblical commentaries, it would be several days' journey. They'd have to stop for the night. They'd have to prepare food, have meals; they'd have to prepare sleeping arrangements, go to sleep. What was the division of labor between men and women? How would she participate?

They were stopped for the night, the activity completed, and she can't sleep. Staring into the sky causes her to recall her childhood nights of wonder and excitement. How different she feels now, just weeks or months later.

◆ ◆ ◆

The Salt Sea (early draft)

Now at this time Mary arose and went in a hurry to the

hill country, to a city of Judah…(Luke 1: 39)

*I lay on the roof as on a raft,
afloat under a white river of stars.
Night's whole territory of night curved over me,
over all the village houses, over
the animals asleep in their pens,
and over all the people asleep on their mats.
The world was wondrous, being inverted,
a place for imagination, for dreams
to play themselves even in waking.*

*I was so childish as a child—just
months ago, thinking nothing
could change, thinking
what I expected to happen
would happen. For days now,
I have been walking, walking away
from my home. Under that roof,
I was no longer at home. I'm no longer
at home in these arms, these legs,
and certainly not with this belly.*

*When I was overshadowed, I was sure,
but sent further away into the hill country,
all the world feels dry and cold.
Now I know the future is not mine.
With the others, I walk into it, a voyage
without shore. We stop for night,
I cook with the other women*

then lay down but do not sleep.
I rub the salt crusting my eyes.
Some tell stories by the fire,
tales we've all heard before.
They laugh, then grow quiet.

A traveler reported a Salt Sea
to the south. Though in water,
you can die, these waters save you.
If you release the hold on your breath,
these waters accept but do not
absorb you, and as if to remind you,
for days, the taste of salt remains.

I lick my lips. And know it is true.
I'm left awake. Time, too, is salty,
and I'm a drop of that sea.

II.

Long before pen goes to paper (or fingers to keyboard), before impressions form and constellate, before what emerges to reveal itself as having poem-potential, the poem begins. It is a long story. Before I could sit down on a winter morning—an image hovering in my mind of a scene with a young woman lying on her flat-roofed home—I needed to be the kind of person in whom such impressions would occur. What relationship to the Bible would lead someone to spin-off from its stories? What kind of writer would adopt another's voice, rather than one's own?

◆ ◆ ◆

After college, after experimenting with pipe smoking and Biblical literalism and poetry workshops, after the community and intensity of new ideas, I was adrift in a self-defining project. I had a pine-plank desk in my parents' basement. All those values talked (and talked and talked) about in late-into-the night sessions where we solved all the problems of the world needed to be aligned with the lived structures and routines of my life after college. After about a year, I came to the end of my work for *The Cable Guide* as a "customization editor," which meant I devoted all skill and subtlety my English studies had developed in me to ensure that the ads for one regional cable company appeared in their edition and not the one for San Luis Obispo. Having saved up my vacation time, I took two weeks off for very different pursuits. The first week, I spent traveling, including a few days with my poet-cousin, Kate, in California, who introduced me to the work of Denise Levertov, Galway Kinnell's *The Book of Nightmares,* and Robert Bly's translation of Rainer Maria Rilke—influences that shape my imagination and work even now, many decades later.

The next week, I went on a seven-day silent retreat at the Christian Brothers' retreat center. I was well acquainted with the place. Periodically, I would attend retreats there as part of the Aspirancy Program, the outreach and formation efforts of the Christian Brothers. All through college,

I met monthly with Brother Richard, my spiritual director, and at least once a year gather in Adamstown with the others for a retreat.

This would be my first extended retreat on my own, my first silent retreat, and my first experience of the Ignatian Spiritual Exercises. Developed by the founder of the Jesuits, St. Ignatius Loyola, these exercises use Christian contemplation to read the Bible or other sacred text (for me, it was the Gospel of Mark), and prayerfully imagine into the stories, thereby being led into meditation in God's presence. I've practiced other forms of the ancient method called *lectio divina*, and they all allow us to participate in and receive teachings from the text in ways that go far beyond "studying" them can.

Despite a regrettable, though brief, period of fundamentalism in college, the meaning of the Bible has not been fixed and determined. The text was first liberated for me by the teaching that the Bible emerges out of the Holy Spirit's on-going revelation within the community (and for the most orthodox, this still means the Roman Catholic Church and the Pope), opening the possibility that further revelation that is not recorded in that document may be given. For example, the ascension of Jesus is described in the Acts of the Apostles, but the Assumption of his mother, Mary, into heaven is affirmed by sacred Tradition. I was raised in this teaching, and only when confronted by fundamentalist Protestant interpretations did I know what it was or how to call it.

Since college, my understanding of the Bible has broadened even further, allowing for a mythic understanding. As

I mentioned before, I was much moved by what the Quaker thinker, Howard Brinton, says about when we engage sacred texts this way: "we are not so much concerned with historical validity or rational consistency with our scientific or philosophic outlook as we are with the inner significance of history, myth, and symbol. Symbol is a language of religion."[254] We seek this "inner significance" through metaphor.

I can't say with any precision how all this influenced the writing of "The Salt Sea," but I'm sure the poem is built on these foundations.

◆ ◆ ◆

I carried Denise Levertov's collections from the 1980s, *Candles in Babylon, Breathing the Waters,* and *A Door in the Hive,* with me for years. From them, I learned her practice of "organic verse," as opposed to a nebulous and utterly subjective "free verse." I also sensed her spiritual evolution, one that allowed her to write "Annunciation," a poem that imagines "the scene" which we all know from paintings and movies: "the room, variously furnished / almost always a lectern, a book."[255] The event is the arrival of the angel Gabriel to announce to Mary that she will be the mother of God. In Levertov's poem, things go differently. Into the room rushes the announcing angel "on solemn grandeur of great wings." Levertov begins with the details that are available to us all, as in all *lectio divina,* but her imagining leads her to a fuller appreciation of the person of Mary, the woman, and the poet is able to counter the tradition.

> *We are told of meek obedience. No one mentions*
> *courage.*
> > *The engendering Spirit*
>
> *did not enter her without consent.*
> *God waited.*
>
> *She was free*
> *to accept or refuse, choice*
> *integral to humanness.*[256]

Levertov's characterization does solidify an understanding of Mary as a woman of distinction not only because of being chosen by God but also because of her choice, something each of us shares with her, in our common "humanness." In doing so, Levertov also manages to re-characterize God, as well. This is no divine rapist, as in the Roman myth of Leda and Zeus, when he is guised as a swan. This God waits, deferring to human choice.

◆ ◆ ◆

These examples prepared me to select from the shelves of some used bookstore a title that may not appeal to others: *The Gospels in our Own Image: An Anthology of Twentieth Century Poetry Based on Biblical Texts.* There's enough in that title to put off whole segments of the reading public. But if each term were a circle in a Venn diagram—poetry, contemporary poetry even, Biblical texts, and the idea that these texts could be made "in our own image," there I would stand in the open space where they all converged.

In his introduction, editor David Curzon says that "All religious traditions develop a literature of imaginative responses to their sacred canon and interpretive embellishments of it."[257] He cites the recent attention to the ancient Jewish practice of *midrash*, noting that it was this tradition that led him to his first anthology.

Curzon presents a passage from the Gospels and then a poem or as many as twelve that respond to it; some counter-argue, some embody or extend, some refine or correct. I immediately recognized T. S. Eliot's "Journey of the Magi," in one of the wise kings' voices, "A cold coming we had of it." It relates the story from their point of view, the encounter leading the speaker to questioning, not conviction: "were we led all that way for / Birth or Death?"[258] Far from my fundamentalist brethren, I had read it aloud to a roomful of Penn Staters in the run-up to Christmas years before. Eliot's poem planted in me the seed of an idea: how can faith in these stories also include profound doubt at the same time? Perhaps that seed prepared me for Brinton's teachings.

Another formative idea came from Curzon's anthology. Each Biblical scene or story or even a single verse could give rise to multiple approaches, divergent responses, alternative interpretations, and a range of tones. Poems originated from a variety of cultures and languages and from across time. Reading more and widely introduced me to the community of writers; this revealed to me that Primo Levi's experience in Auschwitz would lead him to respond very differently to the Annunciation story than Levertov (not in the anthology) or Sylvia Plath (who is). Both Plath and Levi committed suicide.

Perhaps, like these texts or any texts for that matter, my own experiences could be interpreted and responded to in a variety of ways. Life does not impose a fixed and determined interpretation; meanings evolve over time and shift their iridescence depending on perspective.

◆ ◆ ◆

After college and prior to grad school for my creative writing MFA, I would read on my way to work. I drove from the outer edge of Philadelphia up to Bucks County, and I'd have a collection of poems by Rilke or Merwin or Kinnell on the seat beside me. At red lights, I'd open it, absorb a line or whole stanza, then as traffic crept along, I'd tent the book on the passenger seat and savor the image, idea, and phrasing.

Once I landed at Bowling Green, in the glacially scraped flatlands of northwest Ohio, I walked everywhere. And having plucked up a review copy of James Wright's *Above the River: The Complete Poems* from the pile at the *Mid-American Review*, I went back and forth to class, reading. It took some getting used to, reading and walking, but it's amazing how quickly you can get the knack. That's where I came across his poem, "St. Judas" for the first time.

Wright's bit of midrash picks up the Biblical story in the first line: "When I went out to kill myself..." and the sonnet goes on to recount what could transform a betrayer into a saint.[259] Quite a lot of terrain to map in just fourteen lines. Seeing the suffering of another person, Judas forgets the scenes of that day and runs to the stranger's aid. Dropping his rope—his intention to kill himself—the speaker "ignore[s] the uniforms" to tend the man. He knows he is "banished from heaven," but he acts on his compassion, his deep fellow-feeling. Suddenly, though, he recalls the events—and his role in them—that occurred in those scenes: "I remembered bread my flesh had eaten, / The kiss that ate my flesh." This makes him feel skinned alive, "flayed without hope."[260] For those of an orthodox turn of mind, is that enough contrition? What amazes me in Wright's vision of Judas is how readily and completely his character expresses his love and care for another, a stranger. He embodies the parable of the Good Samaritan, and so earns his sainthood.

Such an imaginative twist on a story so fixed in its telling and meaning stunned me. But it also taught me the power of creative transformation, how a poem can, through empathetic imagination, draw the foreign or other close. It takes a deep identification to speak for another, or presumption. But isn't that what all playwrights do? Isn't Shakespeare a poet speaking in any number of voices, identifying with delicate and innocent Desdemona in one scene and then with dastardly Iago the next? Good writing expands a sense of self. Like a deep inhale, it expands the permeable membrane of the self to include even the betrayer, the villain, not for mere entertainment but for insight, revelation, communion.

❧ ❧ ❧

"It is paradoxical that a very sharp sense of the being, the identity of some other being—and in some instances, even an inanimate thing—brings a corresponding heightening and awareness of one's own self, *and* even more mysteriously, in some instances, a feeling of the oneness of the universe…And *both* can be induced."[261]

By the time I hit grad school, Theodore Roethke had become a mentor, what Vera John-Steiner calls "a distant teacher." She describes an "intense and personal kinship […] results when the work of another evokes a special resonance in them."[262] I certainly had experienced that "resonance" with Roethke, and Levertov, Rilke, William Carlos Williams, and other poets. I've never spoken of this bond in terms of "kinship" or family, but of "lineage," in the sense of Zen transmission from teacher to student, transmission that is not bestowed upon as much as awakened in the student.

What Roethke awakened in me was this "sharp sense of the being," which is not a clinical "observation" in order to gather descriptive details. It is a relational dynamic, an arc of energy humming with recognition. And in that heightened awareness, we can pitch lyric language at greater tension, or as he advised himself in his notebooks: "Make the language take really desperate jumps."[263]

The idea that resonant moments of expanded identification could be induced was an opening for me. It deepened my apprenticeship lesson from Rilke (who got it from the sculptor Auguste Rodin) that the artist should not go about mooning and waiting for inspiration, or sitting in coffee shops talking about books and writing. A writer is someone who writes. But here, Roethke is talking about a much more subtle discipline, one that borders on the religious. In fact, he parses his previous statement to say that the identification can be brought about "by intensity of the seeing. To look at a thing so long that you are part of it and it is a part of you."[264] He cites Rilke going to the zoo to observe the animals in this spirit, a practice that resulted in Rilke's 'thing poems" collected in *New Poems 1907 and 1908*. These were collections I read on my way to work, in Edward Snow's brilliant translations. The story of their friendship and contentious working relationship is masterfully told in Rachel Corbett's dual biography, *You Must Change Your Life*. I also practiced this kind of observation, this way into making images in language; perhaps sensing the lines of influence converge added to my sense of finding my lineage.

The feeling of being one with the universe was also familiar, from my spiritual disciplines and traditions. Roethke says it is the "first stage of mystical illumination… the sense that all is one and one is all."[265] To have the myriad objects and welter of experiences cohere in meaningful relation is a profound and comforting sensation. Both the intensity of seeing and the mystical relation to all things, Roethke says, "can be an occasion for gratitude."[266]

All this leads back into poetic practice, too, because the experience is "accompanied by a loss of the 'I,' the purely human ego, to another center, a sense of the absurdity of death, a return to a state of innocence."[267] Having one's sense of self shifted "to another center" allows empathic imagination to draw the other close, but it also invites holding the personal at some remove, allowing for poems that are personal but not strictly autobiographical. Roethke speaks of the "protagonist" in some of his longer sequences, as if it were a character in fiction, and yet so many of the images and symbols emerge from Roethke's life. He was seeking a certain amount of distance in order to "be true to what is most universal" in himself,[268] which may operate in this other center, not in the facts of one's biography.

◆ ◆ ◆

What do I know about being exiled for being pregnant? About being sent away from home or walking into the hill country of Galilee? What do I know of being a God-bearer? Only what I can imagine.

And that is enough.

III.

Theodore Roethke's line "In a dark time, the eye begins to see,"[269] reveals how allowing ourselves to become accustomed to the dark actually allows us to begin to make use of whatever light there is to discern shapes. Anyone who has looked up from the bright screen of their device only to realize they can't make out the faces at a restaurant table knows that lag. It becomes a perfect metaphor for the growth that is possible after or even because of any "dark time." Roethke's poem reflects Roethke's life, and so it includes fear of madness, the death of the self, and the anguished fight to discover and assert one's identity.

Baffled by the meanings when assigned to read Roethke in college, especially "The Lost Son," I took diligent notes. Still, something in them drew me back and still does decades later. Like music I'd turn up and enjoy even when I couldn't even make out the lyrics, I think his poetry's "soundtrack," their tone and rhythms and sonic textures as well as their imagery were compelling enough for me. I "got" enough from them to enjoy them, and following that enjoyment I re-read them again and again.

More than enjoyment, I *needed* "In a Dark Time" as a young man. In it, I had that miraculous sensation of having another person—a stranger, even—speak of my own experience. Reading someone else's words, I could feel and understand my own life. I felt known and understood, a sensation that is sorely lacking in most people's lives. The "I" of the poem could be Roethke or myself; so I read myself in its urgent fear, how I too had felt "in broad daylight the midnight come again."[270] I startled to realize how I too heard "my echo in the echoing wood." And, even though I couldn't tell a heron from a wren, Roethke's correspondences between the natural images and personal struggle were familiar. I nodded in my reading, pausing at the line, "A man goes far to find out what he is." Having one's anguish confirmed by another is not compounded and made worse by knowing there are others who likewise suffer; instead, this relieves the anguish because some part of our pain is feeling alone in it. Perhaps that is why I found so much hope in Roethke's resolution:

A fallen man, I climb out of my fear.
The mind enters itself, and God the mind,
And one is One, free in the tearing wind. ²⁷¹

◆ ◆ ◆

If honesty is to be served, I didn't *want* to know what some part of me did in fact know: "The Salt Sea" is seriously, maybe fundamentally, flawed: *roof/raft/mat* may please the mouth in the saying, but is the mind pleased by the image and idea? When drafting, I can get thrilled by linguistic cleverness and sonic texturing. Afterwards, in the flush of relief and success of a complete draft, I read to appreciate, turning over in my mind those nuggets of phrasing.

However: a niggling: that beginning isn't right. Like a bruise, I didn't want to touch it. Also like something stuck between teeth; the tongue returns to it so often the muscle aches.

"On a raft" and "under a river"? How can she be floating **and** underwater? She may be playing, but that doesn't even make sense.

Question that opening image: sleepless girl sneaks up onto the family's flat roof—on her back, gazing up. The dark of the sky. Stars speckling the whole field of vision— more than are visible now. The depth of her seeing. The "bend" of it, the "arch" of it. *The bowl of night?*

Is she playing games in her imagination, like kids do closing one eye then the other to make the physical world jump back and forth. Does the image change when she imagines she's on a raft? *It occurs to her.*

How would she *feel* recognizing a river above her? Like a fish? In danger of drowning? Is she awake because she's troubled? *She's practicing. Agreeing to what reality offers, what her imagination is creating. Choosing. She chooses.*

The Salt Sea (Version 2)

Now at this time Mary arose and went in a hurry to the hill country, to a city of Judah…(Luke 1: 39)

The whole territory of night curved over me,
over all the village houses, over
the animals asleep in their pens,
and over all the people
asleep on their mats. I would lay on the roof
as on a raft. There I'd scare myself
thinking of all that water
and all who drifted soundlessly below.
To startle myself back, I'd stare up again
at the white river of stars and invert the world:
we were all afloat, all survivors,
all inheritors. The world was wondrous,
a place for imagination, for dreams
to play themselves even in waking.

❖ ❖ ❖

In his essay "The Taste of Self," the poet Stanley Kunitz calls Roethke one of the "superior order of poets"[272] as he analyzes "In a Dark Time" stanza by stanza. Kunitz says the poem is "a lyric process" that seeks "to convey the sensation of the torment of identity."[273] His observations about the images, word choice, and paradoxes in the poem opened up not only what the poem is suggesting about the struggles to claim one's own self, but how the language itself is part of that struggle and claim.

In the end, though, Kunitz says the poem's "mounting intensity" only succeeds through three and a half of its four stanzas. He questions the very resolution I found so rewarding. The stanza starts with another paradox, gives a natural image for the soul's agitation, and then pivots into the ending.

> Dark, dark my light, and darker my desire.
> My soul, like some heat-maddened summer fly,
> Keeps buzzing at the sill. Which I is I?
> A fallen man, I climb out of my fear.
> The mind enters itself, and God the mind,
> And one is One, free in the tearing wind.[274]

First, Kunitz questions the grammar of that rhetorical question, but, more importantly, he questions the tone. "I am more concerned with the clinically analytic tone, which jars on the ear that has been listening to a stranger music" writes Kunitz.

There, feel it? There's the demand of craft: a poem is not a cardboard box, a container to pack content into, a vehicle to convey ideas. Some time after encountering this essay and after reading about poetry's fusion of form and content, I would learn about fresco painting, where colors are mixed directly into plaster, and so the image is not *on* the wall; it is *part of* the wall. For a poem, the meaning is part of the grammar, tone, music; craft means that all the elements of language are arranged to evoke meaning, not simply deliver it. Denise Levertov: "Form is never more than a *revelation* of content."[275]

Kunitz goes on to question the final lines as well. He admits that his own antipathy to religion may be at work, but the ending is not—to use the term bandied about in creative writing workshops—earned. "I am not wholly persuaded by the final couplet, superbly turned as it is. It may be my own deficiency that leads me to resist whatever seems to smack of conventional piety, but I cannot agree that anything in the poem prepares me for so pat a resolution."[276] He is pointing out a complex element of the craft. When form reveals content, it is seamless, whole, coherent. But if there are gaps—variations in form that don't align with variations in meaning—this is felt as unpersuasive or unearned. Creating the positive sensation involves a great many layers of consciousness and structures of language, and the result is a convincing wholeness.

There's a persuasion a work of art works. But it does not argue by claims and evidence and the binding of logic. It appeals to other regions than reason. This sensation of "being convinced" is more apprehended than comprehended. And, as a sudden realization of a whole, a coherent accounting for the relations of all the parts, all the relevant detail needs to be present, and they need to be vivid. The arrangement of those parts needs to suggest the whole, but not give it away. A poem's meaning is not a single statement, to be filled in on a blank line, and it's certainly not restricted to what the author intended. However, a poem does not mean anything anyone wants it to. There is a net of associations, an arc of energy, that catches readers and writer, and it emanates from the language. The feeling of being caught up in and suspended by that net is what convinces.

And I had my first instruction in all these ideas when I had to admit that Kunitz was right about "In a Dark Time." Little in the poem sets us up for the speaker to suddenly take action, to climb. What occasions him not only to enact the will but to surface from his fear-pit? What enables the spaciousness in himself—after being so crowded with self-conscious anguish—to recognize the Other-who-is-within?

◆ ◆ ◆

Once I learned the Dead Sea was called the Salt Sea, I knew my ending.

Days on the road, imagine it: walking through desert wind, the heat being pushed around: travelers' eyes would be crusted with dried tears, lips ringed with dried sweat. The taste of salt on the skin.

But when I sent a friend the poem, she said, "I'm not quite convinced yet of the inner changes, from childishness to … what? that Mary has experienced."

I had established the conclusion before arranging the elements of the poem, and the result was unpersuasive. The deficiency is not merely technical, more than a matter of character development, of pacing the reveal. It's a deficiency of what the poem is really about. I discovered that the whole had too many possibilities to it, and the details arranged meaning into too many shapes.

I knew I needed to discover the central concerns and movements in the poem. And to learn that, I needed to return to the images themselves, to the journey she was on, and let the words and the worlds emerge from them. I had to listen, not to my original ideas or experiences, but to the language itself. It would spark the next insights, if there were to be any.

My friend also questioned the opening images, suggesting, "you might begin the salt imagery with the night sky in the first stanza, where the stars might appear to be salt on a dark cloth, say."

This led me back to other sources.

◆ ◆ ◆

Dead Sea. Sea, source of life. Salt Sea.

Lot's wife, looking back. Etiology as punishment. Sodom and Gomorrah destroyed for immorality, the woman turned into a pillar of salt for nostalgia.

Valley of Salt. Places made barren, as if sown with salt.

After Elijah rides his chariot of fire into the heavens, the next Biblical prophet, Elisha, performs his first miracle: purifying a well. With a cup of salt.

From the Latin *salarium*, what a person is worth in salt: salary.

Covenant of salt.

Infants were rubbed with salt. Good health.

◆ ◆ ◆

The Salt Sea (Version 3)

for my mother

Now at this time Mary arose and went in a hurry to the hill country, to a city of Judah...(Luke 1: 39)

*When I was a girl, just months ago,
I'd lay on the roof as on a raft.
Under me, I'd feel the world sway.
The whole cloth of heaven billowed
over me, curving over my village
and all its houses, the people
tucked up inside, asleep on their mats.
I alone was awake, and I'd wonder
if those who look back become salt,
what are we who look ahead?
For days, with the others, I walked,
walking away from home,
but looking back. Hot wind passed over,
whipping my headscarf, I hunched
under it to protect my eyes,
cover my mouth, hide my skin.
I was so childish as a child, believing
nothing could change, thinking what
I expected to happen would happen.
Now I know: the future is not mine,*

maybe it never was. When overshadowed,
I was certain, but sent away, heading up
into the hill country, the world feels
dry, barren, and the future's a voyage
without shore. With the others
I tack into it. We stop for the night.
I cook with the women, who laugh
how smooth my skin is still.
I serve the meal but do not speak.
I lay down but do not sleep.
I rub the salt crusting my eyes.
Before me stretches night's vast territory.
Bright travelers trace a brief path
then are gone. I remember a pilgrim
once reported a Salt Sea far south.
In its waters, he said, you float
if you release your breath. The waters
accept but do not absorb you.
They do not kill but save you.
The only one awake again,
I gaze into the sky. The prophet's
cup of salt has poured out
across its dark fabric, enough
to rub a newborn with. "Neither death,"
the words return to me,
"nor miscarriage would come
from its waters." I am a boat
with two passengers. I place
both hands on my belly and listen.
In the moonless night, the animals

shift and stamp. On my cracked lips,
I taste of salt. The only one awake,
I'm not alone: Dark as it is,
starlight pours through me,
small as I am. I'm a drop of that sea.

Acknowledgements

I am grateful to the editors of the following periodicals who published my essays over the course of many years. Their work is often driven by passion and commitment, and their hours of diligence is often unpaid.

- Aji Journal, "*The Making of a Poem*"
- BookPress, "*The Sculpture of Real Feelings: The Poetry of Akiko Yosano*" (under the title "Song of Herself")
- Colere: A Journal of Cultural Exploration, "*Hiroshima's Peace Park*"
- Dark Matter: A Journal of Speculative Writing, "*Imagining Creation: A Poet's View of Evolution*" (first delivered at the American Baptist Church in Painted Post, NY)
- Fiction Southeast, "*A Writer, Not Writing*"
- Florida Review, "*Walking in a Flame: The Affirmations of Lucien Stryk*"
- Hiroshima Signpost, "*1995 in the 'City of Peace': Spirit of Boredom or Hope?*"
- Jenny, "*The Memorial Chain*"
- John Bradley's anthology Learning to Glow reprinted "*At the Crossroads: In Hiroshima at the Fiftieth Anniversary*"
- Memoir Journal, "*Apprentice Days*"

- Ontologica, *"Lessons in Totalitarianism"*
- Oracle: A Journal of the Literary Arts, *"Haiku and the Heightening of Awareness"*
- Peace Review, *"At the Crossroads: In Hiroshima at the Fiftieth Anniversary"*
- Scott Minar's anthology The Working Poet II by reprinted *"Apprentice Days"*
- TAB: The Journal of Poetry and Poetics, *"Laying it on the Wire: Delighting in Poetry's Form and Rhythm"*
- The Quarterly Conversation, *"The Secret History of Our 'Enemies'"*
- The Write Launch, *"In Praise of Ointment"*
- War, Literature and the Arts, *"Memories of the Future: The Poetry of Sadako Kurihara and Hiromu Morishita"* (first delivered at the national conference of Associated Writers and Writing Programs [AWP])

Bibliography

Anderson, Maggie. "Long Story," *Windfall: New and Selected Poems.* Pittsburgh: University of Pittsburgh Press, 2000, 21-23.

Armstrong, Karen. *Twelve Steps to a Compassionate Life.* NY: Anchor Books, 2010.

Bacon, Margaret Hope. *Quiet Rebels: The Story of the Quakers in America.* Philadelphia: New Society Publishers, 1985.

Balaban, John. *Ca Dao Viet Nam: Vietnamese Folk Poetry.* Port Townsend, WA: Copper Canyon, 2003.

Spring Essence: The Poetry of Hô Xuân Huong. Port Townsend, WA: Copper Canyon, 2000

"The Invisible Powers," *War, Literature & The Arts*, The David L. Jannetta Lectureship in War, Literature and the Arts United States Air Force Academy, October 13, 2009, https://www.wlajournal.com/wlaarchive/22_1-2/balaban.pdf .

Basho, Matsuo. *Narrow Road to the Interior: And Other Writings.* translated by Sam Hamill, Boston: Shambhala, 2000.

Brinton, Howard. *Friends for 350 Years.* Wallingford, PA: Pendle Hill Publications, 2002.

Brogan, T.V.F. "Cadence." *The New Princeton Encyclopedia of Poetry and Poetics: The Most Comprehensive Guide to World Poetry.* Edited by Alex Preminger, et al. New York: MJF Books, 1993. 158.

"Counterpoint," *The New Princeton Encyclopedia of Poetry and Poetics: The Most Comprehensive Guide to World Poetry.* Edited by Alex Preminger, et al. New York: MJF Books, 1993. 242-3.

Buruma, Ian. *The Wages of Guilt: Memories of War in Japan and Germany.* NY: Farrar, Straus, Giroux, 1995.

Csikszentmihalyi, Mihaly. *Creativity: The Psychology of Discovery and Invention.* NY: HarperPerennial, 1996.

Curdy, Averill. "To the voice of the retired warden of Huntsville Prison (Texas death chamber)," *Poetry* June 2009: 194-5

Dickinson, Emily. *Selected Poems and Letters of Emily Dickinson.* Edited by Robert N. Linscott Garden City, NY: Doubleday, 1959.
de Mello, Anthony. *One Minute Wisdom.* NY: Random House, 1988.
Doolittle, Hilda (HD) "Adonis," Accessed https://www.melodicverses.com/poems/12411/Adonis.
Dunn, Stephen. "At the Smithville Methodist Church," in *The Bread Loaf Anthology of Contemporary American Poetry*, edited by Robert Pack, Sydney Lea, and Jay Parini Hanover, CT: University Press of New England, 1985: 66-68.
Eddy, Gary. "Earning the Language: The Writing of Lucien Stryk," *Zen, Poetry, the Art of Lucien Stryk.* Edited by Susan Porterfield. Athens: Swallow Press/Ohio UP, 1993. 293-313.
Elledge, Jim. "A Review of *Collected Poems,*" *Booklist.* July 1985: 1504. Reprinted in *Contemporary Literary Criticism.* Vol. 37. 159.
Falk, William B. "Radiation Guinea Pigs; Hundreds of Humans Used in Federally Sponsored Tests," *Newsday*, September 29, 1993, Nassau and Suffolk edition. Available online: http//web.lexis-nexis.com/universe...d5=313885e7 e3f7319521c7ff8dbb-c9d8a3.Houston Chronical News Service.
Ferlinghetti, Lawrence. *A Coney Island of the Mind.* NY: New Directions, 1958.
Field, Norma. *In the Realm of a Dying Emperor: Japan at Century's End.* NY: Vintage Books, 1991.
Frost, Robert. "The Secret Sits." Allpoetry.com, accessed 2008, https://allpoetry.com/The-Secret-Sits
Fulton, Alice. "Of Formal, Free, and Fractal Verse: Singing the Body Electric," *Poetry East.* 20-21 (Fall 1986). Reprinted in *Twentieth-Century American Poetics: Poets on the Art of Poetry.* Edited by Dana Gioia, David Mason, and Meg Schoerke. Boston: McGraw Hill, 2004: 470-78.
Gambone, Michael. "Poet and Concubine," *New York Review of Books,* January 28, 2001, https://www.nytimes.com/2001/01/28/books/books-in-brief-fiction-poetry-poet-and-concubine.html.
Goldstein, Joseph. *Mindfulness: A Practical Guide to Awakening.* Boulder, CO: Sounds True, 2013.
Griggs, Jessica. "In Pursuit of Happiness...Daniel Gilbert," *New Scientist*, 210, no. 28, April 16, 2011: 48-49.
Haines, John. "A Hole in the Bucket," *Living Off the Country: Essays on Poetry and Place.* Ann Arbor, MI: University of Michigan UP,

1981: 64-74.
Hamill, Sam. *A Poet's Work: The Other Side of Poetry* Seattle, WA: Broken Moon Press, 1990.
Harper, Michael S. "Remembering Robert E. Hayden." *The Carleton Miscellany.* 28, number 3 (Winter 1980): 231-34. Reprinted in *Contemporary Literary Criticism.* Vol. 37. 152-3.
Hartman, Charles O. *Free Verse: An Essay on Prosody.* Evanston, Illinois: Northwestern UP, 1986.
Hayden, Robert and John O'Brien. "A 'Romantic Realist,'" *Collected Prose.* Edited by Frederick Glaysher. Ann Arbor, MI: University of Michigan Press, 1984. 115-28. Reprinted in *Contemporary Literary Criticism* vol. 37. 150-152.
Hayden, Robert. "A Conversation with A. Poulin Jr.," *Robert Hayden: Essays on the Poetry.* Edited by Laurence Goldstein and Robert Chrisman. Ann Arbor, MI: University of Michigan Press, 2001. 30-40.
Hirsch, Edward. "Mean to Be Free," *The Nation.* December 21, 1985: 685-86. Reprinted in *Contemporary Literary Criticism.* vol. 37: 159-60.
Hopkins, Gerard Manly. *Gerard Manly Hopkins: The Major Works.* Oxford, Oxford UP, 2002.
Huddle, David. "The 'Banked Fire' of Robert Hayden's 'Those Winter Sundays.'" *Robert Hayden: Essays on the Poetry.* Edited by Laurence Goldstein and Robert Chrisman. Ann Arbor, MI: University of Michigan Press, 2001: 251-255.
John-Steiner, Vera. *Notebooks of the Mind: Explorations of Thinking.* Revised Edition. Oxford UP, 1997.
Kaufman, Scott Barry and Carolyn Gregoire. *Wired to Create: Unraveling the Mysteries of the Creative Mind.* NY: Perigree/Penguin Random House, 2015.
Krznaric, Roman, "Six Habits of Highly Empathic People," *Greater Good Magazine*, November 27, 2012, https://greatergood.berkeley.edu/article/item/six_habits_of_highly_empathic_people1
Hirshfield, Jane. *Nine Gates: Entering the Mind of Poetry.* NY: Harper-Perennial, 1998.
Kinnell, Galway. "Report from the U.S.," *Literature Under the Nuclear Cloud: Reports from the Hiroshima International Conference of Asian Writers.* Tokyo: Sanyusha, 1984: 165-170.
Kosakai, Yoshiteru. *Hiroshima Peace Reader.* Translated by Akira and

Michiko Tashiro and Robert and Alice Ruth Ramseyer. Hiroshima: Hiroshima Peace Culture Foundation, 1980.

Kurihara, Sadako. *Black Eggs*. Translated by Richard H. Minear. Ann Arbor, MI: University of Michigan Press, 1994.

Kunitz, Stanley. "The Taste of Self," *A Kind of Order, A Kind of Folly: Essays and Conversations.* Boston: Little Brown & Company, 1975: 87-95.

Langer, Ellen. *On Becoming an Artist: Reinventing Yourself Through Mindful Creativity*. NY: Ballantine, 2005.

Levertov, Denise. *A Door in the Hive* NY: New Directions, 1989.

New & Selected Essays. NY: New Directions, 1992.

The Poet in the World. NY: New Directions, 1973.

Lifton, Robert Jay and Greg Mitchell. *Hiroshima in America: Fifty Years of Denial*. New York: Putnam, 1995.

Liparisi, Joseph A. "A Review of *Collected Poems,*" *Library Journal.* June 1, 1985: 130. Reprinted in *Contemporary Literary Criticism.* vol. 37. 159.

Loori, John Daido. *The Zen of Creativity: Cultivating Your Artistic Life.* NY: Ballantine, 2004.

Mills, Ralph Jr. "Lucien Stryk's Poetry," *Zen, Poetry, the Art of Lucien Stryk.* Susan Porterfield, Ed. Athens: Swallow Press/Ohio UP, 1993: 279-291.

Minear, Richard H. Translator's Introduction to *Black Eggs,* by Sadako Kurihara, trans. Richard H. Minear, 1-38. Ann Arbor, MI: University of Michigan Press, 1994.

Mingyur, Yongey Rimpoche. *The Joy of Living: Unlocking the Secret and Science of Happiness*. NY: Three Rivers Press, 2007.

Mogahed, Dalia. "What It's Like to be Muslim in America." *TED. com*, Last updated February 2016. https://www.ted.com/talks/dalia_mogahed_what_it_s_like_to_be_muslim_in_america?language=en.

Mooneyham, Benjamin W. and Jonathan W. Schooler. "The Costs and Benefits of Mind-Wandering: A Review," *Canadian Journal of Experimental Psychology* 67, no. 1, 2013: 11-18.

Morishita, Hiromu, John Bradley, and Edward A. Dougherty. *Pilgrimage to a Ginkgo Tree*. Trans. Eiko Ishizaki. Hiroshima, Japan: World Friendship Center, 1996.

Morishita, Hiroshi [sic]. Testimonies of the A-Bomb Victims and Voices of Support. 23 February 2007. AtomicBombMuseum. org. <http://www.atomicbombmuseum. com/6_1.shtml>.

Morris, Jim. "Clampdown: The Silencing of Nuclear Industry Workers; Numerous Experiments Done on 'Nuclear Guinea Pigs' for Decades," *The Houston Chronicle*, September, 26, 1993. 2 STAR edition. Available online: http//:web.lexis-nexis.com/universe...d5=afe79c80a6a4cb805482e5c50724a38d.

Muske, Carol. "Little LA Villanelle," *Poetry*, December, 1992, accessed https://www.poetryfoundation.org/poetrymagazine/browse?contentId=38496.

Murray, G. E. "Struck by Lightning: Four Distinct Modern Voices," *Michigan Quarterly Review*. 22, no.4 (fall 1983): 643-54. Reprinted in *Contemporary Literary Criticism* vol. 37. 159-159.

New York Yearly Meeting. *Faith and Practice*. NY: New York Yearly Meeting, 1995.

Oe, Kanzaburo. *Hiroshima Notes*, Tokyo: YMCA Press, 1981.

Ohara, Miyao, editor. and translator. *The Songs of Hiroshima: An Anthology*. Hiroshima: Shunyo-sha Shuppan Company, nd.

Orr, Gregory. *Poetry As Survival*. Athens, GA: University of Georgia Press, 2002.

Owen, Wilfred. *The Collected Poems of Wilfred Owen*. NY: New Directions, 1965.

Pohl, R.D. "Poetics of Activism in Nowak's 'Coal Mountain Elementary,'" *Buffalo News.com*, April 2, 2010. *ArtsBeat*. June 29, 2011, http://blogs.buffalonews.com/artsbeat/2010/04/poetics-of-activism-in-nowaks-coal-mountain-elementary.html

Porterfield, Susan Azar. Introduction to *Zen, Poetry, the Art of Lucien Stryk*. Athens: Swallow Press/Ohio UP, 1993.

"The War Poetry of Lucien Stryk," *The Journal of the Midwest Modern Language Association*. 33, no. 3 (Autumn 2000-Winter 2001): 152-169.

Quayle, Paul. *Hiroshima Calling*. Self published, 1995.

Rexroth, Kenneth. Introduction to *100 Poems from the Japanese*. NY: New Directions, 1959. xi-xxii.

Rilke, Rainer Maria. *Letters to a Young Poet*, trans. Joan M. Burnham, NY: MJF Books, 2000.

Roethke, Theodore. *On Poetry & Craft*. Port Townsend, WA: Copper Canyon, 2001.

Sappho, *The Complete Poems of Sappho*, translated by Willis Barnstone, Boston: Shambhala, 2009.

Seaman, Donna. "*Spring Essence: The Poetry of Ho Xuan Huong* (book review)", *Booklist*, October, 1, 2000, 313.

Shiki, Masaoka. *Selected Poems.* translated by Burton Watson, NY: Columbia UP, 1998.

Snyder, Gary. "Knots in the Grain," *The Real Work: Interviews and Talks 1964–1979.* NY: New Directions, 1980. 44-51.

Strand, Clark. *Seeds from a Birch Tree: Writing Haiku and the Spiritual Journey.* New York: Hyperion, 1997.

Stryk, Lucien. "A World Language of Poetry," *Zen, Poetry, the Art of Lucien Stryk.* Edited by Susan Porterfield. Athens: Swallow Press/Ohio UP, 1993. 48-50.

And Still Birds Sing: New & Collected Poems. Athens: Swallow Press/Ohio UP, 1998.

"Death of a Zen Poet: Shinkichi Takahashi (1901-1987)," *Beneath a Single Moon: Buddhism in Contemporary American Poetry.* Edited by Kent Johnson and Craig Paulenich. Boston: Shambhala, 1991. 283-291.

"The Future of Poetry." *Zen, Poetry, the Art of Lucien Stryk.* Edited by Susan Porterfield. Athens: Swallow Press/Ohio UP, 1993. 55-56.

"Making Poems." *Zen, Poetry, the Art of Lucien Stryk.* Edited by Susan Porterfield. Athens: Swallow Press/Ohio UP, 1993. 25-40.

"Beyond Poetry." *Zen, Poetry, the Art of Lucien Stryk.* Edited by Susan Porterfield. Athens: Swallow Press/Ohio UP, 1993. 57-59.

"What? Why This. Only This." *Singular Voices: American Poetry Today.* Edited by Stephen Berg. New York: Avon, 1985. 259-267.

"U.S. Still Funding 200 Human Radiation Experiments." *The Houston Chronicle,* January 26, 1993, 2 STAR edition. Available online: http//web.lexis-nexis.com/universe...d5=c-9c254ce5958aa 944290f5fbfld43abf.

Takayama, Hitoshi. *Hiroshima In Memoria.* Self published.

Thomas, Lewis. *Late Night Thoughts Listening to Mahler's Ninth Symphony,* NY: Penguin, 1985.

Treat, John Whittier. *Writing Ground Zero: Japanese Literature and the Atomic Bomb.* Chicago: University of Chicago Press, 1995

Turco, Lewis. *The New Book of Forms: A Handbook of Poetics.* Hanover, CT: UP of New England, 1986.

Whitman, Walt. *Complete Poetry and Selected Prose,* edited by James E. Miller, Boston: Riverside Press, 1959.

Wiegers, Michael. "Nine Times out of Ten: John Balaban and the Poetry of Ho Xuan Huong," *The American Poetry Review,* Sept 2000, 6.

Wright, Charles. *Quarter Notes: Improvisations and Interviews*. Ann Arbor: U of Michigan Press, 1995.

Wright, James. "Lying in a Hammock at William Duffy's Farm in Pine Island, Minnesota," *Above the River: The Complete Poems*. NY: Farrar, Straus, and Giroux, 1990. 122.

Yosano, Akiko. *River of Stars: Selected Poems of Yosano Akiko*. Translated by Sam Hamill and Keiko Matsui Gibson (Boston: Shambhala, 1997.

Zajonc, Arthur. "Love As Ethical Insight." *Center for Humans and Nature*. Last Updated August 6, 2014. https://www.humansandnature.org/mind-morality-arthur-zajonc.

Zebrun, Gary. "In the Darkness a Wellspring of Plangency: The Poetry of Robert Hayden," *Obsidian: Black Literature in Review*. 8, no. 1 (Spring 1981): 22-6. Reprinted in *Contemporary Literary Criticism* Vol. 37. 153-154.

Endnotes

1. Kaufman, Scott Barry and Carolyn Gregoire. *Wired to Create: Unraveling the Mysteries of the Creative Mind.* (NY: Perigree/Penguin Random House, 2015), 17.
2. Ibid. 17.
3. Ibid. 21.
4. Levertov, Denise. *The Poet in the World.* (NY: New Directions, 1973), 8.
5. Ibid. 8.
6. Levertov, Denise. *New & Selected Essays.* (NY: New Directions, 1992), 240.
7. Shiki, Masaoka. *Selected Poems,* trans. Burton Watson (NY: Columbia UP, 1998), 46.
8. Ibid 45.
9. Ibid. 61.
10. Basho, Matsuo. *Narrow Road to the Interior: And Other Writings,* trans. Sam Hamill (Boston: Shambhala, 2000), 89.
11. Ibid, 92.
12. Ibid. 27.
13. Ibid. 55.
14. Oe, Kanzaburo. *Hiroshima Notes,* (Tokyo: YMCA Press, 1981), 36.
15. Buruma, Ian. *The Wages of Guilt: Memories of War in Japan and Germany,* (NY: Farrar, Straus, Giroux, 1995), 186.
16. Ohara, Miyao, ed. and trans. *The Songs of Hiroshima: An Anthology.* (Hiroshima: Shunyo-sha Shuppan Company, 1964), 21.
17. Lifton, Robert Jay and Greg Mitchell. *Hiroshima in America: Fifty years of denial.* (NY: Putnam, 1995), 233.
18. Takayama, Hitoshi. "Introduction," *Hiroshima: In Memoriam and Today.* self published, nd.
19. Morishita, Hiromu. *Hiroshima: In Memoriam and Today,* ed. Hi-

toshi Takayama, self published, nd.
20. Falk, William B. "Radiation Guinea Pigs; Hundreds of Humans Used in Federally Sponsored Tests." *Newsday.* 29 Sept 1993. Nassau & Suffolk edition. Available online: http//web.lexis-nexis.com/universe...d5=313885e7 e3f7319521c7ff8db-bc9d8a3.
21. Morris, Jim. "Clampdown: The Silencing of Nuclear Industry Workers; Numerous Experiments Done on 'Nuclear Guinea Pigs' for Decades. *The Houston Chronicle,* 26 Sep 1993, 2 STAR edition. Available online: http//:web.lexis-nexis.com/universe...d5=afe79c80a6a4cb805482e5c50724a38d.
22. Houston Chronical News Service. "U.S. Still Funding 200 Human Radiation Experiments." *The Houston Chronicle,* 26 Jan 1994, 2 STAR edition. Available online: http//web.lexis-nexis.com/universe...d5=c9c254ce5958aa 944290f5fbfld43abf.
23. Kosakai, Yoshiteru. *Hiroshima Peace Reader.* (Hiroshima: Hiroshima Peace Culture Foundation, 1980), 40.
24. Morishita, Hiromu, John Bradley, and Edward A. Dougherty. *Pilgrimage to a Ginkgo Tree.* Ishizaki, Eiko. Translator. Hiroshima, Japan: World Friendship Center, 1996.
25. Minako Goto quoted in Treat, John Whittier. *Writing Ground Zero: Japanese Literature and the Atomic Bomb.* Chicago: University of Chicago Press, 1995, 29.
26. Treat, 32.
27. Ibid., 33.
28. Ibid., 29.
29. Kosakai, Yoshiteru. *Hiroshima Peace Reader.* Akira and Michiko Tashiro and Robert and Alice Ruth Ramseyer, translators. Hiroshima: Hiroshima Peace Culture Foundation, 1980, 31-33.
30. Koichi Tokuno quoted in Treat, 27.
31. Sankichi Toge, quoted in Treat, 26.
32. Hiroko Takenishi, quoted in Treat, 27.
33. Shiro Ozaki, quoted in Treat, 28.
34. Kurihara, quoted in Minear, Richard H. "Translator's Introduction." *Black Eggs.* By Sadako Kurihara. Ann Arbor, MI: University of Michigan Press, 1994: 18.
35. Kurihara, quoted in Minear 17.
36. Treat, 21.
37. Ibid., 21.
38. Ibid., 22.

39. Morishita, Bradley, and Dougherty *Pilgrimage,* 20
40. Morishita, Hiroshi [sic]. "Testimonies of the A-Bomb Victims and Voices of Support." 23 February 2007. AtomicBomb-Museum.org. <http://www.atomicbombmuseum. com/6_1. shtml>, par. 1.
41. Kurihara, quoted in Treat *Writing Ground Zero,* 10
42. Morishita, "Testimonies," par. 2.
43. Kurihara, *Black Eggs,* 53.
44. Minear, "Translator's Introduction" *Black Eggs,* 28.
45. Kurihara, *Black Eggs,* 67.
46. Minear, "Translator's Introduction" *Black Eggs,* 20.
47. Kurihara, "Introduction," *Black Eggs,* 45.
48. Ibid., 45.
49. Kurihara quoted in Minear, "Translator's Introduction" *Black Eggs,* 19.
50. Kurihara, *Black Eggs,* 226-227.
51. Field, Norma. *In the Realm of a Dying Emperor: Japan at Century's End.* NY: Vintage Books, 1991, 179.
52. Kinnell, Galway. "Report from the U.S." *Literature Under the Nuclear Cloud: Reports from the Hiroshima International Conference of Asian Writers.* Tokyo: Sanyusha, 1984, 168.
53. Kurihara, *Black Eggs,* 35
54. Whitman, Walt. "Song of Myself," *Complete Poetry and Selected Prose,* ed. James E. Miller, Jr., (Boston, Riverside Press, 1959), 25.
55. Yosano, Akiko. *River of Stars: Selected Poems of Yosano Akiko,* trans. Sam Hammill and Keiko Matsui Gibson (Boston: Shambhala, 1997), 105.
56. Ibid., 105.
57. Ibid., xii-xiii.
58. Mogahed, Dalia. "What It's Like to be Muslim in America." Last updated February 2016. https://www.ted.com/talks/dalia_mogahed_what_it_s_like_to_be_muslim_in_america?language=en.
59. Yosano. *River of Stars,* 122.
60. Ibid., 122.
61. Ibid., 122-123.
62. Hirshfield, Jane. *Nine Gates: Entering the Mind of Poetry,* (NY: HarperPerennial, 1998), 47.
63. Yosano, *River of Stars,* xiii-xiv.

64. Orr, Gregory. *Poetry As Survival* (Athens, GA: University of Georgia Press, 2002), 1.
65. Ibid., 2.
66. Yosano, *River of Stars*, 75.
67. Ibid., 96.
68. Yosano, *River of Stars*, "A Wish About Poetry," 107.
69. Yosano, *River of Stars*, 100.
70. Owen, Wilfred. *The Collected Poems of Wilfred Owen*. (NY: New Directions, 1965), 31.
71. Zajonc, Arthur. "Love As Ethical Insight." *Center for Humans and Nature*. Last Updated August 6, 2014. https://www.humansandnature.org/mind-morality-arthur-zajonc.
72. New Revised Standard Version (NRSV)
73. Timothy 6: 1-2 (NRSV)
74. De Mello, Anthony. *One Minute Wisdom* (NY: Doubleday), 95.
75. NRSV
76. Penn, William. *Some Fruits of Solitude* (1693), quoted in New York Yearly Meeting (NYYM) *Faith and Practice*, 7.
77. Woolman, John. "Considerations on Keeping Negroes" (1746), quoted in NYYM, *Faith and Practice*, 8.
78. Fox, George, quoted in NYYM *Faith and Practice*, 20.
79. Bacon, Margaret Hope. *The Quiet Rebels: The Story of Quakers in America*, Phila.,: New Society Publishers, 1985, 20.
80. NRSV.
81. Armstrong, Karen. *Twelve Steps to a Compassionate Life*, (NY: Anchor Books, 2010), 97-8.
82. Remarque, Erich. *All Quiet on the Western Front*. This and all the quotations in this essay are from my handwritten notebooks and so the edition I was reading all those years ago is lost to me.
83. Adorno, Theodor. quoted in Steven Helmling *Adorno's Poetics of Critique* available at Google Books, https://books.google.com/books?id=VDnUAwAAQBAJ&pg=PA24&lpg=PA24&dq=%E2%80%9CHegel%27s+statement+in+his+Aesthetics+that+as+long+as+there+is+an+awareness+of+suffering+among+human+beings+there+must+also+be+art+as+the+objective+form+of+that+awareness.%E2%80%9D&source=bl&ots=PEIRY-XPgE&sig=ACfU3U03MrjwEd-wjqZm5CUAupJ1xatqVg&hl=en&sa=X-&ved=2ahUKEwjO35ullP3qAhVEoXIEHTusB8YQ6AEwA-

HoECAoQAQ#v=onepage&q=%E2%80%9CHegel's%20 statement%20in%20his%20Aesthetics%20that%20as%20 long%20as%20there%20is%20an%20awareness%20of%20 suffering%20among%20human%20beings%20there%20 must%20also%20be%20art%20as%20the%20objective%20 form%20of%20that%20awareness.%E2%80%9D&f=false

84. Balaban, John. "The Invisible Powers," *War, Literature & The Arts*, The David L. Jannetta Lectureship in War, Literature and the Arts United States Air Force Academy, October 13, 2009, https://www.wlajournal.com/wlaarchive/22_1-2/balaban.pdf .
85. Ibid., 4.
86. Balaban, John. *Ca Dao Viet Nam: Vietnamese Folk Poetry.* (Port Townsend, WA: Copper Canyon, 2003), 58.
87. Ibid., 59.
88. Ibid., 29.
89. Wiegers, Michael. "Nine Times out of Ten: John Balaban and the Poetry of Ho Xuan Huong," *The American Poetry Review,* Sept 2000, 6.
90. Seaman, Donna. "*Spring Essence: The Poetry of Ho Xuan Huong* (book review)", *Booklist,* October, 1, 2000, 313.
91. Balaban, *Spring Essence*, "Introduction," 5.
92. "*Spring Essence: The Poetry of Ho Xuan Huong* (book review)," *Publishers Weekly*, January 3, 2000. https://www.publishersweekly.com/978-1-55659-148-8.
93. Sappho, *The Complete Poems of Sappho,* trans. Willis Barnstone. (Boston: Shambhala, 2009), 104.
94. Gambone, Michael. "Poet and Concubine," *New York Review of Books*, January 28, 2001, https://www.nytimes.com/2001/01/28/books/books-in-brief-fiction-poetry-poet-and-concubine.html.
95. Balaban, *Spring Essence*, 43.
96. Ibid., 93.
97. Balaban, "The Invisible Powers."
98. Krznaric, Roman, "Six Habits of Highly Empathic People," *Greater Good Magazine*, November 27, 2012, https://greatergood.berkeley.edu/article/item/six_habits_of_highly_empathic_people1.
99. Hamill, Sam. "Only One Sky," *A Poet's Work: The Other Side of Poetry* (Seattle, WA: Broken Moon Press, 1990), 120.

100. Frost, Robert. "The Secret Sits." Allpoetry.com, accessed 2008, https://allpoetry.com/The-Secret-Sits.
101. Dunn, Stephen. "At the Smithville Methodist Church," in *The Bread Loaf Anthology of Contemporary American Poetry*, ed. Robert Pack, Sydney Lea, and Jay Parini (Hanover, CT: University Press of New England, 1985). 66-68.
102. Genesis 31.
103. Brinton, Howard. *Friends for 350 Years*. (Wallingford, PA: Pendle Hill Publications, 2002), 42.
104. Ibid., 42.
105. Ibid., 42.
106. Ibid., 42.
107. Psalm 131, NRSV.
108. Exodus 33:19, NRSV.
109. Isaiah 45:7. The New American Standard Bible puts it this way: "The One forming light and creating darkness, / Causing well-being and creating calamity; I am the LORD who does all these." However, I was assured by a rabbi at Pendle Hill that the Hebrew is not "calamity" but "evil." The idea the God creates evil was a shocking revelation to me.
110. Rilke, Rainer Maria. *Letters to a Young Poet*, trans. Joan M. Burnham (NY: MJF Books, 2000), 35.
111. Thomas, Lewis. "On Matters of Doubt," *Late Night Thoughts Listening to Mahler's Ninth Symphony* (NY: Penguin, 1985), 157.
112. Hopkins, Gerard Manly. "Pied Beauty" *Gerard Manly Hopkins: The Major Works*. (Oxford, Oxford UP, 2002), 132.
113. Ibid., 133.
114. Mooneyham, Benjamin W. and Jonathan W. Schooler. "The Costs and Benefits of Mind-Wandering: A Review." *Canadian Journal of Experimental Psychology* vol 67, issue 1, 2013: 11.
115. Gilbert, Daniel quoted in Jessica Griggs. "In Pursuit of Happiness...Daniel Gilbert." *New Scientist*. 4/16/2011. (v.210 issue 2808): 48-49.
116. Loori, John Daido. *The Zen of Creativity: Cultivating Your Artistic Life*. (NY: Ballantine, 2004), 86.
117. Ibid., 86.
118. Rexroth, Kenneth. "Introduction" *100 Poems from the Japanese*. (NY: New Directions, 1959), xi.
119. Dickinson, Emily. *Selected Poems and Letters of Emily Dickinson*. Ed. Robert N. Linscott (Garden City, NY: Doubleday, 1959), 150.

120. Goldstein, Joseph. *Mindfulness: A Practical Guide to Awakening.* (Boulder, CO: Sounds True, 2013), 82.
121. Ibid., 82.
122. Mingyur, Yongey Rimpoche. *The Joy of Living: Unlocking the Secret and Science of Happiness.* (NY: Three Rivers Press, 2007), 78.
123. Ibid., 78.
124. Csikszentmihalyi, Mihaly. *Creativity: The Psychology of Discovery and Invention.* (NY: HarperPerennial, 1996), 348.
125. Ibid., 349.
126. Langer, Ellen. *On Becoming an Artist: Reinventing Yourself Through Mindful Creativity.* (NY: Ballentine, 2005), 195.
127. Snyder, Gary. "Knots in the Grain" *The Real Work: Interviews and Talks 1964 – 1979.* (NY: New Directions, 1980), 44.
128. Langer, *On Becoming an Artist,* 185.
129. Ibid., 185-6.
130. Ibid., 52-8.
131. Goldstein, *Mindfulness,* 40
132. Mooneyham and Schooler, 14.
133. Carson, Shelley H. *Your Creative Brain* quoted in Scott Barry Kaufman and Carolyn Gregoire *Wired to Create: Unraveling the Mysteries of the Creative Mind* (NY: Perigee, 2015), 39.
134. Goldstein, *Mindfulness,* 40.
135. Ryokan quoted in Goldstein, 40.
136. Snyder, *The Real Work,* 33.
137. Ibid., 34.
138. Loori, *The Zen of Creativity,* 57
139. Kaufman and Gregoire, *Wired to Create,* xii.
140. Ibid., 42.
141. Wright, Charles. *Quarter Notes: Improvisations and Interviews.* (Ann Arbor: U of Michigan Press, 1995), 82.
142. Turco, Lewis. *The New Book of Forms: A Handbook of Poetics.* (Hanover, CT: UP of New England, 1986), 15.
143. Brogan, T.V.F., "Cadence," *The New Princeton Encyclopedia of Poetry and Poetics: The Most Comprehensive Guide to World Poetry* ed. Alex Premiger and T.V.F. Brogan, (NY: MJF Books, 1993), 158.
144. Turco, *The New Book of Forms,* 19.
145. Ibid., 27.
146. Ibid., 26.
147. Quoted in Brogan, "Counterpoint," *The New Princeton Encyclopedia of Poetry and Poetics,* 243.

148. Fulton, Alice. "Of Formal, Free, and Fractal Verse: Singing the Body Electric" *Poetry East.* 20-21 (Fall 1986). Reprinted in *Twentieth-Century American Poetics: Poets on the Art of Poetry.* Ed. Dana Gioia, David Mason, and Meg Schoerke. (Boston: McGraw Hill, 2004), 470.
149. Ibid., 471.
150. Roethke, Theodore. *On Poetry and Craft.* (Port Townsend, WA: Copper Canyon, 2001), 71.
151. Ibid., 78.
152. Ferlinghetti, Lawrence. "Coney Island of the Mind, #15." *A Coney Island of the Mind.* (NY: New Directions, 1958), 30.
153. Doolittle, Hilda (HD). "Adonis," accessed https://www.melodicverses.com/poems/12411/Adonis.
154. Muske, Carol. "Little LA Villanelle," *Poetry*, December, 1992, accessed https://www.poetryfoundation.org/poetrymagazine/browse?contentId=38496.
155. Wright, James. "Lying in a Hammock at William Duffy's Farm in Pine Island, Minnesota." *Above the River: The Complete Poems.* (NY: Farrar, Straus, and Giroux, 1990). 122.
156. Anderson, Maggie. "Long Story." *Windfall: New and Selected Poems.* (Pittsburgh: University of Pittsburgh Press, 2000), 57.
157. Ibid., 58.
158. Ibid., 59.
159. *Pohl, R.D.* "Poetics of Activism in Nowak's '*Coal Mountain Elementary*'" *Buffalo News.Com* 2 April 2010. *ArtsBeat.* June 29, 2011. Accessed http://blogs.buffalonews.com/artsbeat/2010/04/poetics-of-activism-in-nowaks-coal-mountain-elementary.html.
160. *Curdy, Averill.* "To the voice of the retired warden of Huntsville Prison (Texas death chamber)" *Poetry June 2009: 194.*
161. Ibid., 194.
162. Ibid., 195.
163. Quoted in Fulton, "Of Formal, Free, and Fractal Verse," 471.
164. Roethke, *On Poetry and Craft*, 83.
165. Hartman, Charles O. *Free Verse: An Essay on Prosody.* (Evanston, Illinois: Northwestern UP, 1986), 83.
166. Stryk, Lucien. "A World Language of Poetry." *Zen, Poetry, the Art of Lucien Stryk.* Susan Porterfield, Ed. (Athens: Swallow Press/Ohio UP, 1993), 48.
167. Stryk, Lucien. "Making Poems." *Zen, Poetry, the Art of Lucien*

Stryk. Susan Porterfield, Ed. (Athens: Swallow Press/Ohio UP, 1993), 34.
168. Ibid., 26.
169. Mills, Ralph Jr. "Lucien Stryk's Poetry." *Zen, Poetry, the Art of Lucien Stryk.* Susan Porterfield, Ed. (Athens: Swallow Press/Ohio UP, 1993), 279.
170. Stryk, Lucien. *And Still Birds Sing: New & Collected Poems.* (Athens: Swallow Press/Ohio UP, 1998), 284.
171. Strand, Clark. *Seeds from a Birch Tree: Writing Haiku and the Spiritual Journey.* (NY: Hyperion, 1997), 19.
172. Quoted in Susan Azar Porterfield "Introduction." *Zen, Poetry, the Art of Lucien Stryk.* (Athens: Swallow Press/Ohio UP, 1993), i.
173. Stryk, "Why I Write," *And Still Birds Sing,* 158.
174. Mills, "Lucien Stryk's Poetry," 290.
175. Eddy, Gary. "Earning the Language: The Writing of Lucien Stryk. *Zen, Poetry, the Art of Lucien Stryk.* Susan Porterfield, Ed. (Athens: Swallow Press/Ohio UP, 1993), 301.
176. Quoted in Eddy "Earning the Language," 301.
177. Stryk, "Friends," *And Still Birds Sing,* 255.
178. Ibid., 255.
179. Haines, John. "A Hole in the Bucket." *Living Off the Country: Essays on Poetry and Place.* (Ann Arbor, MI: University of Michigan UP, 1981), 65.
180. Ibid., 65.
181. Stryk, Lucien. "Beyond Poetry." *Zen, Poetry, the Art of Lucien Stryk.* Susan Porterfield, Ed. (Athens: Swallow Press/Ohio UP, 1993), 58.
182. Stryk, "Making Poems," 31.
183. Quoted in Mills, "Lucien Stryk's Poetry," 288.
184. Stryk, "Making Poems," 34.
185. Stryk, "The Future of Poetry," 56.
186. Mills, "Lucien Stryk's Poetry," 290.
187. Stryk, Lucien. "What? Why This. Only This." *Singular Voices: American Poetry Today.* ed. by Stephen Berg, editor. (NY: Avon, 1985), 259.
188. Ibid., 259.
189. Ibid., 260.
190. Stryk. "Translating Zen Poems," *And Still Birds Sing,* 238.
191. Stryk, "Note on Translating Japanese Zen Poetry," 51.

192. Stryk, Lucien. "A World Language of Poetry." *Zen, Poetry, the Art of Lucien Stryk*. Susan Porterfield, Ed. (Athens: Swallow Press/Ohio UP, 1993), 49.
193. Stryk, "The Ordinary," *And Still Birds Sing*, 154.
194. Stryk. "What? Why This. Only This," 263.
195. Stryk, "Cherries," *And Still Birds Sing*, 151.
196. Ibid., 151.
197. Stryk, "Awakening," *And Still Birds Sing*, 104.
198. Takahashi, Shinkichi. "Destruction" in Lucien Styk *And Still Birds Sing*, 88.
199. Ibid., 88.
200. Takahashi, "Disclosure," in Lucien Styk *And Still Birds Sing*, 88.
201. Takahashi, "Body," in Lucien Styk *And Still Birds Sing*, 98-99.
202. Stryk, Lucien. "Death of a Zen Poet: Shinkichi Takahashi (1901-1987)." *Beneath a Single Moon: Buddhism in Contemporary American Poetry*, Kent Johnson and Craig Paulenich, editors. Boston: Shambhala, 1991), 290.
203. Stryk, "The Face," *And Still Birds Sing*, 139.
204. Ibid., 139.
205. Stryk, "Return to Hiroshima," *And Still Birds Sing*, 11.
206. Porterfield, Susan Azar. "The War Poetry of Lucien Stryk." *The Journal of the Midwest Modern Language Association*. 33.3 (Autumn 2000-Winter 2001), 161.
207. Stryk, "Return to Hiroshima," *And Still Birds Sing*, 11.
208. Ibid., 12.
209. Porterfield, "The War Poetry...," 164.
210. Stryk, "Return to Hiroshima," *And Still Birds Sing*, 13.
211. Porterfield, "The War Poetry...," 165.
212. Stryk quoted in Porterfield "The War Poetry...," 161.
213. Stryk, "For Helen, on Her Birthday," *And Still Birds Sing*, 303.
214. Ibid., 303.
215. Stryk, "Voyage," *And Still Birds Sing*, 304.
216. Ibid, 305.
217. Ibid, 305.
218. Ibid., 305.
219. Porterfield, Susan Azar. "Introduction." *Zen, Poetry, the Art of Lucien Stryk*. Athens: Swallow Press/Ohio UP, 1993), 13.
220. Hirsch, Edward. "Mean to Be Free." *The Nation*. December 21, 1985: 685-86. Reprinted in *Contemporary Literary Criticism*. Vol. 37, 160.

221. Liparisi, Joseph A. "A Review of *Collected Poems,*" *Library Journal.* June 1, 1985: 130. Reprinted in *Contemporary Literary Criticism.* Vol. 37, 159.
222. Harper, Michael S. "Remembering Robert E. Hayden." *The Carleton Miscellany.* XVIII.3 (Winter 1980): 231-34. Reprinted in *Contemporary Literary Criticism.* Vol. 37, 153.
223. Elledge, Jim. "A Review of *Collected Poems.*" *Booklist.* July 1985: 1504. Reprinted in *Contemporary Literary Criticism.* Vol. 37, 159.
224. Huddle, David. "The 'Banked Fire' of Robert Hayden's 'Those Winter Sundays.'" *Robert Hayden: Essays on the Poetry.* Ed. by Laurence Goldstein and Robert Chrisman. (Ann Arbor, MI: University of Michigan Press, 2001), 251.
225. Ibid., 251.
226. Hayden, Robert. "Those Winter Sundays," *Collected Poems.* ed. Frederick Glaysher, (NY: Liveright, 1997), 41. This poem is also available on the Poetry Foundation's website with annotations: https://www.poetryfoundation.org/poems/46461/those-winter-sundays.
227. Huddle, "The 'Banked Fire,'" 253.
228. Murray, G. E. "Struck by Lightning: Four Distinct Modern Voices." *Michigan Quarterly Review.* XXII.4 (fall 1983): 643-54. Reprinted in *Contemporary Literary Criticism* Vol. 37, 158.
229. Hayden, Robert. "A Conversation with A. Poulin Jr." *Robert Hayden: Essays on the Poetry.* Ed. by Laurence Goldstein and Robert Chrisman. (Ann Arbor, MI: University of Michigan Press, 2001), 31.
230. Ibid., 32.
231. Ibid., 27.
232. Hayden, "Middle Passage," *Collected Poems*, 48. This poem is also available on the Poetry Foundation site with audio of the poet reading it.
233. Ibid., 51.
234. Ibid., 48.
235. Ibid., 52.
236. Ibid., 49-50.
237. Ibid., 49.
238. Ibid., 50-1.
239. Ibid., 52.
240. Ibid., 52.
241. Ibid., 53.

242. Hayden, "Frederick Douglass," *Collected Poems*, 62. Also available at the Poetry Foundation's site, with audio.
243. Hayden, "[American Journal]," 192.
244. Ibid., 192
245. Ibid., 193.
246. Ibid., 194.
247. Ibid., 194.
248. Ibid., 192.
249. Ibid., 195.
250. Ibid., 195.
251. Ibid., 194.
252. Zebrun, Gary. "In the Darkness a Wellspring of Plangency: The Poetry of Robert Hayden." *Obsidian: Black Literature in Review*. 8.1 (Spring 1981): 22-6. Reprinted in *Contemporary Literary Criticism* Vol. 37, 154.
253. Luke 1: 39-40 (NRSV).
254. Brinton. *Friends for 350 Years*, 42.
255. Levertov, Denise. "Annunciation," *A Door in the Hive* (NY: New Directions, 1989), 86.
256. Ibid., 86.
257. Curzon, David. "Introduction," *The Gospels in Our Image: An Anthology of Twentieth-Century Poetry Based on Biblical Texts.* (NY: Harcourt, Brace and Co., 1995), xxvii.
258. Eliot, T. S. "Journey of the Magi," *The Waste Land and Other Poems.* (NY: Harcourt, Brace & World, 1962, 69-70.
259. Wright, James. "St. Judas," *Above the River: The Complete Poems.* (NY: Farrar, Straus, & Giroux, 1990), 84.
260. Ibid., 84.
261. Roethke. *On Poetry & Craft*, 40.
262. John-Steiner, Vera. *Notebooks of the Mind: Explorations of Thinking.* Revised Edition. (London: Oxford UP, 1997), 54.
263. Roethke, *On Poetry & Craft*, 76.
264. Ibid., 40.
265. Ibid., 41.
266. Ibid., 40.
267. Ibid., 41.
268. Ibid., 53.
269. Roethke, Theodore. *The Collected Poems of Theodore Roethke.* (NY: Anchor Books, 1975), 231.
270. Ibid., 231.

271. Ibid., 231.
272. Kunitz, Stanley. "The Taste of Self" *A Kind of Order, A Kind of Folly: Essays and Conversations.* (Boston: Little Brown & Company, 1975), 88.
273. Ibid., 88.
274. Roethke, "In a Dark Time," *Collected Poems,* 231.
275. Levertov, Denise. *The Poet in the World.* (NY: New Directions, 1973), 13
276. Kunitz, "The Taste of Self," 94-5.

Apprentice House is the country's only campus-based, student-staffed book publishing company. Directed by professors and industry professionals, it is a nonprofit activity of the Communication Department at Loyola University Maryland.

Using state-of-the-art technology and an experiential learning model of education, Apprentice House publishes books in untraditional ways. This dual responsibility as publishers and educators creates an unprecedented collaborative environment among faculty and students, while teaching tomorrow's editors, designers, and marketers.

Outside of class, progress on book projects is carried forth by the AH Book Publishing Club, a co-curricular campus organization supported by Loyola University Maryland's Office of Student Activities.

Eclectic and provocative, Apprentice House titles intend to entertain as well as spark dialogue on a variety of topics. Financial contributions to sustain the press's work are welcomed. Contributions are tax deductible to the fullest extent allowed by the IRS.

To learn more about Apprentice House books or to obtain submission guidelines, please visit www.apprenticehouse.com.

Apprentice House
Communication Department
Loyola University Maryland
4501 N. Charles Street
Baltimore, MD 21210
Ph: 410-617-5265
info@apprenticehouse.com • www.apprenticehouse.com

www.ingramcontent.com/pod-product-compliance
Lightning Source LLC
Chambersburg PA
CBHW070528090426
42735CB00013B/2905